TEXAS POLITICS: A READER

Second Edition

TEXAS POLITICS: A READER
Second Edition

Edited by
Anthony Champagne
and Edward J. Harpham
The University of Texas at Dallas

W. W. Norton & Company
New York • London

Copyright © 1998, 1997 by W. W. Norton & Company, Inc.

All rights reserved
Printed in the United States of America
The text of this book is composed in Berthold Walbaum Book
Composition by PennSet, Inc.
Manufacturing by The Courier Companies, Inc.
Book design by Jack Meserole

Library of Congress Cataloging-in-Publication Data
Texas politics : a reader / edited by Anthony Champagne and Edward J.
 Harpham.—2nd ed.
   p. cm.
 Includes bibliographical references.
 ISBN 0-393-95878-7 (pbk.)
 1. Texas—Politics and government—1951–   I. Champagne, Anthony.
II. Harpham, Edward J.
JK4816.T47   1998
320.9764—dc21   97–42845

W. W. Norton & Company, Inc., 500 Fifth Avenue, New York, N.Y. 10110
http://www.wwnorton.com
W. W. Norton & Company Ltd., 10 Coptic Street, London WC1A 1PU

2 3 4 5 6 7 8 9 0

Contents

PART I Texas and the Nation

1 The Changing Political Economy of Texas 3
—ANTHONY CHAMPAGNE AND EDWARD J. HARPHAM, University of Texas at Dallas

2 The Texas Constitution 16
—LAWRENCE W. MILLER, Collin County Community College

3 Texans in Congress: The Changing Nature of the Texas Congressional Delegation 32
—JAMES W. RIDDLESPERGER, JR., AND JOANNE CONNOR GREEN, Texas Christian University

PART II Institutions

4 The Texas Governor: Weak or Strong? 51
—CHERYL D. YOUNG AND JOHN J. HINDERA, Texas Tech University

5 Leadership, Power, and Emerging Partisanship in the Texas Legislature 66
—GREGORY S. THIELEMANN, University of Texas at Dallas

6 Judicial Selection in Texas: Democracy's Deadlock 88
—ANTHONY CHAMPAGNE, University of Texas at Dallas

PART III Politics

7 Party Identification and Public Opinion in Texas, 1984–1994: Establishing a Competitive Two-Party System 107
—JAMES A. DYER, JAN E. LEIGHLEY, AND ARNOLD VEDLITZ, Texas A&M University

8 Texas Elections 123
—JAMES CARTER, Sam Houston State University

9 Gender and the Campaign for Governor 140
—JEANIE R. STANLEY, Political Consultant and
Coauthor of *Claytie and the Lady*, The Woodlands

10 The Party System in Texas 156
—PAUL LENCHNER, Texas A&M University—
Commerce

11 The Texas Trial Lawyers Association:
Interest Group Under Siege 177
—CHARLES P. ELLIOTT, JR., Texas A&M University—
Commerce

PART IV   Policies

12 Taxes in Texas 197
—BERNARD L. WEINSTEIN, University of North Texas

13 Education Reform in Texas 213
—CLARK D. THOMAS, U.S. Department of Health and
Human Services, Dallas

14 Welfare Reform and the New Paternalism in Texas 233
—EDWARD J. HARPHAM, University of Texas at Dallas

PART I

Texas and the Nation

1
The Changing Political Economy of Texas

ANTHONY CHAMPAGNE AND EDWARD J. HARPHAM
UNIVERSITY OF TEXAS AT DALLAS

As the twentieth century draws to a close, Texas is in the midst of a great transformation. The land of cowboys and cotton, wildcatters and oil, and Sam Rayburn and Lyndon Johnson finds itself at the end of one age and the beginning of another. No longer can Texas be considered a backwater rural state whose primary industries are tied to the land. No longer is oil the primary lubricant of the state's economy. No longer is winning the Democratic primary tantamount to being elected to office.

Fewer than one in five Texans now live in rural communities. Cotton, cattle, and oil remain important sectors of the Texas economy, but they are not the only important sectors. Over the past decade, Texas has developed a diversified economy with a significant high-tech component geared to a world economy. Similarly, the popular image of a Texan as a drawling, rural Anglo does not fit the state's demographic portrait in the late 1990s. The proportion of Texans of Hispanic ancestry is increasing. Last, but certainly not least, the politics of a single-party, Democratic state has gone the way of the Old South as a Republican party based in the suburbs has grown in strength at all levels of government.

Understanding Texas's great transformation means coming to terms with three dimensions of change: economic, demographic, and political.

ECONOMIC CHANGE

Among the most important features that shape the economy of Texas are its size and diversity. The second-largest state in the Union (after Alaska), Texas comprises 7 percent of the total water and land area in the United States. It is as large as New England, New York, Pennsylvania, Ohio, and Illinois combined, and covers almost 167 million acres of land area and over 3 million acres of inland water. Texas has a coastline of 367 miles and a 773-mile border with Mexico. Geographically, Texas spans three distinct regions: the Gulf Coastal Plains, the Interior Lowlands, and the Great Plains.[1] Not surprisingly, the history of the state's economy is complex.

By the beginning of the Civil War, the Texas economy had become

---

1. Dallas Morning News, *Texas Almanac 1994–95* (Dallas: Belo, 1993) pp. 107–9.

dependent on the production and sale of one commodity: cotton.[2] Cotton production, in turn, was based on the large-plantation system and slave labor. Virtually the entire crop was sold outside the state and almost all other goods were imported. The Civil War and Reconstruction brought an end to the slave-based cotton economy. A new mercantile class arose to replace the planters as the social foundation of the cotton industry. By 1874, cotton production had returned to the prewar levels of 500,000 bales a year. This figure rose to 1 million bales in 1878 and 1.5 million bales in 1884, making Texas the primary producer of cotton in the United States.

As the cotton industry expanded in the latter third of the nineteenth century, a new industry tied to the land grew in importance: cattle. The building of the railroads and the development of the state's infrastructure linked this industry to growing consumer markets in the North and the Midwest, quickly making Texas one of the leading producers of livestock and their products.

The discovery of oil at Spindletop, near Beaumont on the Gulf Coast, in January 1901 changed forever the landscape of the Texas economy. By 1902, Texas was supplying 20 percent of the oil used in the United States; that figure would rise to 50 percent by the 1960s. Oil production and oil-related industries expanded following the First World War. But it was the discovery of a massive oil field 170 miles north of Spindletop in 1930 that secured Texas's oil-based future. Home of the largest known oil reserve in the United States (until the discovery of a larger one in Alaska in the late 1960s), Texas attracted thousands of individuals seeking their fortunes in the oil business. Large pools of risk capital found their way into the Texas economy and a petrochemical industry began to grow along the Gulf Coast.

World War II accelerated many of these changes. During the war, Texas was the home of numerous military bases, as well as the center of such war-related industries as petrochemicals, electronics, aircraft, and metals. In the years following the war, Texas became the second-largest defense contractor, after California.[3]

The average rate of growth in Texas's economy was a robust 6.3 percent from 1946 to 1951. Although that average rate fell 3.2 percent from 1951 to 1961, it remained 0.5 percent above the national average. Between 1961 and 1971, and again between 1971 and 1981, the average rate of growth remained a healthy 4.4 percent. In the latter period, the rate of growth exceeded 5 percent for five of the ten years, and exceeded 6 percent for three of those years. Texans liked to claim that ingenuity and entrepreneurialism lay at the heart of their state's economic boom in the

---

2. The following discussion is drawn from *Forces of Change: Shaping the Future of Texas,* comp. John Sharp (Austin: Texas Comptroller of Public Accounts, 1993), vol. 1, chap. 3.
3. See *Forces of Change,* chap. 5; Neal R. Pierce and Jerry Hagstrom, *The Book of America: Inside Fifty States Today* (New York: W. W. Norton, 1983), pp. 623–24.

late 1970s. But something much more fundamental lay behind Texas's success story: booming world oil prices.

In 1971, the price of crude oil stood at less than $5 a barrel. Two oil embargoes in the 1970s drove energy prices up quickly and stimulated the Texas economy. By 1981, when energy prices on the world market peaked at $35 per barrel, oil and oil-related businesses were responsible for 26 percent of the gross state product. Real estate prices in key urban areas, such as Houston and Dallas–Ft. Worth, shot up. Some visionaries began to speak of Texas as having an economy that could never go into recession. The price of oil, it was projected, would go to $70 or even $80 a barrel in coming years, assuring the state prosperity well into the future. Those projections were overconfident, however.

World oil prices began a downward spiral in 1982, bottoming out on March 31, 1986, when the price of oil fell below $10 a barrel. As the price of oil fell, other sectors of the state's economy began to suffer. Speculative real estate deals and large construction projects first slowed down, then came to a halt. Loan defaults began to rise and banks began to fail. In the 1980s, 370 banks failed in the state of Texas. What followed was an economic free fall. Between 1981 and 1991, Texas went through two serious recessions, one in 1982 and another in 1986–87. The average annual rate of economic growth limped along at 1.7 percent, the lowest since World War II. Meanwhile, Texas's contribution to the U.S. gross national product fell from 8.2 percent in 1982 to 6.6 percent in 1989. While Texas remained the third-largest state economy in the nation, it was a troubled one.

As the 1990s proceeded, the pivotal role of oil in the Texas economy continued to recede. Oil production had peaked in 1972, when 1.3 billion barrels worth $4.5 billion were pumped out of the ground. The dollar value of annual oil production had peaked in 1981, when the 945 million barrels produced $32.7 billion. By 1992, however, barrel production had fallen to 642 million barrels worth only $11.8 billion. More revealingly, oil was only responsible for 12 percent of the gross state product by the early 1990s. It was estimated that approximately 146,000 oil-related jobs had been lost throughout the 1980s.[4]

Texas emerged slowly from the economic malaise of the 1980s with a much more diversified economy. New service industries began to replace oil as the linchpin of economic growth in the state. For the most part, Texas escaped the economic recession of the early 1990s. From 1990–93, Texas led the ten most populous states in job creation by adding 373,000 new jobs.[5] It is significant that these jobs were primarily in service-related industries. The percentage of the gross state product grounded in ser-

---

4. Production figures as drawn from *Texas Almanac 1994–95*, p. 609. Job figures are drawn from *Forces of Change*, chap. 5.
5. *Texas Almanac 1994–95*, p. 440.

vices rather than goods rose from 57 percent in 1980 to 72 percent in 1993. The bulk of future job expansion is expected to be in the service sector.

What will the Texas economy look like as it continues to move away from its dependence on oil? It is difficult and perhaps even foolhardy to speculate. Certainly the cotton farmers and the cattle ranchers couldn't have imagined in their wildest dreams the oil-based economy that defined the state for much of the twentieth century. We can, however, point to three distinct trends that are moving the economy into the future.

First, there is the trend toward a broad diversification of the economy. For the first time in its history, the Texas economy is beginning to look more like the national economy. No longer will one or two industries define the state's interests or distinguish those interests from those of the nation as a whole. Increasingly, Texas will find itself riding the wave of economic development alongside the rest of the nation. Inevitably, the economic issues concerning most Texans will come ultimately to resemble those of most other Americans.

Second, economic power will continue to move away from the extraction-based industries of oil and agriculture found in rural areas to the service-oriented and high-tech industries found in urban and suburban environments. Well into the foreseeable future, the economy of Texas will be dominated increasingly by the "core triangle" region—the area between Houston, San Antonio, and Dallas–Ft. Worth. This core triangle encompasses only 10 percent of the state's land, but it already includes 60 percent of the state's population. More important, it is the center of the state's high-growth and high-tech industries.

The third key factor defining the future of the Texas economy may well lie outside both the state and the nation. Its central location in the United States and the long border it shares with Mexico place Texas in a strategic location for international trade. The value of exports from Texas has grown rapidly over the past few years, rising from $19.7 billion (or 7 percent of U.S. exports) in 1987 to $45.3 billion (9.7 percent of U.S. exports) in 1993. The vast majority of this trade was with Mexico. Indeed, approximately half of all U.S. exports to Mexico come from Texas. The passage of the North American Free Trade Agreement (NAFTA) in 1993 should accelerate the link between Texas and the international economy. By lowering trade barriers on twenty thousand goods, services, and financial commodities among the United States, Mexico, and Canada, NAFTA created a single market of 370 million people and $6.3 trillion. Much as oil restructured the Texas economy throughout the twentieth century, NAFTA may restructure it in new and unpredicted ways in the twenty-first.

Changing Demographics

Contrary to the assumptions of the framers of the 1876 Constitution, Texas would not remain a rural state. By the early part of the twentieth

TABLE 1.1

The Changing Face of Texas, 1850–1992

	1850	1900	1950	1990	1996*
Population (millions)	.213	3.05	7.71	17.00	19.0
Urban	4%	17%	63%	80%	NA
Rural	96	83	37	20	NA
Anglo	72%	80%	87%	61%	57%
Black	28	20	13	12	12
Hispanic	NA	NA	NA	25	29
Other	NA	NA	NA	2	2

NA=not available.
Sources: *Statistical Abstract of the United States: 1994* (Washington, DC: U.S. Department of Commerce, Bureau of the Census, 1994); Dallas Morning News, *Texas Almanac 1994–95* (Dallas: Belo, 1995).
* estimated.

century, the percentage of the population living in rural areas had begun a dramatic decline. At the same time, Texas began experiencing overall population growth. As shown in Table 1.1, nearly 83 percent of the more than 3 million people living in Texas in 1900 resided in rural areas. As the century progressed and oil redefined the state economy, the rural character of Texas changed. By 1950, slightly more than 37 percent of the population remained rural, and by 1960 only one in four Texans lived in the country. According to the 1990 census, only one in five Texans now lives in a rural area, an almost complete reversal of the 1900 pattern.

Texas is now the country's second most populous state, with an estimated 19 million residents in 1996. During the boom decade of the 1970s, the population of Texas expanded by more than 27 percent. Growth in the 1980s was much more irregular; although the state's population increased by 19.4 percent, much of the growth was concentrated in the early years of the decade. From 1980 to 1983, the state's population increased approximately 3.1 percent annually. This fell in the mid-1980s to an average annual growth rate of 0.3 percent due to a souring economy. Between 1988 and 1990, population growth increased modestly to 1.1 percent annually. The first four years of the 1990s showed an accelerated population expansion, as the total population grew by 6.2 percent between 1990 and 1993. As the economy continued to recover after the oil debacle, population growth has continued its upward climb.

Much of the population growth in Texas has been due to a net immigration from other states as well as from other countries. Three out of every ten people living in Texas were born outside the state. In the 1970s, the vast majority of immigration (74.2 percent) came from other states, while only 25.8 percent was international. In the 1980s, however, these numbers reversed; only 23.8 percent of new Texans came from other states, while 76.2 percent came from other nations. The U.S. Bureau of the Census estimates that between 1990 and 1993 this trend continued; more than 25,000 Americans moved to Texas from other states, while approximately 226,000 immigrated to Texas from foreign countries. In the early 1990s, 68 percent of Texas's population growth was due to natural causes (births minus deaths in the state), while 25 percent was due to international migration and 13 percent to national migration into the state.[6]

These demographic patterns have produced major shifts in Texas's racial and ethnic composition. Once an overwhelming majority in the state, the proportion of the population that was Anglo fell to 57 percent in 1996. Texas has become considerably more ethnically diverse than the nation as a whole.

Since Reconstruction, African-Americans have made up a prominent, although declining, percentage of the population of the state, the greatest numbers being concentrated largely in the east. The proportion of African-Americans in Texas dropped steadily from 20.4 percent in 1900 to only 11.6 percent in 1996. Like the rest of Texas, the African-American population has urbanized, especially in the Dallas–Ft. Worth and Houston-Galveston-Brazoria areas. In Dallas–Ft. Worth, the African-American population is 14.3 percent of the total population and in Houston-Galveston-Brazoria, it is 17.9 percent.[7]

In contrast to the African-American population, the proportion of Hispanics in Texas has increased significantly, particularly in recent years. Reliable information on the number of Hispanics in Texas and the nation prior to 1950 is incomplete. In 1980, 21 percent of the population was Hispanic. By 1996, this number had risen to 29 percent. Almost 78 percent of Hispanic Texans live in metropolitan areas, while only a little more than 6 percent live in suburban and almost 16 percent live in nonmetropolitan areas. The vast majority of Hispanics reside in south and west Texas, although larger numbers have found their way into other parts of the state. Dallas County, for example, is now the home of more than 315,000 Hispanic residents, who make up 17 percent of the county's total population.[8]

Important socioeconomic changes have accompanied these shifts in the state's demographic profile. As shown in Table 1.2, personal per capita income rose marginally throughout the 1980s and early 1990s. Relative to the rest of the nation, however, Texas's ranking fell from twentieth

---

6. *Texas Almanac 1994–95*, p. 393; *Statistical Abstract of the United States: 1994* (Washington, DC: U.S. Department of Commerce, Bureau of the Census, 1994), pp. 28–29.
7. *Texas Almanac 1994–95*, pp. 303–6. Texas Department of Human Services, *DHS at a Glance* (Austin: 1996), pp. 4–5.
8. *Texas Almanac 1994–95*, p. 186.

TABLE 1.2

Per Capita Income in Texas and the United States, 1980–1995
(in constant 1992 dollars)

	1980	1990	1995
Texas	16,821	18,027	19,204
United States	16,991	20,090	21,188

Source: *Statistical Abstract of the United States: 1996* (Washington, DC: U.S. Department of Commerce, Bureau of the Census, 1996), p. 453.

to thirty-first between 1980 and 1993. In 1980, per capita personal income in Texas was approximately 99 percent of that of the nation. In 1990, it fell to 90 percent, recovering to 91 percent by 1995. It is even more disturbing that the median household income fell in Texas both in real dollars as well in relation to the nation as a whole. (See Table 1.3)[9]

Growing inequality appears to be one of the distinguishing characteristics of Texas as it enters an era of economic and demographic transformation. Poverty statistics appear to bear this out. In 1980, more than 2.4 million Texans lived in poverty—15.7 percent of the state's population.[10] This had increased to 2.7 million people by 1990 and to more than 3 million by 1992. Between 1990 and 1992, the proportion of the population living in poverty had risen from 15.9 percent to 17.8 percent, a startling increase in such a short period of time. Moreover, both figures were above the national poverty rates (13.5 percent in 1990 and 14.4 percent in 1992). The largest increases were among minority groups. In 1990, 33 percent of all Hispanics and 31 percent of all African-Americans lived in poverty.[11] Among the poorest regions in the nation were rural southern counties with large Hispanic populations, such as Starr, Maverick, and Dimmit counties, where poverty rates hovered between 30 and 40 percent of the population.

TABLE 1.3

Median Household Income in Texas and the United States, 1984–1994
(in constant 1994 dollars)

	1984	1988	1992
Texas	32,841	31,272	30,755
United States	31,972	34,106	32,264

Source: *Statistical Abstract of the United States: 1996* (Washington, DC: U.S. Department of Commerce, Bureau of the Census, 1996), p. 465.

9. *Statistical Abstract 1994*, pp. 456, 468.
10. For a further discussion of how poverty is measured, see Chapter 14 in this volume.
11. *Texas Almanac 1994–95*, p. 306.

It is likely that the demographic transformation of Texas will continue well into the next century as the overall population continues to grow at a steady rate. Texans will become more urbanized, suburbanized, and ethnically diverse. Moreover, as baby boomers age, the population as a whole will be older. In 1992, only 10.2 percent of the population of Texas was over the age of 65. It is projected that by 2030, this figure will increase to 20 percent. Along with the other demographic changes taking place in Texas, the aging of the population will change the face of the state and will place new demands on both the private and the public sectors.

Political Change

In 1949, the well-known political scientist V. O. Key described Texas politics as a "modified class-politics" where the "anxieties of the newly rich" and the "repercussions of the New Deal in Texas" pushed politics into a battle between conservatives and liberals.

> In 40 years a new-rich class has risen from the exploitation of natural resources in a gold-rush atmosphere. By their wits (and, sometimes by the chance deposit in eons past of an oil pool under the family ranch) men have built large fortunes from scratch. Imbued with faith in individual self-reliance and unschooled in social responsibilities of wealth, many of these men have been more sensitive than a Pennsylvania manufacturer to the policies of the Roosevelt and Truman Administration.[12]

The one-party "establishment" politics chronicled by Key and others was built on oil. The sharp ideological cleavages between liberals and conservatives were reinforced by finely honed political personalities. Political conflict remained firmly within the Democratic Party, however. For most of the century, the Republican Party was a nonentity in state politics and could be safely ignored by Democratic candidates up and down the ticket as well as within the state legislature.[13]

There were two notable exceptions to the monopoly on political power held by the Democratic Party from Reconstruction through the 1970s. In the 1950s, conservative Democrats bucked the liberals in the national party and supported Dwight D. Eisenhower for president under the banner of "Democrats for Eisenhower." In the 1960s, Republican John Tower, an unknown professor from a small state university, was able to win a special election for the U.S. Senate and to hold on to the seat in later, regular elections. But these were exceptions to the rule. Well into the 1970s, winning the Democratic primary was tantamount to winning the November election in Texas, be it for the office of county judge or governor.

Establishment politics in Texas was challenged in the early 1980s as

---

12. V. O. Key, Jr., *Southern Politics* (New York: Vintage, 1949), p. 255.
13. See for example George Norris Green, *The Establishment in Texas Politics: The Primitive Years, 1938–1957* (Westport, CT: Greenwood, 1979).

the Republican Party fielded its first successful candidate for governor since Reconstruction, William Clements, who won in 1982. The establishment slowly unraveled throughout the decade as more Republicans began to run for offices across the state and as the oil economy went into decline. By the middle of the 1990s, the era of one-party politics was over, although it was not yet clear exactly what sort of politics would replace it. Three changes are restructuring politics in Texas: the increas-

TABLE 1.4

Texas Election Results, 1980–1996

	1980	1982	1984	1986	1988	1990	1992	1994	1996
Texas house									
Democratic	114	114	98	94	93	93	91	89	82
Republican	35	36	52	56	57	57	58	61	68
Texas senate									
Democratic	23	26	25	25	23	22	18	17	14
Republican	7	5	6	6	8	9	13	14	17
U.S. Congress									
Democratic	19	22	17	17	19	19	21	19	16
Republican	5	5	10	10	8	8	9	11	14

Source: *Statistical Abstract of the United States: 1982, 1989, 1994, and 1996* (Washington, DC: U.S. Department of Commerce, Bureau of the Census, 1982, 1989, 1994, and 1996).

ing prominence of the Republican Party at all levels of government, an expanding role for women and minorities in politics and government throughout the state, and the growing influence of money in political campaigns.

No longer can Republicans be considered the also-rans in an election. Republican candidates have carried the state in five of the last seven presidential elections and have won three of the state's last five gubernatorial races. More significantly, Republican influence in both houses of the state legislature and in the U.S. Congress continued to grow throughout the 1980s. As Table 1.4 documents, between 1980 and 1996 Republicans increased their seats in the state house from 35 to 68 and in the congressional delegation from 5 to 14. In 1996 the Republicans became the majority party in the state senate by capturing seventeen seats.

The 1994 election revealed how much Texas politics had changed over the previous fourteen years. Besides picking up one seat in the state senate, two seats in the state house, and two seats in Congress, Republicans won the governor's office and a second seat in the U.S. Senate. They also won the three seats on the Texas Railroad Commission that were up for election and four out of five statewide judicial elections. Raul Gonzalez, an incumbent with no opposition, was the only Democratic candidate to win a statewide judicial race in 1994. For the first time since

Reconstruction, the Republican Party also demonstrated electoral power farther down the ballot. In Houston, for example, Republicans swept Democrats from local courthouse offices.[14] In Dallas County, the sole Democratic candidate to win a district judge race in November 1994 switched to the Republican Party in February 1995. He was joined by thirty other local Democratic officials across the state.

To be sure, the Democratic Party in Texas remains a powerful force. Democrats continue to control the state house, the congressional delegation, and half of the nonjudicial statewide offices in Texas. But the party's monopoly on power in the state probably is broken forever. The danger remains that the Democratic Party, like the oil economy, might find its position in the state further eroded as the century comes to a close.

A second major change that is redefining politics in Texas is the growing influence of minorities and women. For the first half of the century, African-Americans were effectively excluded from politics in Texas through such mechanisms as the all-white primary (declared unconstitutional in 1944). Civil rights and voting rights legislation enacted by Congress in the 1960s and 1970s guaranteed a place for African-Americans in Texas's political life. An increasing number of African-Americans were elected to office in the 1980s and 1990s. In 1982, there were only 207 black elected officials in all levels of government in Texas. This rose to 300 in 1988 and to 472 in 1993. In 1993, there were 18 black members serving in either the U.S. Congress or in the state legislature, up from 14 in 1982. The most notable increase, however, was at the local level, where the number of black city and county officials rose from 89 in 1982 to 150 in 1988 to 323 in 1993.[15]

As with African-Americans, the number of Hispanics holding public office has grown in recent years. By 1993, more than 2030 Hispanics held public office in Texas, including 38 state legislators and executive officials.[16]

Women are also participating in state government and politics much more than in the past. In 1992, Texas elected Ann Richards, its first female governor since the 1920s and 1930s, when "Ma" Ferguson ran in the place of her husband. In 1994, the first female senator from Texas, Republican Kay Bailey Hutchinson, was elected. But these highly visible elections tell only part of the story. Throughout the 1990s, women won important positions at all levels of government in Texas. In 1995, 3 women were elected to Congress from Texas, 33 women to the state legislature, and 5 women to other statewide offices. It is perhaps more

14. Bruce Nichols, "Harris County Voters Oust 8 of 10 Minority Judges," *Dallas Morning News*, 11 November 1994, p. 1A.
15. *Statistical Abstract of the United States: 1982* (Washington, DC: U.S. Department of Commerce, Bureau of the Census, 1982), p. 261; *Statistical Abstract 1994*, p. 285.
16. *Statistical Abstract 1994*, p. 285.

significant that women held more than 25 percent of county courthouse offices and almost 24 percent of municipal offices in the state.[17]

The importance of minorities and women to the changing politics of Texas extends beyond officeholding. They are also playing pivotal roles in electoral politics. Ann Richards's defeat of Clayton Williams in the 1990 gubernatorial election was due in no small part to the overwhelming support she received from African-Americans and Hispanics, as well as the large number of women who abandoned the Republican Party's gaffe-prone candidate, who had made a joke about rape to reporters during the campaign.

The politics of ethnicity and sex, however, can cut both ways, as Richards learned to her chagrin in 1994. Minority turnout in 1994 was approximately 5 percent higher than in 1990. According to exit surveys, as in 1990, Richards was the overwhelming choice of minority voters, receiving 97 percent of the African-American vote and 78 percent of the Hispanic vote. But she lost the election because of her inability of make inroads in the white vote. Her support among white voters fell from 42 percent in 1990 to 35 percent in 1994. Not only did fewer women vote for Richards in 1990, but male support for her candidacy collapsed. Exit polls showed that 67 percent of white male voters supported the Republican candidate, George Bush, Jr., while only 31 percent backed Democratic incumbent Richards. According to one analyst, the 336,000-vote difference between the two was due to the new white voters that had been added to voting rolls in northern and eastern Texas.[18]

The third change that is remaking political life in Texas is the growing influence of money. Money has long been the lifeblood of politics in America as well as in Texas. But its importance has become intensified in recent years. Urbanization and the rapid expansion of the population have broken up the old style of personal politics that once dominated Texas life. A new style of politics, revolving around the mass media in general and television in particular, has made campaigning for offices from the courthouse to the statehouse an expensive affair. In addition to the intensifying two-party competition, three factors have made money a necessary precondition to a successful political career in the state.

Texas law requires that all campaign contributions be reported, although there are no limits (excepting judicial races) to the contributions. This has enabled interest groups and private individuals to funnel enormous amounts of money to candidates of their choice. A 1994 study released by the American Tort Reform Association found that trial law-

---

17. *Statistical Abstract 1994*, p. 285; Sam Attlesey, "Texas Women Progressing in Politics but Lag behind U.S.," *Dallas Morning News* 23 August 1995, p. 1A.
18. See James E. Garcia, "Bush Faces Problem of Reaching Minorities after Giving Governor-elect Little Support," *Dallas Morning News* 12 November 1994, p. B1; Sam Attlesey, "White Men Put Bush in Office, Analysis Shows," *Dallas Morning News* 12 December 1994, p. 44A.

yers gave $8.8 million to statewide political and judicial races in Texas over the last four years, not including congressional races. A *Dallas Morning News* study found that medical, chemical, manufacturing, and insurance interests had donated $6.9 million to political candidates since 1990, while oil and gas interests had given $5 million.[19]

Certain individuals have become high rollers in the game of politics through their individual contributions. According to Wayne Slater of the *Dallas Morning News*, more than a dozen Texans contributed between $250,000 and $1 million to candidates between 1990 and 1994. Chicken magnate "Bo" Pilgrim has given $399,000 to numerous candidates in both parties since 1990. In one notorious example of influence peddling, Pilgrim distributed checks for $10,000 on the floor of the Texas senate two days before a vote on a workers-compensation bill that he favored. Others have been more discriminating in their actions. Tyler oil executive Royce Wisenbaker has given $400,500 to Democratic political candidates since 1990. Dallas investors Peter and Edith O'Donnell have given more than $361,000 to Republican candidates.[20]

Money donated at the right time can play a major role in determining the outcome of a campaign. At the end of her 1990 race for governor, Ann Richards was running short of cash. Texas trial lawyers raised almost a million dollars in the final weeks of the campaign, enabling Richards to launch a last-minute media blitz reminding voters what her opponent, Clayton Williams, really stood for.[21]

The total amount of money raised by candidates in Texas has become staggering in recent years. Since 1990, gubernatorial candidates have collected more than $60 million in campaign donations, and candidates for lieutenant governor have attracted more than $10.7 million. Even races farther down the ticket have become expensive affairs. Between 1990 and June 1994, candidates for the Texas Supreme Court and for the Texas Railroad Commission have collected more than $11.2 million and $7.4 million, respectively.[22]

There is little likelihood that big money will stop flowing into Texas political campaigns soon. If anything, the flow of money will intensify as Republicans and Democrats fight to redefine the terrain of Texas political life in the coming years.

---

19. Wayne Slater, "Attorneys Dismiss Report on Funds, Assail Business Interests," *Dallas Morning News* 14 September 1994, p. 14A.
20. Wayne Slater, "Fuel for the Political Fires: Handful of Contributors Wields Big Influence on Statewide Campaigns," *Dallas Morning News* 3 June 1994, p. 1A.
21. Wayne Slater, "Richards Campaign Takes in Big Gifts from Trial Lawyers," *Dallas Morning News* 5 March 1994, p. 1A.
22. Wayne Slater, "Fuel for the Political Fires: Handful of Contributors Wields Big Influence on Statewide Campaigns."

Conclusion

The essays in this book were commissioned with an eye toward providing an insight into the many changes that are restructuring political and economic life in Texas. There are numerous texts that do a good job of providing students and general readers an overview of the basic governmental institutions and political processes found in Texas. Their primary concern is to describe the institutions and processes of government in the state. Our goal here is considerably different. By encouraging our authors to offer new and potentially controversial themes regarding government in Texas, we have sought to encourage new insights and different perspectives on the state's institutions, politics, and policies. As we have argued in this chapter, Texas is in the midst of a great transformation at the end of the twentieth century. New economic, demographic, and political forces are restructuring the state in novel and unexpected ways. If our book helps students and general readers gain a better understanding of the significance of this great transformation of Texas government, we will have accomplished our goal.

2
The Texas Constitution

Lawrence W. Miller
Collin County Community College

The national government and the states have constitutions that establish a basic framework for government. Laws are then passed and rights are defined within the boundaries of these documents. Like the U.S. Constitution, the Texas Constitution was written in a particular historical context with certain goals in mind.

Texas's governing document is the Constitution of 1876. It was written at the end of Reconstruction as a reaction to the radical Republican government of E. J. Davis. The goal of the framers of that document was to insure that no one as powerful as Governor Davis could ever again hold office. The constitution signaled the return of Democratic control of the government and, along with that control, a weak governor and a decentralized state government.

The constitution was a creature of a rural state dominated by populist white farmers who believed that if government was weak, if taxes were low, and if they were left alone by government, they and the state would prosper. That philosophy is still the governing principle of the Texas Constitution, although it is debatable whether such a principle is appropriate in the diverse, urban state that Texas has become.

Texas is unusual in that its constitution is so lengthy and detailed that much policymaking must occur through the process of constitutional amendment rather than simply by lawmaking. For example, if Texas were to have an income tax or to change its system for selecting judges, those changes would not come from statutes enacted by the legislature, but would have to be constitutional amendments voted upon by the people.

Although the Texas Constitution has lasted more than 120 years, it has been the subject of much criticism. It is an unusually detailed document that places numerous limitations on policymaking. Its emphasis on lawmaking through constitutional amendment not only makes it very difficult to make policy, but also makes it very easy for the legislature to avoid responsibility for controversial actions by leaving the decision to the amendment process. The great stress in the constitution upon decentralization also makes it very difficult for officials to accomplish their programs or to be assigned accountability for policy failures. The governor shares power with several other statewide elected officials who have independent power bases, such as the *lieutenant governor, the attorney general, and the comptroller. The quest for decentralization and a weak governor has even led to the creation of one of the few elected regulatory agencies, the Texas Railroad Commission.*

It has been more than two decades since there was a serious effort to rewrite the Texas Constitution. That effort ended with failure. In spite of the document's many flaws, it has satisfied the people of Texas enough that no one believes that another effort at rewriting the constitution is likely.

This chapter explains the framework of organization under which Texas is governed and provides a foundation for the remaining discussions of Texas politics and policy.

A Constitution should be short and obscure.[1]

Napoleon Bonaparte, 1803

If Napoleon Bonaparte's statement about constitutions is to be taken at face value, then those persons responsible for drafting the present Constitution of the State of Texas failed miserably. The 28,600 word document (not including amendments) is neither brief nor obscure. In 1876, this constitution became Texas's sixth.[2] By the end of 1995, the constitution had been amended more than 360 times and contained more than 76,000 words,[3] making it more than six times longer than the U.S. Constitution and the third-longest state constitution in the nation.

Scholars believe that constitutions should be flexible, concise, and dedicated to the fundamental principles of government.[4] The Texas Constitution fails all three tests. The state constitution was described by two scholars as an "ill-organized, forbiddingly written document. As bedside reading, it would be a Texas-sized sleeping pill."[5] Another scholar states that "having to read the Texas constitution is 'cruel and unusual punishment'—and prohibited by the eighth amendment of the U.S. Constitution."[6] The current state constitution is the last of six efforts over a forty-year period (1836–1875) to draft a state constitution. The United States Constitution, described by Franklin D. Roosevelt as ". . . the most marvelously elastic compilation of rules of government ever written,"[7] was ratified almost ninety years prior to 1876. Why then didn't the framers of the Texas Constitution learn from the efforts of their pred-

---

1. Said by Napoleon Bonaparte at the Conference of Swiss Deputies, January 29, 1803. *The Columbia Dictionary of Quotations* (Microsoft Bookshelf '95, Microsoft Corporation).
2. This does not include the constitution of Coahuila y Tejas, which became effective in 1828. This constitution was adopted after Mexico revolted from Spain and each state (Texas was united with Coahuila) drafted its own constitution.
3. *The Book of the States* (Lexington, KY: The Council on State Governments, 1995).
4. David Saffell, *State Politics* (Reading, MA: Addison-Wesley, 1984), pp. 23–24.
5. Kim Quaile Hill and Kenneth R. Mladenka, *Texas: Politics and Government* (New York: Macmillan, 1993), p. 26.
6. Leon Blevins, *Texas Government in National Perspective*, 2nd ed. (New York: McGraw-Hill, 1993), p. 2–15.
7. Said by Franklin D. Roosevelt in a radio broadcast, March 2, 1930. *The Columbia Dictionary of Quotations* (Microsoft Bookshelf '95, Microsoft Corporation).

ecessors? This question and the prospects for change are examined in this chapter.

The United States Constitution

On May 25, 1787, the framers of the U.S. Constitution met in Philadelphia for the "sole and express purpose" of revising the Articles of Confederation. Twelve states sent delegates (because they feared that the convention would weaken states' powers to relieve debtors of their debts, Rhode Island was the only state not to send a delegate) and many of the delegates are well known to scholars and to the general public. James Madison, George Washington, Alexander Hamilton, Elbridge Gerry, and Benjamin Franklin were all in attendance. At the opening session, Washington was elected chairman of the convention, the delegates decided to meet in secret, and the Virginia Plan became the basis for discussion. Hence, the decision was made to scrap the Articles altogether, draft a new constitution, and form a new government.

Background and Experience

The state legislatures chose seventy-four delegates to the convention, but only fifty-five attended. Half were lawyers, most were planters or merchants, many were college graduates, and all were independently wealthy.[8] They were practical men guided by extensive experience in governing. Forty-two of the delegates had served in the Continental Congress and more than forty had held high offices in state governments. As all educated men of their day, the framers had read and been influenced by the writings of Aristotle, Plutarch, John Locke, David Hume, and Montesquieu: however, the delegates were guided more in their deliberations by experience than theory. John Dickinson, a delegate from Delaware, went so far as to state that "experience must be our only guide."[9]

Consensus

The founders shared many ideas about government. They believed in a social contract; that government originated as an implied agreement between the people and the government, and that the people gave up part of their liberty to the government in exchange for the protection of their remaining liberties. They believed in a republican form of government, a government by representatives of the people. Delegates held a cynical view of human nature and believed that concentration of power was dangerous: therefore, they wanted to divide power to check and balance the avarice of people. The founders also favored a "balanced"

---

8. For background information on the Founding Fathers see Charles A. Beard, *An Economic Interpretation of the Constitution* (New York: The Free Press, 1986).
9. Max Farrand, *The Framing of the Constitution of the United States* (New Haven: Yale University Press, 1913), p. 204.

TABLE 2.1

Advantages and Disadvantages of Monarchy, Oligarchy, and Democracy

Type of Government	Advantage	Disadvantage
Monarchy	Efficiency	Tyranny
Oligarchy	Knowledgeable Participants	Rule for Self-Interest
Democracy	Popular Participation	Mob Rule

or "mixed" government. They wanted to incorporate the advantages found in a monarchy, oligarchy, and a democracy while countering the disadvantages. (See Table 2.1)

With this division of power in mind, the members of the convention created three branches of government to parallel the three types of government. The executive branch represents the monarchy, the judicial branch represents the oligarchy, and the legislative branch represents democracy. To avoid the disadvantages of each type of government, John Adams (who was ambassador to England and not at the convention), in a pamphlet circulated in Philadelphia several weeks before the convention,[10] argued for a system of separation of powers through checks and balances as the best guarantee of a free government.

Conflict and Compromise

Disagreements over representation, slavery, voter qualifications, and trade tied up the convention most of the summer of 1787 and threatened to scuttle ratification of the Constitution. Sharp conflict between the large states and the small states over how the new Congress would be constituted deadlocked the convention. Small states feared domination by the large states, while the large states wanted a strong central government under their control. The "Great Compromise" resolved this issue by creating a bicameral legislature with one house based on population and the other based on equality. If the new House of Representatives was to be based on population, then how would the slaves be counted? Southern states wanted slaves to be counted to boost their representation, while delegates from the North didn't want slaves to be counted at all. This conflict was resolved by the "Three-fifths Compromise." Representation and taxation were to be based on population, and all slaves would count as three-fifths of a person. This number (three-fifths) was used once before by the Confederation Congress in requesting money from the states, so to the delegates, this seemed a logical solution to the dispute. Qualifications for voting and for holding office were other important conflicts resolved at the convention. Many of the delegates believed that only men of property should be voters and officeholders. However,

10. John Adams, *A Defence of the Constitutions of Government of the United States of America* (London: C. Dilly, 1787). James Madison later argued this point in *The Federalist Papers*, No. 51 when he wrote that "Ambition must be made to counteract ambition. . . ."

the delegates could not agree on specific property qualifications, so they left both issues up to the states. The last conflict was over trade. Southern states, with their agricultural economy, favored free trade: Northern states sought protection, via tariffs, from goods manufactured in England. The delegates compromised by allowing import but not export taxes.

Conclusion

On September 17, 1787, after 109 days of meetings, the U.S. Constitution was signed by thirty-nine of the original fifty-five delegates. Most of the delegates were not particularly pleased with the finished product. Much of their displeasure revolved around the major compromises of the convention. The nature of compromise is that no party receives exactly what they desire: hence, neither party to a compromise is particularly pleased with the final result. The Northern states believed that they had given too much to the South, whereas the South believed the opposite. The same was true between big and small states, and between agricultural and industrial areas. When the Constitution went to the states for ratification, these issues, along with accusations that the Constitution was created to ensure control by the economic elite and that the new document did not contain a bill of rights, threatened to defeat ratification. Although the Constitution was eventually ratified by the necessary nine states in specially called state conventions, John Marshall, who later became Chief Justice of the United States, may have been correct when he suggested "in some of the adopting states, a majority of the people were in opposition."[11]

CONSTITUTIONS OF THE STATE OF TEXAS

Between 1835 and 1876, Texans drafted and ratified six constitutions, each reflecting the politics of the period and the history of the state.[12] The first was in 1836, when Texas proclaimed independence from Mexico and declared itself an independent republic. The second was adopted in 1845, when Texas joined the United States. This constitution lasted for sixteen years, until the outbreak of the Civil War and Texas's secession from the Union. Because Texas was no longer a member of the Union, it drafted a constitution in 1861 for admittance to the Confederacy. With the defeat of the Confederacy, the implementation of presidential Reconstruction, and the declaration by President Andrew Johnson that the insurrection in Texas had ended, a fourth constitution was drafted in 1866. When the radical Republicans gained control of the U.S. Congress fol-

11. Quoted in Charles A. Beard, *An Economic Interpretation of the Constitution* (New York: The Free Press, 1986), p. 299ff.
12. The politics and the history of Texas are intertwined. Two good books on the history (and therefore the politics) of the state are T. R. Fehrenbach, *Lone Star: A History of Texas and the Texans* (New York: Macmillan, 1968) and Robert A. Calvert and Arnoldo De Leon, *The History of Texas* (Arlington Heights, IL: Harlan Davidson, 1990).

lowing the elections of 1866, they implemented a more punitive brand of Reconstruction, one that necessitated the drafting of another state constitution in 1869. The last constitution was drafted in 1875, after the end of Reconstruction.

The Constitution of the Republic of Texas (1836)

On March 2, 1836, at Washington-on-the-Brazos, Texas declared independence from Mexico and established an interim government under a constitution that was drafted in less than three weeks. Most of the delegates to this convention were from the South and the constitution reflected the American influence, being similar to the U.S. Constitution. It was brief and flexible, and provided for a bicameral legislature and an elected chief executive. After the Texas War for Independence was won, the people of Texas overwhelmingly ratified the constitution for the Republic of Texas. The leading figures in this new nation were experienced American politicians. Sam Houston, who was elected president, had served in the U.S. Congress and later as governor of Tennessee, and the vice-president, Mirabeau Lamar, had served in the state legislature of Georgia. When Texans ratified the 1836 Constitution, they also overwhelmingly approved a referendum calling for annexation to the United States. However, in 1836, the United States was not ready to annex Texas. If Texas was admitted, it would come in as a slave state, and President Andrew Jackson feared a hostile Northern reaction. Another problem was Mexico. General Santa Anna had signed the Treaty of Velasco, ending the war between Texas and Mexico. However, when Santa Anna returned to Mexico City, he repudiated the treaty. Hence, Mexico still claimed Texas. The United States, by annexing Texas, risked war with Mexico—a war they were not prepared to fight. Texas, therefore, remained an independent republic until 1845.

The Statehood Constitution (1845)

By the 1840s, annexation became more acceptable to the people of the United States, who believed that the future of the country was tied to westward expansion. When James K. Polk won the presidential election of 1844 with a platform of Manifest Destiny, or the inevitable expansion of the United States to the Pacific, the annexation of Texas became a reality. John Tyler, the lame-duck president, recommended that Congress pass a joint resolution of annexation. The resolution quickly passed in both houses of Congress and, on March 3, 1845, Texas was asked to join the United States. There were, however, some unusual provisions in the annexation agreement: Texas could divide itself into as many as five states[13]; Texas was responsible for paying off its foreign debt; the Texas flag could fly at the same height as the U.S. flag; and Texas would retain

---

13. This provision, long forgotten, was the basis for an interesting novel. See Alan R. Erwin, *The Power Exchange* (Austin, TX: Texas Monthly Press, 1979). In 1991, a member of the Texas House of Representatives from the panhandle resurrected this provision and, somewhat tongue in cheek, called for the division of Texas.

title to its public lands (unclaimed land primarily in western Texas), which would be sold to pay off its debt. When Texas agreed to these terms, the new state drafted a new constitution—the Constitution of 1845. When this constitution was ratified by the voters and approved by Congress, Texas became the twenty-eighth state.

According to some historians and political scientists, the Constitution of 1845 was well written, appropriately designed, and the best constitution ever produced by the state.[14] The delegates were "exceptionally able men,"[15] experienced in politics and in public affairs. They drafted a document that borrowed heavily from the constitutions of other Southern states and from the constitution of the Republic of Texas. The legislature would meet biennially, homestead rights were protected, and public schools were funded. The governor and lieutenant governor were elected, but could only serve two consecutive terms, and other state officials were appointed by the governor with senate approval. In 1850, influenced by Jacksonian democracy, the voters of the state amended the constitution to call for the election of most state officials. This constitution worked well and was considered a model for its time. Many provisions from the 1845 Constitution were incorporated into subsequent state constitutions, including the present state constitution.

The Constitution for the Confederacy (1861)

In December 1860, a group of political leaders called on the voters to send two delegates from each representative district to a state convention to be held in January 1861. By a vote of 152 to 6, this convention passed a resolution, later ratified, calling for secession from the Union. Texas was admitted to the Confederate States of America, and a new constitution was drafted that was little different from the Constitution of 1845. All references to the United States of America were replaced by Confederate States of America, public officials were required to declare their allegiance to the Confederacy, and the institution of slavery received greater protection. This constitution, like its predecessor, is considered to be, organizationally and structurally, a good constitution.

The Constitution of Presidential Reconstruction (1866)

Abraham Lincoln's plan for bringing the Southern states back into the Union featured the Ten-Percent Plan: that is, if 10 percent of the people who had voted in the 1860 presidential election would swear their allegiance to the United States, then that state could elect their own state government. Andrew Johnson succeeded to the presidency upon Lincoln's assassination, and began to implement this lenient plan. Johnson appointed A. J. Hamilton as provisional governor of Texas, whose task

14. See Fred Gantt, Jr., *The Chief Executive in Texas: A Study in Gubernatorial Leadership* (Austin, TX: University of Texas Press, 1964), p. 24, and Rupert N. Richardson et al., *Texas: The Lone Star State*, 6th ed. (Englewood Cliffs, NJ: Prentice-Hall, 1993), pp. 150–151.
15. Richardson et al., *Texas: The Lone Star State*, 6th ed., p. 150.

it was to restore civil government. In February 1866, Governor Hamilton called for an election to select delegates to a convention to draft a new state constitution. Delegates to this convention represented both the unionist and secessionist factions. As required by the national government, the delegates to this convention abolished slavery and repudiated both the ordinance of secession and the war debt: they did barely enough to gain readmission to the United States. The Constitution of 1845 was slightly modified by amendments, and was resurrected as the Constitution of 1866. In June 1866 the new constitution was ratified, a new governor was elected, and two months later the legislature convened. In late August, President Johnson proclaimed the insurrection to be over, and Texas was back in the United States.[16]

The Constitution of Congressional Reconstruction (1869)

In the November elections of 1866, the radical Republicans (Northern Republicans who chafed at the leniency of presidential Reconstruction) gained control of the U.S. Congress. They insisted on more punitive measures and on removing the former Confederate leaders from state governmental positions. In March and April of 1867, Congress passed additional Reconstruction Acts that divided the South into military districts with a military leader superior to civil officials, required all voters to take an oath of allegiance to the United States, prevented ex-Confederates from voting, and demanded new state constitutional conventions that would be open to voters of both races. The military governor of Texas, General Philip Sheridan, appointed E. M. Pease as provisional governor, and he called for the convening of a constitutional convention in Austin on April 1, 1868. Ninety delegates, ten of whom were African-American, and many of whom were carpetbaggers (Northerners who moved South for personal gains after the war), drafted a constitution that, according to two scholars, included provisions that present-day reformers would like to see in today's document.[17] These provisions included annual legislative sessions, the power for the governor to appoint other state officials, and greater power at the state level (and less at the local). "The convention assumed considerable responsibility beyond the writing of a constitution and spent much time chartering railroads, gathering evidence of lawlessness in East Texas, debating proposals for the sale of a portion of the state to the United States, and dealing with the inappropriate conduct of its own members."[18] The convention adjourned until after the November elections and reconvened in December. The moderate faction, under the leadership of A. J. Hamilton,

---

16. In 1868, the United States Supreme Court in *Texas v. White* ruled that secession was unconstitutional. Hence, the states of the Confederacy had never really left the Union.
17. Richard Kraemer and Charldean Newell, *Essentials of Texas Politics*, 4th ed. (Minneapolis, MN: West Publishing, 1989), p. 17.
18. Richardson et al., *Texas: The Lone Star State*, 6th ed., p. 233.

was able to thwart the radicals and their leader, E. J. Davis. Unable to stop the moderates, the radicals endorsed the constitution and Davis ran for governor, defeating Hamilton by fewer than 800 votes out of more than 79,000 ballots. The gubernatorial election was close (and likely corrupt), but the vote on ratifying the new constitution was an overwhelming 72,000 in favor of the document and fewer than 5,000 opposed. In March 1870, President Ulysses S. Grant signed an Act of Congress that brought military rule in Texas to an end. Reconstruction, at least officially, was over.

The Constitution of 1876

To many Texans, Reconstruction continued after 1870. The Texas Legislature, which included two African-Americans (of thirty) in the senate and nine (of ninety) in the house, was dominated by supporters of Governor Davis. The legislature enacted two bills dealing with lawlessness: a state police and a state militia were created, both under the control of the governor. The governor was also given the power to fill vacancies at the city, county, district, and state levels. The election for congress that should have been conducted in 1870 (and that Davis feared would elect Democrats) was postponed until November of 1872. The office of state printer was created for the printing of official matters. While giving the citizens better access to governmental affairs, it also created a press that was subsidized by (that is, sympathetic to) the government.

In September 1871, a taxpayers convention met in Austin to protest the high salaries of government officials, violations of the state constitution, and the allegation that the Davis administration was bankrupting the state. In a special election held in October 1871, Democrats elected four of their candidates to the U.S. Congress. In the presidential election of 1872, U. S. Grant, running for reelection, lost Texas to the Democratic candidate, Horace Greeley. In 1872, Texans also elected a Democratic majority to the state legislature where, in 1873, they repealed many of the oppressive laws enacted by the previous Republican-dominated legislature. By 1873, newspapers across Texas began calling for the convening of a constitutional convention. While Governor Davis ignored these pleas, Democratic members of the legislature introduced a joint resolution providing for the election of delegates to a convention. This resolution overwhelmingly passed the house, but was killed in the senate.[19] In 1873, Democrat Richard Coke defeated Governor Davis by more than two to one, but the governor refused to leave office, claiming that there had been rampant voter fraud. When President Grant refused to intervene and the local militia took the side of the newly elected governor, E. J. Davis beat a hasty retreat. In 1874, the Democrats were able to gain

---

19. See Seth S. McKay, *Seven Decades of the Texas Constitution of 1876* (Lubbock, TX: Texas Technological College Press, 1943), pp. 49–50.

control of the state judiciary, and by 1875, the last vestige of the Republican administration was the Constitution of 1869. Most Texans believed that this too needed to be replaced.

Background and Experience

In 1874, Democratic precinct, county, and district conventions overwhelmingly approved resolutions calling for a constitutional convention. Newspapers began campaigning for a convention, and Governor Coke, who initially was opposed to the calling of a convention, suggested that three delegates be elected from each of the thirty senatorial districts. After much debate and numerous attempts to modify Coke's plan, it was approved by both houses. Delegates were elected in August 1875, and the convention assembled in Austin on the first Monday in September.[20]

Of the ninety delegates, seventy-six were Democrats and fourteen were Republicans. The average age of the delegates was forty-five, and seventy-two of the men were immigrants from other Southern states; nineteen were from Tennessee. About fifty of the delegates had come to Texas between 1840 and 1870, and had first-hand experience of Reconstruction. Some historians say that five (others say six) African-Americans served as Republican delegates. There is some disagreement as to the occupational backgrounds of the delegates: one source lists thirty-three lawyers, twenty-eight farmers, three merchants, three physicians, two editors, two teachers, two mechanics, one minister, and one postmaster.[21] Many had held high ranks in the Confederate Army and three had been U.S. Army officers.

Several of the delegates were well known, and several others were to become well known. John H. Reagan had been Postmaster General of the Confederacy and would later become a member of the U.S. House, U.S. Senate, and Chairman of the Texas Railroad Commission. Other delegates included John "Rip" Ford, best remembered as the Texas Ranger captain who marched on the state capital and convinced Governor Davis to leave office without a fight; Thomas Nugent, who became the Populist Party candidate for governor in 1892 and 1894; and Lawrence "Sul" Ross, Indian fighter, later governor of the state and president of Texas A&M University.

About one-third of the delegates had served in the Texas legislature; two had served in the state legislatures of Tennessee and Mississippi; three had legislative experience at the national level (two delegates had represented Texas and one had represented the Territory of Kansas); and two delegates had served in the Congress of the Confederate States of America. At least eight members had judicial experience, and many others had experience in local politics. Eleven (or twelve) delegates had

20. S. S. McKay, *Seven Decades of the Texas Constitution of 1876*, pp. 65–67.
21. J. E. Ericson, "The Delegates to the Convention of 1875: A Reappraisal," *Southwestern Historical Quarterly*, vol. 67 (July 1963), p. 24.

experience at previous state constitutional conventions: one had been a member of the 1845 convention, eight or nine had been delegates at the convention (1861) that drafted the constitution for Texas's admission into the Confederacy, one was a delegate at the 1866 Presidential Reconstruction constitutional convention, and one had been a delegate at the radical Republican convention of 1869.[22]

Between one-third and one-half of the delegates were members of the Patrons of Husbandry (the Grange), a farmer's organization that favored frugality and antimonopolistic business practices. The economic panic of 1873 increased statewide membership in this organization, and it became a powerful economic as well as political force. "Retrenchment and Reform" were the bywords of the organization. Members favored low taxes and limited governmental services, wanted regulation of the railroads, banks, and other corporations, favored a very limited public school system, and wanted a poll tax as a suffrage requirement.

Were the delegates to the state convention, like those who had been in attendance in Philadelphia, well versed in the writings of the great philosophers? Probably not. Were they experienced in governmental affairs? Yes, but not to the same extent as the drafters of the U.S. Constitution. Texans who had been uninvolved in decision-making now had an opportunity to draft a state constitution to their liking. The abilities of the delegates have been reinterpreted and reanalyzed. In 1875, the *San Antonio Herald*, commenting on the delegates, wrote "We know that the convention has relatively but a few able men in its composition, but those we deem very able, with sound clear judgment."[23] However, in 1963, J. E. Ericson claimed that the members of the 1875 convention were "a much abler group of men . . . than is generally conceded. Their background and training compares favorably with that of the delegates to any previous constitutional convention held in Texas. If their product is inferior, then the cause must lie elsewhere."[24]

Goals and Objectives

The most pressing goal of the convention delegates was to restrict the power of the state government. During the radical Republican regime many Texans could not participate in the government because they had engaged in insurrection against the Union. Many, if not most, Texans believed that excessive tax money was spent to fund inappropriate government activities, such as promoting railroad construction and excessive funding of public schools. The public debt during the Davis administration had increased twenty times over what it had been in 1866. Hence, many of the delegates had a strong desire to hobble the powers of government.

22. J. E. Ericson, "The Delegates to the Convention of 1875: A Reappraisal," p. 25.
23. Quoted in Richardson et al., *Texas: The Lone Star State*, 6th ed., p. 246.
24. J. E. Ericson, "The Delegates to the Convention of 1875: A Reappraisal," p. 27.

Because many of the delegates were members of the Texas Grange, a second goal of the convention was to further the interests of the agrarian population. The farmers were dependent upon the banks for loans and for the railroads to transport their product to market, so they wanted the government to limit the powers of these interests. Grangers also wanted to reduce the power of state government and place most of its power at the local level.

The economic depression that began in 1873 was not yet over by 1875. Many of the delegates had suffered severe economic hardship and had a difficult time reconciling the vast amount of government spending with their own personal economic situation. They wanted the government to be as economical as they themselves had to be.

The government designed by the 1875 convention reflected the delegates' personal situations and experiences. Hurt by the actions of the previous government, banks, and the railroads, and in the middle of a severe depression, the delegates created a new constitution that was a reaction to their problems.

The New Constitution

The state constitution drafted in 1875 was longer and more detailed than previous state constitutions. Many items previously left to the discretion of the legislature became a part of the law of the state. Provisions in the constitution placed limits on governmental power and authority by spelling out citizens' rights in relation to the government. Reacting to the centralization of power in the Davis administration, the constitution specifically required separation of powers and a series of checks and balances.

The legislative branch was to consist of a senate of thirty-one members and a house never to exceed one hundred and fifty. The legislators were to meet in biennial sessions and their salary was reduced. The powers granted to the legislative branch along with their limitations were spelled out in great detail: being a member of the Texas Legislature was not to be a highly sought-after profession. The executive branch provided for seven officials, six of whom were to be elected by the people of the state, and thus were independent of the governor. The governor could veto legislation and could item veto sections of an appropriations bill, but the two houses could override the veto by a two-thirds vote. Governors could call out the militia, declare martial law, call special sessions of the legislature, and fill vacancies subject to senate approval. Like the legislature's powers, the executive's powers were set forth in great detail. The governor was given the responsibility to "execute the laws," but not the power to do so. Contrary to provisions in the 1869 Constitution, the judicial article provided for the election, rather than the appointment, of all judges by popular vote.

Responsibility for education became decentralized. Local control of education was a way for white landowners to avoid paying for the education of African-American students. Schools were to be segregated and compulsory education was eliminated. The convention wrote very detailed laws regarding railroad competition, established freight and passenger rates, provided for homestead grants, and gave incentives for the construction of railroad lines.

The constitution was approved by the delegates with little opposition, and was ratified by voters almost three to one. The delegates achieved most of their objectives, which were guarantees of a low tax rate, limitations on the power of the government, restrictions on banks and railroads, and greater responsibility falling on local officials. All of these were popular measures in Texas of the 1870s: unfortunately, the constitution was time-bound to that era. Moving Texas from the nineteenth century to the twentieth, and now into the twenty-first, falls on the amending process rather than the legislative process.

Amending the Constitution

In 1943, Seth McKay wrote that the Constitution of 1876 had not been a great success. Of the thirty-three sessions of the legislature to that date, thirty-one had proposed constitutional amendments.[25] This situation has not improved in the fifty-three years since Professor McKay's book was published, and efforts to replace this constitution have, thus far, been unsuccessful. Hence, the fundamental law for the State of Texas is kept up to date not by custom, usage, and interpretation, but by the amending process. An amendment is proposed by a member of the legislature and must be approved by two-thirds of the total membership of the house and senate. The amendment is then placed on the ballot for the electorate: a majority vote is needed for approval. Unlike some states (for example, California), there is no opportunity for citizens to force constitutional amendments on the ballot, because Texas does not have an initiative procedure.

Through 1995, the voters of the state had approved 365 of the 554 proposed constitutional amendments. In 1987, an all-time record was achieved: the electorate was asked to approve twenty-eight amendments. The need for amendments is unquestioned, as Texas continues to be pressured by changing demands brought about by urbanization, industrialization, technological advances, and the need for social services. This need, as Table 2.2 shows, is increasing in intensity. Since 1981, the state constitution has been amended successfully an average of almost nine amendments per year. This rate is considerably greater than the rates for previous eras, and shows no sign of decreasing. When the voters of the state are asked to decide constitutional amendments, voter turnout is low—particularly if the election is a special election just to vote on pro-

25. S. S. McKay, *Seven Decades of the Texas Constitution of 1876*, p. 183.

TABLE 2.2

Amendments to the Constitution of 1876

Years	Number Proposed	Number Adopted	Average Number Adopted Per Year
1879–1900	31	17	0.81
1901–1920	55	21	1.05
1921–1940	91	47	2.35
1941–1960	78	59	2.95
1961–1980	151	98	4.90
1981–1995	148	123	8.20
Total	554	365	

posed amendments. If amendments are at the bottom of a general election ballot, far fewer people vote for (or against) the amendments than vote for people running for offices at the top of the ballot. One reason for voter apathy is easy to explain by reading some of the amendments that voters have been asked to ratify. In 1937, an amendment was added that gave Harris County special taxing powers; in 1968, an amendment was added that allowed Dallas County to issue bonds for road construction; in 1991, voters were asked to approve clear title on approximately 4,400 acres in Fort Bend and Austin counties. The number of amendments dealing with workman's compensation is legendary. What do all of these amendments have in common? They are all examples of policymaking by constitutional amendment. The voters of the state are doing the jobs that should probably be done by the members of the state legislature.

Prospects for Reform

Calls to revise the Constitution of 1876 began fairly soon after its ratification, but it was not until 1974 that a convention was held, and those efforts ended in failure. In 1973, the legislature created a thirty-seven-member Constitutional Revision Commission to make recommendations to members of a constitutional convention, composed of members of the Texas Legislature, that was to meet the following year. The revision commission proposed a draft of a new constitution and this draft became the basis for debate in 1974. Not long after the convention was convened in January 1974, it became obvious that special interest groups who were protected by the 1876 Constitution were going to make drafting a new constitution very difficult. Justices of the Peace feared that a requirement that all state judges be attorneys would cost 90 percent of them their jobs. The interests of Texas A&M and the University of Texas were wrapped up in protecting the Permanent University Fund, and the highway lobby was concerned about the Highway Trust Fund. The major battle, however, was over "right-to-work"—a somewhat misnamed law that prohibits union membership as a condition of employment. Business-backed legislators wanted the state's right-to-work law to be included in the new constitution, whereas labor leaders were vehemently opposed. As the clock ran out on the delegates, the proposed constitution failed to obtain the necessary two-thirds majority needed to pass by only three votes. Critics have long suspected that a major problem with the 1974 constitutional convention was that the members of the legislature were the delegates. With primaries and general elections facing most of the delegates, they did not want to alienate the major benefactors in their districts. Hence, they fell into the same trap as did the delegates to the 1875 convention—they attempted to draft a document that was detailed, rather than general. The delegates also were hampered by weak leadership from the governor's office. The incumbent did not take an active leadership role.[26]

Not wanting their efforts at constitutional reform to go to waste, in 1975 the legislators voted to present the failed constitutional revision effort to the voters as a series of eight constitutional amendments. Voters in 250 of the 254 counties rejected all eight of the amendments.

After the debacle of 1974–1975, it is no wonder that involvement in constitutional revision is not high on the lists of legislators. There are certainly more votes out there for "getting tough on crime" or "providing a quality public school education" than for something as mundane as revision of the fundamental law of the state. There has been no political leadership to revise the constitution and there has been very little talk from the public about constitutional revision. Other than the League of Women Voters, which has consistently shown an interest, no other group has come forth to push for revision. Most members of the general public must be pleased with the current state constitution, satisfied with the piecemeal revisions that have been occurring for the past 120 years, or they don't care. Texans are generally suspicious of change, and recent political scandals (for example, Watergate and Iran-Contra) have done nothing to alleviate skepticism toward politicians. There is no guarantee that the political forces of the 1990s would be any more successful than those of the 1870s in drafting a constitution that followed the guidelines for a good constitution.[27]

Conclusions

Why didn't the framers of the Texas Constitution learn from their predecessors, particularly those who wrote the United States Constitution? There are several explanations.

26. For a good account of the 1974 constitutional convention, see Janice May, *The Texas Constitutional Revision Experience of the '70s* (Austin, TX: Sterling Swift, 1975).
27. The problems of constitutional revision today are similar to those in 1928. See S. D. Myres, Jr., "Mysticism, Realism, and the Texas Constitution of 1876," *Southwestern Political and Social Science Quarterly*, vol. 9 (September 1928), pp. 166–173.

The framers of the U.S. Constitution were living under a weak national government, the Articles of Confederation, whereas the delegates to the 1875 Texas Constitutional Convention had just lived under what they believed to be a tyrannical government, the regime of E. J. Davis. The purposes were different for the delegates to these two conventions. The delegates in Austin wanted to create a system that shackled governmental power. They were not interested in creating a long-lasting model constitution, but were looking for a short-term "fix." Soon after they adjourned there was general agreement that another constitution was needed. In Philadelphia, the delegates were looking for something more long lasting. Soon after the U.S. Constitution was drafted, Benjamin Franklin wrote, "Our new Constitution is now established, and has an appearance that promises permanency. . . ."[28] Many of the delegates in Philadelphia might have been surprised that their handiwork would survive more than 200 years, and the delegates in Austin would likely be very disappointed that their effort had survived for 120 years.

A second explanation for the vast difference between the two constitutions pertains to the nature of compromise. The delegates to the Texas constitutional convention did not need to compromise their principles. An overwhelming majority of these delegates were single-minded in their contempt for government. They didn't have to worry about giving in to proposals that were much different from what they themselves wanted. Hence, their purpose, the limitation of government, was achieved. Nor were they concerned about ratification. Most of the people in the state felt the same way about government as did the delegates. The drafters of the U.S. Constitution, however, had serious disagreements over substantive issues. This forced them to compromise their principles and mute their personal ideologies. The result was a series of statements which were general in nature, general enough to pass the convention, and general enough to be ratified by the states.

It is not likely that the Texas Constitution will be substantially revised in the foreseeable future. Efforts to draft a new constitution have failed and there is little hope for anything but continued piecemeal changes to the document. If the amending of the Texas Constitution continues along its current pace, it will become the nation's second-longest by the year 2000. However, Alabama's constitution is currently more than double the size of the Texas Constitution, so Texans will have to settle for "We're Number Two."

---

28. A letter from Benjamin Franklin, November 13, 1789, *The Columbia Dictionary of Quotations* (Microsoft Bookshelf '95, Microsoft Corporation).

3
Texans in Congress: The Changing Nature of the Texas Congressional Delegation

JAMES W. RIDDLESPERGER, JR., AND JOANNE CONNOR GREEN
TEXAS CHRISTIAN UNIVERSITY

In 1960 Senator Lyndon Baines Johnson sought House Speaker Sam Rayburn's approval before he agreed to accept the vice-presidential nomination. Rayburn was initially very reluctant to agree. He preferred, he told Johnson, for he and Johnson to continue running the government from Capitol Hill.

There is an element of exaggeration in Rayburn's claim, but not much. When Lyndon Johnson was majority leader of the Senate and Sam Rayburn was Speaker of the House of Representatives, Texans had extraordinary influence over the national government. Although that power in Congress is lessened today, as the following chapter points out, it is still significant.

Texas is a large and wealthy state, but state government cannot be understood without understanding how the state fits into the national picture. A state with significant congressional influence can benefit from national policies in all sorts of ways—from large and expensive public works projects, to government contracts, to military bases, to funding formulas for social welfare programs that benefit the state. Without power in Washington, no matter how well run a state is, that state can be a loser. A state must have voices in Washington, especially in positions of power in the Congress where the state's interests can be protected and advanced.

At one time, Texas greatly benefited from being a one-party state. With the Democratic Party in power during the New Deal era and with a strong seniority system operating in Congress, Texas could secure congressional committee and subcommittee chairs along with congressional leadership positions. As the New Deal era declined, one-party Democratic politics in Texas also declined.

Much as in the era of Johnson and Rayburn, Texans hold powerful positions in Washington. Richard Armey is majority leader of the House of Representatives, and Bill Archer has advanced after years in a minority role to the chair of the House Ways and Means Committee. Texas Republicans may not have mastered Congress as did Johnson and Rayburn, but they are forces to be reckoned with on Capitol Hill.

It is interesting that in this era of distrust of the national government and talk of national budget cuts, Texas Republicans in Congress seem to be interpreting their role much as did the old Democratic power brokers: bring home the bacon, federal dollars, and government projects to Texas.

The following chapter explores Texans in Congress—their roles, their power, and how that power affects the state.

The relationship between national and state governments is important. States receive a large portion of their revenues from the national government, as illustrated by the fact that Texas received 29 percent of its governmental revenue from the national government in 1995.[1] Local governments, such as cities, and independent school districts also benefit from direct federal financial aid. In addition, the national government awards huge contracts for various governmental projects in the states, such as defense spending dollars, which can have a major impact on the economic growth, and thus the tax revenue, of a state. The national government spent a little more than 15 billion defense dollars in Texas in 1987, ranking Texas third among the states.[2] The national government finances, either alone or with state contributions, many works projects that can improve the quality of life in a state, such as the building of water reservoirs or interstate highways.

The amount the federal government may spend in a state is determined by a variety of factors, one of which may be the relative strength of the state's congressional delegation. A recent illustration of winning and losing federal dollars was the Superconducting Supercollider, a project that would have cost $8 billion to build and would have brought $270 million a year afterward for its operation. The project was to be built near Waxahachie, in central Texas. Texas won the original federal contract after competition with at least thirty other states, in part because of the size and power of its congressional delegation (and with support from President George Bush, also a Texan). When, just a few years later, the Congress was looking for ways to cut spending, it was able to cancel that project despite the unified opposition from the Texas delegation. The difference came in part because of the diminished strength of the delegation, due to the departure of House Speaker Jim Wright and the resignation by Senator Lloyd Bentsen to become the Secretary of the Treasury. Wright's last congressional vote before his resignation was for the appropriation of money for the Supercollider.[3]

In this chapter we discuss the Texas congressional delegation, beginning with a short overview of the twentieth-century history of the delegation. We then assess data that illustrate how the delegation has changed over time, and, finally, we address the changing nature of the

---

1. Stefan D. Haag, Rex Peebles, and Gary Keith, *Texas Politics and Government* (New York: Longman, 1997), p. 523.
2. James R. Anderson, *Bankrupting America: The Tax Expenditures of the Pentagon by Congressional District* (Lansing, MI: Employment Research Associates, 1989), p. 8.
3. See *Congressional Quarterly Almanac, 1989*, (Washington, D.C.: Congressional Quarterly Press, 1990), p. 40; Michael Barone and Grant Ujifusa, *The Almanac of American Politics 1994*, (Washington, D.C.: National Review, 1993), p. 1224.

delegation and the role that the 1994 elections had in altering its character.

Texas Congressional Leaders in the Twentieth Century

The Texas congressional delegation has had a large presence in leadership during the twentieth century, with five powerful chamber leaders, including three Speakers of the House of Representatives, a Senate Majority Leader, and a House Majority leader. This leadership is more than any other state's, with the possible exception of Massachusetts, which has also been home to three speakers. Such success stems from the fact that these leaders went to Congress at early ages, were recognized as very able legislators, and came from a strong and unified delegation.

The first Speaker of the House from Texas was John Nance Garner, a Democrat from rural Uvalde, in southwestern Texas. Garner served as speaker from December 7, 1931, to March 1933. During his short tenure in office, "Cactus Jack" was notable for two accomplishments. First, he pushed incumbent Republican President Herbert Hoover's relief program to address problems stemming from the Great Depression. Passage came with bipartisan support, in part because of the tradition established by Garner's predecessor of having a social meeting, known affectionately as "The Board of Education," at the end of business every day to discuss compromises between the parties. At this meeting, the good-natured debate often centered on whether the bourbon would be consumed over ice or in tap water. (Garner preferred the latter, because it was the closest he could find to the "branch" water of Texas.) Garner's second major accomplishment was pushing through Congress a Democratic public works program that was vetoed by the conservative president. Later, a compromise bill was put into law. His short tenure as speaker ended when he became vice president under Franklin D. Roosevelt, a position he retained for eight years.[4]

Texas's next Speaker of the House, Sam Rayburn, had, in contrast to Garner's short tenure, a term as leader in Congress that lasted from the time that he became majority leader in 1937 until late 1961. During those twenty-four years, he served as majority leader from 1937 to 1940, as minority leader thereafter when Republicans controlled the chamber, and as speaker from September 1940 to January 1947, from January 1949 to January 1953, and from January 1955 until his death November 16, 1961. Rayburn was perhaps the most powerful congressional leader of the twentieth century, both in terms of years served and with respect to his leadership style. Although Joseph Cannon, who served as speaker earlier in the century, may have exerted more iron-fisted control over the House of Representatives while leader, Rayburn was very influential and he

---

4. See Marquis James, *Mr. Garner of Texas* (New York: Bobbs-Merrill, 1939), pp. 119–30; Bascom N. Timmons, *Garner of Texas* (New York: Harper, 1948), pp. 131–51.

served seventeen years as speaker to Cannon's eight years. "Mr. Sam," as Rayburn was called, served as speaker during World War II and the Korean War, and as the Cold War began. Although international policy was a national focal point, Rayburn never forgot that his first job was to represent his Bonham constituency in northeastern Texas. His contributions to the district and the state included the building of farm-to-market roads, rural electrification, construction of Lake Texoma and other reservoirs, and the development of major military bases.[5] Rayburn, a lifelong close friend of his predecessor Garner, continued to preside over the "Board of Education" and led the Texas congressional delegation in weekly luncheons that were served in the speaker's chambers. The lunches originally included all members of the Texas delegation, but after Dallas elected arch-conservative Republican Bruce Alger to Congress in 1954, the sessions officially became the Texas Democratic delegation luncheons in order to exclude Alger, whom Rayburn found obnoxious.[6] Rayburn was a loyal Democrat known for his sound political judgment and mastery of House rules as well as his ability to persuade members to his views.

For a period of years between 1953 and 1961, as Rayburn was the leader of Democrats in the House, his protégé Lyndon B. Johnson was in charge of Democrats in the Senate, first as minority leader from 1953 to 1955, and thereafter as majority leader. Like Garner in the House, Johnson left to become vice-president, in his case under President John F. Kennedy. Like Rayburn, Johnson's period of leadership in the Senate was critical; he not only had the title of leader, but was clearly the dominant force in Senate politics during the years of his leadership. He had a difficult task, for he served at a time when there was a Republican president, Dwight D. Eisenhower. Johnson worked with Eisenhower on occasion, and sometimes around him, as when the Senate passed Johnson's version of the 1957 Civil Rights Act, perhaps his greatest single accomplishment.[7] Johnson was able to manipulate the outcome of votes through his ability to make even those who did not necessarily agree with him vote to pass bills, a technique known then as simply the "Johnson Treatment." Johnson, like Rayburn, saw part of his duties as delivering federal dollars to his constituents, and the two worked so efficiently that an adage was that, had they remained in control of Congress much longer, the whole state of Texas would have been under water, a reference to their active pursuit of the building of lakes and

---

5. See Anthony Champagne, *Congressman Sam Rayburn* (New Brunswick, NJ: Rutgers University Press, 1984), pp. 52–6.
6. D. B. Hardeman and Donald C. Bacon, *Rayburn: A Biography* (Austin: Texas Monthly Press, 1989), p. 417.
7. See Donald W. Jackson and James W. Riddlesperger, Jr., "The Eisenhower Administration and the 1957 Civil Rights Act," in *Reexamining the Eisenhower Presidency*, ed. Shirley Anne Warshaw (Westport, CT: Greenwood, 1993), pp. 85–101.

reservoirs. Perhaps the best measure of Johnson's leadership came from one of his most bitter political opponents, Republican Barry Goldwater, whom Johnson defeated in the presidential election of 1964. Goldwater recalled: "He was a very good majority leader. He worked the Senate. . . . When Lyndon Johnson said 'This is going to be legislation,' you knew you weren't going to leave until it *was* legislation, until it was finished".[8]

The most recent Speaker of the House from Texas was James C. Wright of Fort Worth. Wright ascended to the speakership on January 6, 1987, and served until his resignation on May 31, 1989. He had served the previous decade as majority leader. Wright saw himself as a disciple of Sam Rayburn, selecting Rayburn's birthday as the occasion for his swearing in. But things had changed in Washington. The new speaker presided over an increasingly partisan House and there was a Republican president, Ronald Reagan. Wright was quite partisan, and he sought to serve as strongly as had Rayburn. Wright had built his reputation in Congress through his service on the Public Works Committee, bringing projects into the state and his district. He saw such activities as a high calling, simply a matter of being a faithful public servant. As Wright entered congressional leadership, though, the nature of the Texas delegation was changing. Instead of being a largely rural state such as the one known to Garner and Rayburn, Texas was a modern, urbanized state. And, in contrast to the one-party Democratic state his predecessors had represented, Texas had become a diverse state with a growing Republican presence. The unified delegation that had sponsored and supported Garner and Rayburn no longer existed. Wright's leadership in the House was to be short-lived, and he was forced to resign after only a little more than two years as speaker.[9]

In 1994, Texas became home to the new House majority leader, Congressman Richard Armey of the 26th district, when the Republicans took control of the House of Representatives. Armey, unlike previous Texas chamber leaders, is a Republican. Until his election to the House in 1984, he was an economics professor at the University of North Texas. He has become known for his strong conservative voice and his promotion of the 1994 Contract with America, of which he was a principal author. He also gained national attention with his support for closing excess military bases through the work of a bipartisan commission, his effective opposition to President Clinton's national health care plan, and his backing of a "flat-rate" federal income tax. By 1997, he was recognized by most observers as a very strong majority leader, and the *Wall Street Journal*

---

8. Goldwater, quoted in Merle Miller, *Lyndon: An Oral Biography* (New York: Putnam, 1980), p. 231. See also Rowland Evans and Robert Novak, *Lyndon B. Johnson: The Exercise of Power* (New York: New American Library, 1966).
9. Wright had to resign because of a series of ethics charges levied against him. See John M. Barry, *The Ambition and the Power: The Fall of Jim Wright* (New York: Viking, 1989).

characterized him as "one of his party's most prolific and effective idea machines".[10]

The powerful figures in the Texas delegation have not been limited to these chamber leaders; many others have had significant positions of power, including a number of committee chairs in both chambers. Most of them were Democrats, such as committee chairmen J.J. "Jake" Pickle and Jack Brooks in the House of Representatives and Lloyd Bentsen, one of the most admired members of the U.S. Senate and Finance Committee Chair, who became Secretary of the Treasury under President Bill Clinton. Following the 1994 election, Democrats Kika de la Garza and Henry B. Gonzalez lost the chairs of their respective committees when the Republicans took control. Yet the transition also allowed Texans in the Republican Party to assume leadership positions.

POWER OF THE TEXAS DELEGATION

Having the positions of chamber leaders is one measure of the power of the Texas delegation, but there are others as well. Since becoming a state, Texas has represented a formidable force in Congress. Its sheer geographic size and large population guarantee this, but exactly how powerful is the delegation in Congress? The measure of power and influence in Congress is complicated; several factors are consequential in assessing a state's power in the national legislature. These include the size of the state's delegation, the partisan unity and composition of the delegation, the number of leadership posts, including committee chairs, that the delegation commands, and the success of the delegation in directing federal funds into the state. Each of these factors will be addressed in turn.

Texas Delegation Size

Perhaps the largest controversy in the drafting of the U.S. Constitution was the basis of according representation in the national legislature. Less populous states wanted equal representation for all states, whereas more populous states preferred representation based on population. The Great Compromise resulted in today's system—a bicameral national legislature with equal representation in one chamber and representation based upon population in the other. Because every state is equally represented in the Senate, the size of a state's population is not a factor in determining senatorial influence. However, given its population base, Texas has an advantage in the House of Representatives. The Constitution requires that a census be taken every decade for the purpose of apportioning the House of Representatives. In virtually every reapportionment since

---

10. Michael Barone and Grant Ujifusa, *The Almanac of American Politics 1996* (Washington, D.C.: National Journal, 1995), pp. 1327–29.

TABLE 3.1

Relative Size of the Texas Delegation in the U.S. House of Representatives

Year	Number in Texas Delegation	Total Size of House	Texas's Share of Total Membership
1852	2	234	.9%
1862	4	241	1.7
1872	6	292	2.1
1882	11	325	3.4
1892	13	356	3.7
1902	16	386	4.1
1912	18	435	4.1
1922	18	435	4.1
1932	21	435	4.8
1942	21	435	4.8
1952	22	435	5.1
1962	23	435	5.3
1972	24	435	5.5
1982	27	435	6.2
1992	30	435	6.9

Source: Kenneth C. Martis and Gregory A. Elmes, *The Historical Atlas of State Power in Congress, 1790–1990* (Washington, DC: Congressional Quarterly Press, 1993).

Texas became a state, it gained seats in the national legislature.[11] While the size of the delegation has grown consistently, so has its size in relation to the membership of the house. In 1852, Texas had two members out of 234 members in the House of Representatives (constituting roughly 1 percent of total membership). By 1932 the proportion of the Texas delegation increased to 4.8 percent (see Table 3.1). In the 1990 reapportionment cycle, Texas held nearly 7 percent of the seats in the House of Representatives: this percentage of votes makes the Texas delegation a significant force in Congress.

A second implication directly related to the congressional delegation size is its role in presidential elections. Because the number of electoral college votes is based on the number of representatives a state has in Congress, those states with more representatives are given more prominence in presidential politics, and perhaps accorded more influence with presidential candidates (and the eventual president) as a result. The electoral college size has been established at 538 (the number is based on 435 representatives, 100 senators, and three electors from the District of Columbia). A presidential candidate must have a majority, or 270, votes in the electoral college to claim victory. Texas currently has 32 electors

11. Kenneth C. Martis and Gregory A. Elmes, *The Historical Atlas of State Power in Congress, 1790–1990* (Washington, D.C.: Congressional Quarterly Press, 1993). The 1920 reapportionment was delayed nearly ten years by rural interests who feared losing representation in the House of Representatives.

—more than 11 percent of the total needed. This total of votes means that aspiring presidential candidates will solicit support from Texas consistent with its being the second-most populous state. The importance of Texas's role can be illustrated by the state's record in presidential voting. Since 1932, there have been sixteen presidential elections. Over that sixty-five-year period, Texas voters have failed to cast their electoral votes for the winner only three times, in 1968, 1992, and 1996. Political scientists have attempted to assess the overall importance of each state in presidential elections, and have concluded that large states such as Texas have a much more important role in presidential politics than their proportion of the electoral vote would indicate.[12]

Disproportionate Power Accorded to the Texas Delegation

Throughout this century Texas has held prominence and power in Congress. In part, the influence can be attributed to the growing absolute size of the delegation, but other factors are relevant. The historical cohesiveness of the delegation as well as a common bonding factor—a general sense of pride in the state and a common denominator of wanting to advance causes of importance to all Texans—are important. Such spirit is illustrated by this statement made by former Speaker Jim Wright (a member of Congress for thirty-four years):

> . . . there has always been a high degree of collegiality in this [the Texas] delegation. I believe more than in any other delegation the Democratic delegation so long in power, and surely for these last forty consecutive years, has followed a practice in which we've had enough Democratic members to have some member of our delegation on every major committee. Those members assumed a responsibility to look out for the interests of the constituents represented by their Texas colleagues even though they might disagree on matters of principle with those individual members. Whenever a Texan had a problem relating to the parochial interests of his constituents he always had a champion, an intercessor and a friend on whatever committee the bill or the proposition came under. That actually applied without any regard to whether the members agreed with one another on philosophy. Our delegation always has been heterogeneous . . . but we have been able to work together when the interests of Texas were concerned. Because of that I think we have probably been the strongest and the most effective delegation in Congress.[13]

Further anecdotal evidence of the unity can be found in the Democratic delegation's long-standing tradition of having weekly lunches together, a tradition that has endured since the beginning of the tenure of Sam Rayburn. Those lunches led to a cohesiveness among Texans which in turn resulted in a strength greater than their numbers alone would

---

12. George Rabinowitz and Stuart Elaine Macdonald, "The Power of the States in U.S. Presidential Elections," *American Political Science Review* Vol. 80 (March 1986), pp. 65–87.
13. Authors' interview with James C. Wright, January 20, 1995, Fort Worth, Texas.

have given them. Former Speaker Wright summed up the disproportionate strength of the Texas delegation: "The very fact of a weekly meeting even though it was a Democratic group only, the very fact of someone always being on a major committee, the additional fact that Texas had adopted a habit of electing people for long periods of time gave our delegation great strength—far greater strength, I believe, than any other delegation even including California and New York which were larger."[14]

The delegation continues to work together on issues of importance to the state, even as the partisan divisions within the delegation grow more profound. For example, members of the delegation joined together early in 1997 to try to save the National Weather Service Office in Fort Worth. While they were ultimately unsuccessful, the example illustrates that state interests sometimes cross party lines.[15]

Committee Chairs, Congressional and Party Leaders

Texas has historically held a great number of standing committee chairs. When Sam Rayburn was asked why Texas always managed to have so many committee chairs, more than any other state, he replied, "we pick 'em young, we pick 'em honest, we send 'em there and we keep 'em there."[16] In virtually every Congress since 1958, Texas has had at least two members serving as chairs of standing committees in Congress. For much of this time period, committee chairs had great power over their area of legislative specialization. Even following the congressional reforms of the 1970s, which served to make the institution more democratic and decentralized (by creating independent, sovereign subcommittees), committee chairs remained powerful actors in the legislative game. Texans held many powerful committee chairs. This, coupled with the disproportionate number of congressional leaders hailing from Texas, made the delegation one of the nation's more important ones. Texans have held leadership posts throughout the modern congressional era. During the entire period Texans held multiple committee chairs, the high point coming in the late 1960s when five Texans chaired House committees.

Texas's Share of Federal Government's Spending

One way to test a delegation's power is to examine how successful the members are in representing their state in the allocation process of federal domestic spending. This "bringing home the bacon" sheds some light on the effectiveness of the delegation. An analysis of this type is rather complicated. One substantial factor complicating the matter is that a significant portion of the federal government's expenditures in states is determined by factors beyond the delegation's ability to influence. Ex-

---

14. Authors' interview with James C. Wright.
15. Michael E. Young, "U.S. Weather Service Office Might Close," *Dallas Morning News*, February 16, 1997, pp. A39 and A44.
16. As quoted by James C. Wright, authors' interview.

TABLE 3.2

Texas's Share of Federal Expenditures

Year	Percent of U.S. Population	Share of Federal Tax Burden	Share of Federal Domestic Spending
1970	5.44%	4.78%	5.89%
1974	5.53	5.1	5.31
1978	5.53	5.5	5.1
1982	6.4	6.9	5.32
1986	6.92	7.3	5.7
1990	6.8	6.06	5.81

Source: Michael Barone, Grant Ujifusa, and Douglas Matthews, *The Almanac of American Politics* (New York: Dutton, various years).

amples of this include most welfare expenditures. Rather than indicating the success of the delegation, they stem from demographic characteristics of the state (for example, the number of people living in poverty and the number of people seeking federal assistance). Further complicating this analysis is the fact that a seemingly ideal measure, per capita spending (federal spending gauged for population), is a poor measure because it consistently favors the geographically large yet less populated states, such as Alaska and Montana. Neither of these states would be seen as having historically powerful delegations, yet their states receive a disproportionate amount of federal per capita spending, which would seem to indicate the opposite. However, analysis of expenditures can shed light onto the complex question of congressional delegation power.

Table 3.2 displays the data in a form that counters some of the problems with state economic distribution analysis by presenting the information as percentages to allow comparisons. Texas does not fair exceptionally well with regard to government expenditures in relation to its percentage of the population or with regard to its share of the federal tax burden, despite the overall effectiveness of its congressional delegation. In 1990, Texas composed approximately 6.8 percent of the nation's population and contributed about 6 percent of the federal taxes, yet received only 5.8 percent of the federal government's expenditures. Twenty years ago the picture was a bit different. In 1970, the share of the expenditures exceeded the state's share of the tax burden as well as the proportion of the national population.

Another way to examine the delegation's success in obtaining federal government money without examining per capita spending as an absolute measure is to compare per capita spending in light of the state's size. When comparing Texas to other large states, the per capita spending is comparable.[17] These findings could be partly the result of changing federal budgetary politics and less of a reflection on the success of

17. See *Statistical Abstract of the United States: 1994* (Washington, D.C.: U.S. Department of Commerce, Bureau of the Census, 1994).

Figure 3.1

Partisan Composition of the Texas Delegation Since 1952

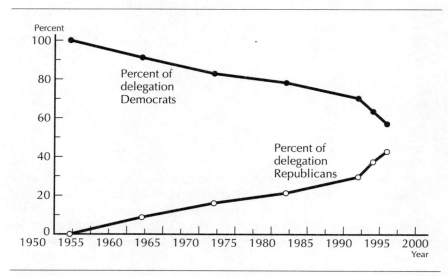

Source: *Congressional Directory* (Washington, D.C.: U.S. Government Printing Office, 1952, 1962, 1972, 1982, 1992, 1994, 1996).

the Texas delegation's efforts in bringing the federal money to their state. As more and more of the federal government's domestic budget is composed of nondiscretionary spending, it will become more and more difficult for a state's delegation to represent it in the budgetary process.

Changing Nature of the Texas Delegation

While the Texas delegation has become larger, it has also become more diversified along partisan lines. Since 1952, more and more Republicans have been elected to office (see Figure 3.1). The changing partisan composition has many implications for the power of the Texas delegation in Congress. If the two parties were ideologically at odds, the overall influence accorded to the delegation might decrease because the delegation would be divided, making it difficult to maximize on the advantage accorded by its absolute size. As a whole the delegation remains relatively conservative, but the ideological stances of the delegation have been changing. Analysis of the average ideological rating of the delegation over the past twenty years reveals some interesting patterns. The average ideological rating, as measured by scores calculated by the Americans for Democratic Action (ADA), has become less conservative than in ear-

FIGURE 3.2

Average Ideological Rating—
Texas Delegation, Democratic Delegation, and Republican Delegation

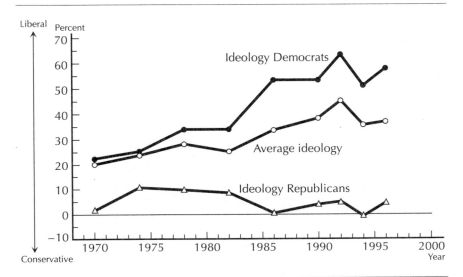

Source: Michael Barone, Grant Ujifusa, and Douglas Matthews, *The Almanac of American Politics* (New York: Dutton, various years). 1996 data from *ADA Today: A Newsletter for Liberal Action*, (Washington) vol. 51, no. 1.

lier periods (see Figure 3.2). The ADA rates members of Congress by their votes on key issues, with scores varying from 0 (most conservative) to 100 (most liberal).[18] For example, the average ideological score of the delegation in 1970 was 20.5. By 1992, the average score for the delegation reached its height, at 44.4. In 1994, the rates dipped to scores comparable to 1988 and 1990 scores, but they have more recently been rising again. The liberalizing trend may appear to indicate that the delegation was becoming uniformly less ideologically conservative. However, if one examines the ideological scores along partisan lines, a different picture emerges.

On average, Democrats are scoring higher in more recent years than

18. Americans for Democratic Action ratings were obtained from Michael Barone, Grant Ujifusa, and Douglas Matthews, *The Almanac of American Politics* (New York: Dutton, 1972); Barone, Ujifusa, and Matthews, *The Almanac of American Politics 1976* (New York: Dutton, 1975); Barone, Ujifusa, and Matthews, *The Almanac of American Politics 1980* (New York: Dutton, 1979); Barone and Ujifusa, *The Almanac of American Politics 1984* (Washington, D.C.: National Review, 1983); Barone and Ujifusa, *The Almanac of American Politics 1988* (Washington, D.C.: National Review, 1987); Barone and Ujifusa, *The Almanac of American Politics 1992* (Washington, D.C.: National Review, 1991); and *ADA Today* (Americans for Democratic Action) vol. 50, no. 1, pp. 9–10.

they had in the past, indicating that more liberal individuals are being elected to Congress, or that those already there are behaving differently than they had before. Such movement mirrors trends among all Southern Democrats in the House of Representatives. Part of the explanation might be that there were internal pressures from the Democratic leadership for party members to show more national party loyalty.[19] An alternative hypothesis for the polarization of ideology scores focuses on the changing nature of partisans in the South. As Southern Democrats became more like Northern Democrats (largely because of the defections to the Republican Party of the truly conservative, made possible with the emerging two-party competition), the voting behavior of Southern Democrats came to be more similar to that of their northern and western colleagues.[20] It will be interesting to see if Southern Democrats will revert to more conservative ways now that the Democrats do not control the House. In addition, the Republican members of Congress are very conservative, having average ideology scores that hover under 10. In 1996, the average Republican ADA rating was 4.6 and in 1995 it was 0.4. Texas Democrats and Republicans are becoming more polarized along ideological lines; however, the groups have common ground because by national standards, they are both relatively conservative.

The delegation has also become diversified in gender. The first woman elected to the modern Congress from Texas was Barbara Jordan in 1972. Representative Jordan was the first African-American elected from the South, the first African-American member of the Texas senate, and the first woman to be elected president pro tempore of the Texas senate.[21] Representative Jordan, a remarkable person, paved the way into political life for many women. One of the nine current female senators, Kay Bailey Hutchison, hails from Texas, and three of the fifty-one female representatives, Sheila Jackson Lee, Eddie Bernice Johnson, and Kay Granger, are Texans. Research has shown that the introduction of women into a legislative body changes the policy preferences and output of the institution.[22] Although the proportion of women of the Texas delegation to the House of Representatives is below the aggregate national average

---

19. David W. Rohde, "Something's Happening Here; What It Is Ain't Exactly Clear: Southern Democrats in the House of Representatives," in *Home Style and Washington Work: Studies of Congressional Politics*, ed. Morris P. Fiorina and David W. Rohde (Ann Arbor, MI: University of Michigan Press, 1989), pp. 137–63.
20. David Rohde, *Parties and Leaders in the Postreform House* (Chicago, IL: University of Chicago Press, 1991), pp. 45–8.
21. Michael Barone, Grant Ujifusa, and Douglas Matthews, *The Almanac of American Politics* (New York: Dutton, 1973), p. 1003.
22. See for example, Sue Thomas and Susan Welch, "The Impact of Gender on Activities and Priorities of State Legislators," *Western Political Quarterly* vol. 44 (June 1991), pp. 445–56; Sue Thomas, "The Impact of Women on State Legislative Policies," *Journal of Politics* vol. 53 (1991), pp. 958–76; Rebecca Tillet and Debbie Krafcheck, *Factsheets on Women's Political Process* (American Council of Life Insurance and National Women's Political Caucus).

(approximately 12 percent of the House is female compared with only 10 percent of the delegation), the fact that one of the nine female senators is from Texas is a positive sign with regard to the diversification of the delegation. Given the general concern of the population over the fact that women still remain the most underrepresented group in American politics, the continued diversification of the delegation will be significant in shaping Texas's role in the future.

Texas is an ethnically diverse state: 11.9 percent of Texans are of African-American heritage and 25.4 percent are of Hispanic origin. The Texas delegation has begun to reflect that diversity: as of 1997, it includes five Hispanic representatives (six until the death of Congressman Frank Tejeda in early 1997) and two African-Americans. Although minority representation in Congress is not proportional to the population, it is at an all-time high. One reflection of diversity is the election in 1992 of Henry Bonilla, the first Republican minority representative from Texas.

The 1996 Election and Beyond

In November 1994, the general election brought about a change of power in Congress. For the first time in forty years, the Republican Party took control of both chambers of the national legislature. At first glance, such a turn of events might be seen as bad news for Texas, since the House of Representatives delegation is still controlled by Democrats. However, this is not the case, and with the continued dominance of the Republican Party in Congress following the 1996 election, the situation remains positive for Texans in Congress. Both Texas senators are Republicans, and the House majority leader is Republican Richard Armey of Flower Mound. In addition, Republican Bill Archer of Houston continues to hold the reins of arguably the most important committee in Congress, the House Committee on Ways and Means, and Tom DeLay is the majority whip, third in power among House Republicans. With Republicans taking such important positions of leadership, Texas actually appears to have increased its influence in Congress. The Washington insider newspaper *Roll Call* rates the power of state delegations in Congress. Despite the loss in recent years of Jim Wright (through resignation), Lloyd Bentsen in the Senate (through his stepping up to head the Department of the Treasury), Jake Pickle (through retirement), and Jack Brooks (through defeat in the 1994 election), the overall power rating of the state delegation went up in 1994 with the 104th Congress. After California, Texas ranks as having the second-most powerful delegation in Congress. Such status is perhaps fitting, because Texas has become the second-most populous state in the union. The movement to second place was a step up from third in the 103rd Congress. However, in the 105th Congress, the delegation slipped in power from second place back to third, as there were eight retirements by veteran members in 1996, several of whom held high-ranking committee positions.[23]

The nature of the delegation, however, has changed dramatically in two ways. First, there is much more division within the delegation than ever before. As mentioned above, the previous source of influence of Texans in Congress came from the group solidarity as well as from its absolute size and having members in leadership positions. Now, with seventeen Democrats and thirteen Republicans in the House delegation[24] and two Republicans in the Senate, and the increasingly liberal ideology of Texas Democrats, that solidarity may very well be a thing of the past. Instead of working together, Texans in Congress might well be working at cross purposes.

The Texans in new leadership positions also define the representative role in a different way than did leaders in the past. Rather than the Garner, Rayburn, Johnson, and Wright models of "bringing home the bacon," these leaders focus more on pursuing national agenda issues. Said Armey of pork barrel politics, "I think that tradition is over in American politics."[25] Such statements may also reflect that the current Texans in leadership represent more affluent suburban districts where federal spending is not as crucial, unlike the rural districts of Garner and Rayburn or the urban district of Wright. For example, the median household income in the Republican leaders' suburban districts are as follows: $40,533 in Armey's district, $42,157 in Archer's district, and $40,654 in Delay's district, all significantly above the national average of $30,000.[26] As a result, their constituents would benefit from a tax reduction such as Representative Armey's "flat tax" proposal rather than federal pork barrel legislation. In other words, these representatives have constituency interests in mind just as did previous leaders, but the policies they propose take a slightly different form.

Another note of interest is that the old Texas strategy of electing people young and keeping them there for a long time is under challenge from two fronts. First, the movement to limit terms in Congress, one which has great current support, would mean that the tactics that got House speakers Garner, Rayburn, and Wright to their positions, and current majority leader Armey and Ways and Means Committee Chair Bill

---

23. Benjamin Sheffner, "After Revolution, Who Has Clout?" *Roll Call* (January 23, 1995), pp. B8–9. Sheffner, "Which States Carry the Clout in the Post-Dole Congress?" *Roll Call* web site, www.rollcall.com/refdes/clout.html.
24. We consider Frank Tejeda's district to be Democratic since most analysts believe it will remain under control of the Democrats. The partisan distribution is seventeen Democrats and thirteen Republicans following the December 1996 special elections mandated by the Supreme Court ruling that found several Texas minority access districts to be unconstitutional.
25. Ron Hutcheson, "Texas Maintains Clout on Capitol Hill," *Fort Worth Star Telegram* (December 11, 1994), p. A16.
26. Michael Barone and Grant Ujifusa, *The Almanac of American Politics 1996* (Washington, D.C.: National Journal, 1995), pp. xxxvi, 1283, 1318, and 1329.

Archer to theirs, might no longer work. If members of Congress can serve a limit of twelve years, the technique of "paying dues" as a strategy for reaching the top might be supplanted by other techniques. Even if term limits are not implemented, the tradition of a one-party state no longer exists. It might be that senators and representatives will find it increasingly difficult to remain in Congress for long periods of time.

No matter what changes come as a consequence of the changing Congress, Texas is assured of having a position of influence. Both parties now seem to be developing leaders, and the increase in population assures a strong delegation in the future. The traditions of John Nance Garner, Sam Rayburn, Lyndon Johnson, and Jim Wright are now in the past, but their legacies of Texas leadership in Congress may foreshadow the accomplishments of the new generation of Texas leaders.

PART II

Institutions

4
The Texas Governor: Weak or Strong?

CHERYL D. YOUNG AND JOHN J. HINDERA
TEXAS TECH UNIVERSITY

THE MANY TEXAS EXECUTIVES

Texas has several statewide elective officials who perform executive functions and they all have more or less independent power bases. The reason for these multiple power levers in Texas politics goes back to the state constitution, which incorporated fears of a powerful state executive and so divided power among many points. Because of that constitutional goal, Texas has eight statewide elected officials who primarily perform what could be called executive or administrative functions. In addition, there are eighteen statewide judicial offices encompassing the Texas Supreme Court and the Texas Court of Criminal Appeals, and one statewide office that is primarily legislative, the office of lieutenant governor. These statewide offices are listed in Figure 4.1.

The administrative officers include the governor, the attorney general, the comptroller of public accounts, the commissioner of the general land office, the commissioner of the agriculture department, and three railroad commissioners.

It would be possible to have a stronger governor by having fewer administrative officers. The governor would campaign statewide and would appoint the officers necessary to run all the departments of government. If elected officers were desired, candidates for statewide offices could run on slates led by the gubernatorial candidate. Candidates for offices on the slate below that of governor would then be dependent on the governor for their election.

Rather than the executive officers being part of a team, they have often proven to be competitors: it has been common in recent years for the governor and the attorney general to be political rivals. In Texas, the power of the governor is such that the gubernatorial budget is widely ignored by the legislature. Because the lieutenant governor and the speaker have independent power bases, their views matter greatly in the legislature and the governor's voice is accordingly weakened. In the Texas Legislature, there is no leadership position in the house or senate whose duties include carrying out the governor's programs.

As the following chapter points out, however, the office of governor is not powerless. In addition to being the most visible state officer and being

FIGURE 4.1

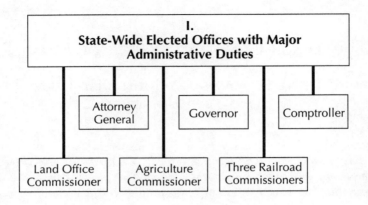

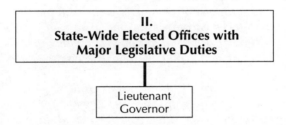

The Speaker is elected from a district like other representatives and is then elected Speaker by a majority of the members of the Texas House of Representatives

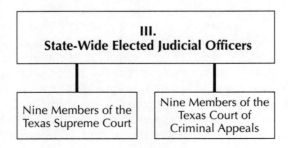

able to veto legislation, the governor has extraordinary powers of appointment. Indeed, it is that power of appointment that enables the governor to impose a policy agenda upon the bureaucracy. Governor Ann Richards, for example, appointed approximately 2,400 people to state boards, commissions, executive positions, and vacant judicial posts. Some of these positions are of minor importance, but some are of great importance and visibility. Taken together, these appointments can have major effects on state policy. Governor Richards, for example, appointed a gay person to the Funeral Service Commission, which regulates funerals in Texas; the appointment was in response to concerns about how funeral directors were handling bodies of AIDS victims. One appointment that Governor Richards made to the University of Texas Board of Regents, which governs the University of Texas, was clearly to provide financial expertise in the university's handling of its endowment funds.

Thus, although Texas governors are not as powerful as they are in many states, they are not powerless: that is why the battles for the governor's office in Texas are very expensive and hard-fought. The powers of the governor are explored further in this chapter.

Since Reconstruction, the powers of the governor of Texas have been considered weak, especially when compared to the powers of other state governors or of the Texas Legislature.[1] Using several different measures, researchers have consistently found the Texas governor lacking in both formal and informal power. In fact, a 1983 study of gubernatorial appointment, budget, removal, and organizational powers ranked the Texas governor 49th in the nation.[2] Only South Carolina's governor was considered less powerful. The Texas governor also ranked 49th in a 1990 study of gubernatorial authority. In that study, only the governor of Rhode Island was found to be less powerful.[3]

Over the years, Texas governors have offered conflicting assessments about the lack of formal powers. Governor O'Daniel claimed state agencies could ignore his requests and could tell him to "go jump into the lake."[4] Governor Allan Shivers agreed with O'Daniel, saying that the position was "something of a paper tiger."[5] However, Governor Shivers's attitude changed somewhat after he left office. As the former governor of Texas, Shivers said that "if the governor has prestige, i.e., stands

1. Richard H. Kraemer and Charldean Newell, *Essentials of Texas Politics* (St. Paul, MN: West Publishing Company, 1980), p. 97.
2. Virginia Gray, Herbert Jacob, and Kenneth N. Vines, eds., *Politics in the American States: A Comparative Analysis*, 4th ed. (Boston: Little, Brown 1983), pp. 458–59.
3. Thad L. Beyle, "Governors" in *Politics in the American States*, 5th ed. Virginia Gray, Herbert Jacob, and Robert B. Albritton, eds. (Glenview, IL: Scott Foresman, 1990), p. 228.
4. Kenneth R. Mladenka and Kim Quaile Hill, *Texas Government: Politics and Economics* (Belmont, CA: Wadsworth, Inc., 1986), p. 140.
5. Fred Gantt, Jr., *The Impact of the Texas Constitution on the Executive* (Houston, TX: Institute for Urban Studies, University of Houston 1973), p. 7.

high with the public, he can be persuasive with other officers who would hesitate to face an open break with him."[6] Governor Price Daniel agreed with Shivers's later statement, saying that most independently elected state officers "will work on nearly anything that is for the good of the state, and they will help the governor in his program."[7]

Are the dismal perceptions of the Texas gubernatorial institution accurate? Or are the governor's powers underestimated? The following analysis of the institution and the image of the Texas governor suggests that at least the potential for political power exists in the elaborate organizational scheme called the "executive branch" of Texas.

THE EXECUTIVE BRANCH INSTITUTION

Several provisions in the Texas Constitution suggest that the governor's low power rankings are inaccurate. Article IV of the post–Civil War Constitution of 1876 delegates to the governor the following significant judicial, legislative, and administrative responsibilities and powers:

Judicial:
1. to grant reprieves, commutations of punishments, and pardons
2. to remit fines and forfeitures upon recommendation of the Board of Pardons and Paroles
3. to revoke conditional pardons

Legislative:
1. to convene special sessions of the legislature for specific purposes[8]
2. to deliver to the legislature a biennial report on the condition of all public money required to be raised by taxes
3. to approve or veto any bill passed by the legislature[9]
4. to appoint with the advice and consent of the state senate replacements for any vacancies in state or district elective office, except the legislature, until the next general election

Administrative:
1. to issue a writ of election to fill vacancies in the state legislature, U.S. House of Representatives, or U.S. Senate
2. to appoint (with the advice and consent of the state senate) state officials and members of state boards, commissions, and task forces
3. to serve as commander in chief of the state's military.

---

6. Fred Gantt, Jr., *The Chief Executive in Texas: A Study in Gubernatorial Leadership* (Austin, TX: University of Texas Press, 1964), p. 117.
7. Ibid., p. 116.
8. Governors frequently call special sessions for the legislature. Governor Price Daniel called eight, John Connally called two, Preston Smith called four, Dolph Briscoe called two, and Bill Clements called three.
9. The governor has the line item veto, which allows him or her to delete specific program expenditures without vetoing an entire bill. In contrast to the federal executive, the governor does not have a pocket veto. A pocket veto allows an executive to block a bill by refusing to sign it before the legislature adjourns.

The original 1876 provisions have been enhanced by a 1972 amendment replacing the governor's two-year term with a four-year term. In addition, the Texas Constitution does not limit the number of terms a governor can serve.

The 1876 Constitution, however, did create a plural executive, thus limiting some of the formal powers of the governor and eliminating many other opportunities for exertion of informal power. Texas's variation on the plural executive theme is characterized by an inordinate number of the state-wide elections for the following executive offices:

1. The lieutenant governor, with only 25 employees, is often considered the most influential position in Texas government. The lieutenant governor's influence arises from his or her constitutional and statutory responsibilities to direct legislative business in the senate, chair both the Legislative Budget Board and Legislative Council, function as vice-chair of the Legislative Audit Committee, and serve as a member of the Legislative Redistricting Board. The lieutenant governor is part of the senate committee on appointments, breaks roll call ties, assigns bills, and serves as acting governor when the governor is out of state. The lieutenant governor's budget is allocated within the annual appropriation of the state senate, which in 1997 was almost $24 million.
2. The attorney general defends the constitution and laws of Texas, represents the state in litigation, issues legal opinions upon request, and serves as legal counsel to the governor and every other entity in the executive branch. The attorney general's office employs over 3,600 people divided into 14 different litigation divisions. The attorney general's 1997 budget was almost $251 million.
3. The comptroller of public accounts is the state's tax administrator and tax collector. As such, the comptroller heads an agency of 2,843 employees and a 1997 budget of over $168 million. The comptroller is responsible for accounting for all state funds and for providing any budgetary research required for revenue estimation and certification. The comptroller assumed greater responsibilities in state investments and excise tax collection when the State Treasurer's Office was abolished in 1996.
4. The commissioner of the General Land Office (GLO) supervises and holds title to almost 12 million acres of land; inventories rare and endangered plants and animals; promotes conservation programs; administers the repository of all original land grants, patents, and other documents; and helps veterans buy land and homes in the state. The GLO employs 6,009 individuals and had a 1997 budget of over $38 million.
5. The commissioner of agriculture supervises the more than 540 employees of the Department of Agriculture, which promotes the sales

of agricultural commodities. The Department regulates the distribution, use, and disposal of pesticides. It also controls the quality of seed sold in the state. The Department provides various financial and commercial services to agricultural businesses. Its 1997 budget was almost $23 million.
6. The three elected members of the Railroad Commission and its over 840 employees regulate the railroads, surface mining, and the oil and gas industry. With a 1997 budget of over $47 million, the commission protects property rights, natural resources, and the general environment.[10] This relatively inconspicuous agency is generally considered one of the most powerful institutions in the state.

The plural executive arrangement described above is not unusual. In fact, 43 states directly elect their attorneys general, 42 elect their lieutenant governors, 38 elect their treasurers, and 37 elect their secretaries of state.[11]

When an executive branch is filled with so many independently elected officers, the chief executive may actually be a ruler without a kingdom. One executive branch officer can not depend upon the loyalty of any other because each elected officer has a different constituency. The voters who elected the governor do not always have the same ideas about oil and gas policy as do the voters who elected the railroad commissioners. In addition, members of the plural executive do not necessarily share the same party affiliation. When members of the plural executive are opposition partisans, the governor is not able to use party leadership to coordinate diverse interests. Members of the plural executive have their own reelection campaigns to consider. Often, members of the plural executive have ambitions for the governorship themselves. When Attorney General Jim Mattox decided to run in the Democratic gubernatorial primary in 1990 against Ann Richards, even partisanship could not keep their campaign civil. Often some members of the plural executive have more job experience than the governor. That longer tenure may confer more organizational power. For example, Lieutenant Governor Bob Bullock has served in the state legislature, as comptroller, as Texas secretary of state, and as a long-time lieutenant governor. His fears about encountering a new governor are probably slight.

The existence of a plural executive indicates a weak governor and a competitive executive branch. Each member of the plural executive has the potential to exert considerable political clout and economic influence independent of the governor. If unified, these officeholders can depreciate the power potential of the 196 employees and $79.5 million budget available to the Governor's Office. However, these independently elected

---

10. Marilyn P. Duncan, ed. *Guide to Texas State Agencies*, 9th ed. (Austin, TX: L. B. J. School of Public Affairs, The University of Texas at Austin, 1996).
11. John A. Straayer, Robert D. Wrinkle, and J. L. Polinard, *State and Local Politics* (New York: St. Martin's Press, 1994), p. 125.

officers do not often work in unison against the governor as they are just as competitive with each other as they are with the governor. The possibility of a strong plural executive is further weakened by the constitutional provisions previously mentioned and by the importance of the governor's image in the public's mind.

Additionally, if plural executive officers were as powerful as their descriptions suggest, why would so many of them leave their posts to run for and/or become governor? Governors James Hogg and Preston Smith left the lieutenant governorship to run for governor. Governor Beauford Jester abandoned the Railroad Commission to assume the post. Before becoming governor, Mark White was the state's attorney general. His ascension to the governor's mansion involved tough primary challenges from fellow Democrats—and fellow plural executive members—Land Commissioner Bob Armstrong and Railroad Commissioner Buddy Temple. The governorship has even lured some Texans from Washington, D.C. Joseph D. Sayers, for example, left Congress to become the first Texas governor of the twentieth century. Price Daniel even left the U.S. Senate to successfully run for the governorship.

THE EXECUTIVE BRANCH IMAGE

The governor is the most visible political figure in the state. In contrast to the formal organization of the executive branch, the image of the Texas governor has historically signified strength and leadership. The informal qualifications for the job suggested by history are that the governor should be white, Anglo Saxon, Protestant, male, conservative, active in the Democratic party, involved in civic affairs, trained as an attorney, and experienced in state government. As a state symbol, on the other hand, the governors are expected to personify several other traits of which Texans are very fond. Texans expect their governors to be independent and to have integrity. Texans also seem to appreciate a gubernatorial exhibition of the rough, aggressive persona of the Texas cowboy, or even the Texas cowgirl. That caricature helps to endear most governors, male or female, to the general public.

The image of a strong governor endures and fosters great folklore that Texans have passed on for generations. Governor and former President of the Republic of Texas Sam Houston guided Texas through its admission to the United States and then through the difficult pre–Civil War years. Governor E. J. Davis was such a strong governor that his dictatorial abuses of power actually led to the 1876 Constitution's provisions for a plural executive.[12] Although controversial, governors James "Farmer Jim" and Miriam "Ma" Ferguson were both popular because of the bravado they exuded even after Farmer Jim became the first, and

---

12. Eugene W. Jones, Joe E. Ericson, Lyle C. Brown, and Robert S. Trotter, Jr., *Practicing Texas Politics*, 6th ed. (Boston: Houghton Mifflin Company, 1986), p. 289.

only, Texas governor to be impeached and convicted.[13] Texas governors Allan Shivers and John Connally are more recent examples of governors with a strong image. According to James E. Anderson, "if strength is measured by the force of their personalities, respect from legislators, and accomplishing what they desired," governors Shivers and Connally were as powerful, it not more powerful, than other states' governors who enjoyed greater formal grants of political and administrative power.[14] In fact, Governor John Connally's image reached superhuman status among Texans when he survived a bullet wound during the 1963 assassination of President John F. Kennedy in Dallas.

Even the most recent officeholders have continued the trend of strong images. Governor Ann Richards pushed the state legislature to consider one of her pet projects, school finance reform. At present, Governor George W. Bush emanates the strong governor image in his dealings with the state legislature and in his pursuit of national recognition for the state and for himself.

Is the Governor Weak or Strong?

As Texas enters the twenty-first century, the Texas governorship remains challenged by the independently elected members of the plural executive. The governor must still rely on informal powers to accomplish his or her goals and have substantial bargaining, leadership, and persuasion skills in order to achieve anything while in office. However, a number of recent changes have occurred that suggest an invigoration of the governorship. These changes involve the governor's activities: (1) in national party politics; (2) with the media; (3) as chief administrator; (4) with the budget; and (5) with appointment powers.

National Politics

Recent Texas governors have sought greater visibility in national politics. Democrat Ann Richards and Republican George W. Bush each played prominent roles in their respective national party conventions. Both were stationed on "the big platform" during prime time television coverage. Both gave speeches before the convention delegates and to national audiences. Both have been touted as potential presidential or vice presidential candidates. Involvement in national politics and in the national party organization increases the governor's power as chief of the state party organization. It also provides the governor with a bigger stage for performance of his or her symbolic role as ceremonial chief of state.

---

13. Rupert N. Richardson, Ernest Wallace, and Adrian N. Anderson, *Texas: The Lone Star State*, 4th ed. (Englewood Cliffs, NJ: Prentice-Hall, Inc., 1981), pp. 377–79.
14. James E. Anderson, Richard W. Murray, and Edward L. Farley, *Texas Politics: An Introduction*, 4th ed. (New York: Harper and Row, 1984), p. 197.

The Media

As Texas governors have taken more prominent positions in national politics, state and local media interest in the office and the officeholder has been resuscitated. Governor W. Lee "Pappy" O'Daniel was the first real media governor. His radio program featured the Light Crust Doughboys and advertised not only his Hillbilly Flour, but also his gubernatorial aspirations.[15] Years later, governors William "Bill" Clements and Mark White instituted weekly press conferences and a monthly television program, entitled "The Governor's Report." Governor White believed so strongly in the power of the media that he spent $200,000 on commercials urging citizens to write their legislators about a particular utility regulation he wanted passed.[16] In his first term, Governor George Bush has prompted media attention to his administration in several ways. He has established within the Executive Office a Communications Office to manage his media relations. The Communications Office schedules interviews, writes press releases, and prepares speeches for both the governor and Mrs. Bush. Governor Bush has also cultivated local press attention by making numerous appearances in towns and cities across the state. He has also made several appearances on national television shows, such as "The CBS Sunday Morning Show.

The Administration

Texas governors have increased their power relative to the legislature as well as other elected members of the executive branch through an enlargement of their role as chief administrator. Recent governors have made more efficient use of their office budgets while at the same time increasing their office staff. Those administrative units provide valuable support to the governor. They allow for a more immediate connection with the governor's constituents and ensure that the governor's policies are promptly and properly implemented by state agencies and commissions. The offices advise the governor on problems and develop policy options. They also serve as the governor's primary liaisons to state agencies, commissions, and the state legislature.

The Budget

The governor is the chief budget officer for the state. As such, he or she has a mixed bag of powers and opportunities that are growing. The governor is charged with the responsibility of preparing a state budget for legislative consideration and must also review agency financial reports twice a year. Governor Bush has an Office of Budget and Planning to help him perform these duties. The governor's budget office works

---

15. Richard Morehead, *Fifty Years in Texas Politics: From Roosevelt to Reagan, from the Fergusons to Clements* (Burnet, TX: Eakin Press, 1982), p. 31.
16. Wendell M. Bedichek and Neal Tannahill, *Public Policy in Texas*, 2nd ed. (Glenview, IL: Scott Foresman and Company, 1986), p. 221.

with the legislative budget office in issuing joint budget instructions to state agencies and conducting joint budget hearings.

Texans have contemplated the governor's budgetary role in the past. In 1981, Texas voters had an opportunity to increase the governor's budgetary power. However, voters rejected a constitutional amendment to create a State Finance Management Committee. The members of that committee would have been the governor, lieutenant governor, house speaker, and house and senate budget committee chairs.[17] In 1987, the legislature bypassed voters and gave the governor direct budget execution authority. Governor Bush can now respond to fiscal emergencies by reallocating existing appropriations in a number of ways. He can direct agencies to spend appropriations for purposes other than those statutorily defined and change the timing of an agency's appropriations. The governor can even transfer appropriations from one state agency to another. The 1987 legislative authorization actually allows for more active gubernatorial management of state appropriations than would have been the case had the 1981 amendment passed. According to the 1987 legislation, the governor does not have to sit on a committee with other members of the plural executive, nor does he have to share budgetary authority with them.

Appointments

A fifth, and perhaps the most important, area in which the Texas governor is asserting more power is through appointments to state commissions. Over 4,000 appointment opportunities occur during a governor's four-year term. Some positions are critical to the functioning of the state. Other appointments, such as those to the Texas State Board of Plumbing Examiners, may only be salient for certain constituencies.

The governor appoints boards and commissions that regulate admission into over twenty-seven different occupations, including chiropractors, funeral directors, plumbers, polygraph examiners, private investigators, and pest control professionals. The governor's appointments to public health and welfare agencies handle a wide range of public policies involving the needs of such groups as the aged, the disabled, and the homeless. There are also appointments to business agencies, conservation agencies, public safety boards, ethics commissions, public employee agencies, finance bodies, technology agencies, education agencies, energy boards, and cultural bodies.

Through the ability to appoint various commission members, commission chairs, and agency executive directors, the governor has many opportunities to informally influence many types of policies. Most commissions are composed of nonsalaried members appointed by the governor with the advice and consent of the senate. Senate approval is

---

17. Eugene W. Jones, Joe E. Ericson, Lyle C. Brown, and Robert S. Trotter, Jr., *Practicing Texas Politics*, 6th ed. (Boston: Houghton Mifflin, Company, 1986), p. 299.

usually essential. Even if the governor makes an appointment when the legislature is not in session, senate approval must still be garnered. Recess appointments must be submitted for confirmation to the senate within ten days after the senate convenes for either a regular or special session. Besides the requirement of senate approval, the governor's appointments are typically for six-year terms, which overlap the governor's four-year term. These staggered terms prevent the governor from appointing a majority on any commission until late in his or her first term. Some commissions require appointees from specific occupational groups. For example, the governor appoints nine of the thirty members of the Council on Offenders with Mental Impairments. Four of those nine appointees must have expertise in mental health, mental retardation, or development disabilities. One of those four must be a psychiatrist. Of the other five appointees, one must be a criminal defense attorney, one a representative from a pretrial services agency, and one a criminal justice system expert. In addition, some commissions require members with specific demographic characteristics. Two of the eighteen members of the Texas Commission on the Arts, for example, must live in counties with less than 500,000 residents. Some appointees must come from professional lists supplied by organizations. For example, each of the fourteen members of the Health Professions Council must come from a different health care organization. Finally, most appointments have express conflict of interest and lobbying restrictions so that, for example, the members of the Texas Alcoholic Beverage Commission may not have any financial connections with any liquor business.

The Texas governor also makes an important appointment that most state governors do not. In Texas, the governor appoints the secretary of state, an elected position in thirty-seven states. Once considered a "glorified keeper of certain state records," the secretary of state is now a much more significant member of the plural executive.[18] The secretary of state not only cares for the Great Seal of Texas but also affixes the governor's signature on proclamations, commissions, and certificates. More importantly, the secretary of state performs several political and economic functions that are fundamental sources of political power. He or she registers lobbyists, certifies elections, and administers campaign reporting and disclosure laws. The secretary also administers the Uniform Commercial Code, issues corporate charters, and publishes the *Texas Register*.

Most governors understand the relevance of the appointment power. Governor Ann Richards lobbied the legislature in order to secure the power to appoint the commissioner of education, a health and human services commissioner, and the executive director of the Department of

---

18. Kenneth R. Mladenka, and Kim Quaile Hill, *Texas Government: Politics and Economics* (Belmont, CA: Wadsworth, Inc., 1986), p. 145.

Commerce. All three positions have a considerable impact on the well-being of the state of Texas and its citizenry. The commissioner of education supervises the Texas Education Agency and the largest 1997 budget of any Texas agency, $10,647,732,800. The commissioner serves a four-year term that overlaps with the term of the governor who appointed him or her. The health and human services commissioner directs 79 employees and a budget over $5 million. During a two-year term, the commissioner coordinates budget requests and strategic planning from every major health and human services agency in the state. Both the education and health and human services commissioners receive the highest salary provided a state employee, $156,014. The director of the Department of Commerce also serves a two-year term, working with over 300 employees and a 1997 budget of over $335 million. The Department of Commerce administers a variety of economic development programs dealing with trade, job training, music, film, enterprise zones, and tourism.

Until 1980, the governor could only terminate members of his or her personal staff of about 500 employees. If the governor wanted an agency commissioner removed, she or he had to rely on either the state legislature or the state courts. People whom the governor had nominated were removable only through impeachment, address, or *quo warranto* proceedings. Impeachment, the most common form of removal, did not even require the governor's involvement since the proceeding began and ended in the legislature. The second most common form of removal, the address, required marginal involvement on the part of the governor. An address could be accomplished only if the governor successfully convinced the legislature to remove a district or appellate judge from office. If two-thirds of both legislative chambers agreed, the judge was removed. In a *quo warranto* proceeding, the least common form of removal, the governor had only a spectator's role. The attorney general began the legal procedure while the courts carried out the actual removal.[19]

In 1980, the legislature gave the governor greater power to remove members of state boards and commissions. The governor can now remove appointees. If the appointment originally required senate confirmation, the governor must show cause and get the approval of two-thirds of the state senators voting.[20] If the appointment did not require senate confirmation, the appointee can be removed by the governor without senate involvement.

---

19. Kraemer and Newell, 1980, p. 103.
20. James W. Lamare, *Texas Politics: Economics, Power, and Policy*, 2nd ed. (St. Paul, MN: West Publishing Company, 1985), p. 137.

The Appointment Power

The ability to make appointments to over 125 executive branch agencies is a major source of power for the governor. Each appointment, however, does not have equal weight. Any variation from the typical organizational structure indicates either an increase or decrease in overall gubernatorial power.

The typical arrangement for a bureaucratic organization in Texas involves an agency and a commission. The agency is composed of the full-time staff and is charged with the actual implementation of public policy. Usually, an executive director manages the day-to-day operations of the agency. The executive director is normally selected by a commission, the agency's governing body. The commission does not get involved with daily management activities, but it does supervise the overall planning and production of the agency. Most commissions are composed of six or nine members, who are appointed to six-year terms by the governor with the advice and consent of the senate. Most commissions are led by chairpersons who are specifically designated by the governor.

Nearly all of the executive branch agencies were created by the state legislature, not the Texas Constitution. They were organized under statutory laws, such as the Agricultural Code, Health and Human Services Code, and Alcoholic Beverages Code. Consequently, the agencies were not created simultaneously and are not uniform in their structure. Sometimes, the governor acquires more statutory authority over the governance and management of executive branch agencies. Sometimes the governor is granted less authority.

The governor has the greatest degree of power when he or she is the commission's chairperson and appoints commission members and the agency's executive director. Less than 2 percent of Texas executive branch agencies are arranged this way. The governor has slightly less organizational power when he or she selects the commission's chairperson and members, but not the executive director. Almost half of the state's agencies are organized this way. A third agency configuration gives the governor the power to appoint commission members who in turn select their chairperson and the agency's executive director. This occurs in about 30 percent of all agencies. About 10 percent of the agencies are arranged so that the governor appoints some, but not all, of the agency's commissioners. When this occurs, the governor usually shares appointment powers with the lieutenant governor, the speaker of the house, and/or a professional organization.

The Influence of the Governor's Appointment Power

The image of the strong Texas governor is becoming much more of a reality than the plural executive arrangement would suggest. Much of the increase in real power derives from the governor's appointment and removal powers. Through increases in the number of appointments and enlargment of commission jurisdictions, the governor is now able to counter the power of other members of the plural executive.

The governor can invade the jurisdiction of the attorney general in several ways. The governor chairs the Criminal Justice Policy Council, an agency charged with creating a more effective and efficient criminal justice system. The governor can also impose upon the powers of the attorney general through appointments to the Commission on Jail Standards, the Texas Juvenile Probation Commission, the Texas Commission on Law Enforcement Officer Standards and Education, the Council on Offenders with Mental Impairments, and the Council on Sex Offenders Treatment. The attorney general does not even serve as an *ex officio* member of any of these organizations.[21]

The comptroller of public accounts must also endure gubernatorial intrusions into his or her areas of expertise. The governor chairs both the Texas Bond Review Board and the State Council on Competitiveness. The governor also appoints members to the Finance Commission, the Texas Public Finance Authority Commission, the State Depository Board, and the State Securities Board. Each bureaucracy can claim, or exert some influence over, the general jurisdiction of the comptroller.

Similarly, the commissioner of the General Land Office and the commissioner of agriculture must suffer gubernatorial intrusions. Through appointments to the State Preservation Board, the Texas Parks and Wildlife Department, the Texas Water Development Board, and the Texas Natural Resource Conservation Commission, the governor is able to influence the activities of the General Land Office. As chair of the State Preservation Board, the governor can exert direct influence over the very building in which the General Land Office is housed. The commissioner of agriculture is similarly influenced by the governor's appointments to the Texas Food and Fibers Commission, Agriculture Resources Protection Authority, and Structural Pest Control Board.

Through the Committee on Energy Policy, the governor is even able to counter some of the authority the Railroad Commission exerts over energy policy. Created in 1993, the committee works with the Texas Energy Coordination Council to develop state energy policies and encourage research. The committee is composed of eight members: the governor, the lieutenant governor, the speaker of the house, the land

---

21. An *ex officio* member is a member of a commission by virtue of his or her office and does not require an appointment or further confirmation proceedings.

commissioner, the chair of the house committee on energy resources, the chair of the senate natural resources committee, a public utility commissioner, and one member of the Railroad Commission.

The influence of the governor may appear to be modest if the focus is exclusively on the policy adoption or policy implementation stages of the policy process. If however, the agenda setting and policy formulation stages are acknowledged, the governor appears much more powerful. Appointments to commissions and selection of commission chairpersons and/or agency executive directors enable the governor to have a great deal of influence over: (1) what policy problems appear on an agency's agenda; and (2) what policy solutions are formulated for those problems. If the governor can control the formative stages of the policy process, domination in the latter stages may be less critical. The governor may have already set the tone of the policy before it is even adopted, much less implemented.

5
Leadership, Power, and Emerging Partisanship in the Texas Legislature

Gregory S. Thielemann
University of Texas at Dallas

At first glance, the Texas Legislature looks like many other state legislatures. It is divided into two houses based upon single-member districts. The house of representatives comprises 150 members, each elected for two-year terms. The senate comprises 31 members serving overlapping four-year terms (see Figure 5.A). Regular legislative sessions begin on the second Tuesday in January on odd-numbered years, the years following general statewide elections. Sessions are limited by the constitution to 140 days, although the governor has the power to call special sessions to take up particular issues of pressing public concern. State legislators are paid $7,260 per year plus a per diem, salaries that are among the lowest in the nation, reflecting the desire of Texans to keep the job a part-time one.

Like most other states, legislators come from one of two parties (the Republicans and the Democrats). Each house is organized into a committee system that structures the way in which legislative business is conducted. A speaker of the house is elected by the house members to be its legislative leader, while the lieutenant governor, elected by a statewide popular vote, runs the senate.

First glances, however, can be deceiving. Neither the house nor the senate acts like the typical state legislative body nor, for that matter, like either U.S. house of Congress. This essay explores some of the reasons why the Texas legislature is unique and identifies forces of change that may eventually make it more mainstream. Traditionally, the Texas house and senate have been highly centralized legislative bodies with an unusually powerful speaker and lieutenant governor running each body in a nonpartisan manner. Neither the house nor the senate is organized along strict party lines, due in part to the historical dominance of the Democratic Party in the legislature. The speaker of the house, for example, traditionally has been elected not along partisan lines, but with the help of a bipartisan coalition of house members. As a result, supporters from both political parties have been rewarded by the speaker with desirable committee assignments. In contrast to other legislative bodies across the nation, Republicans as well as Democrats have been appointed to chair key legislative committees and to play leading roles in the legislative process.

FIGURE 5.A

The Texas Legislature

This figure provides a breakdown of the party membership in the Texas house and senate following the 1996 general election. Since the election there have been minor changes due to shifts in party affiliation. Unlike the U.S. Congress, there are no organized majority leadership positions. Along with the bipartisan committee system, this helps to centralize the power of both the speaker of the house and the lieutenant governor.

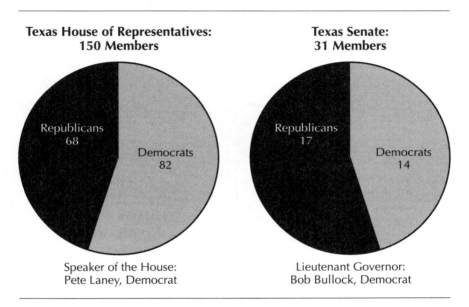

Centralized power based upon bipartisanship does not mean that the speaker or the lieutenant governor can pass all the legislation that they support. It does mean, however, that they can block most legislation that displeases them. A legislator who wishes to pass a bill may draft the bill, introduce a bill drafted by a lobbyist, or use the services of the Texas Legislative Council. Special committees will often be appointed to study important issues, some of which may be taken up in future legislation.

A member of either house of the legislature may introduce any bill during the first sixty calendar days of a regular session. After that any bill, other than a local bill, that does not relate to a matter declared by the governor to be an emergency must have the consent of four-fifths of either the house or the senate (see Figure 5.B). Introduced bills are then referred by the speaker or the lieutenant governor to appropriate committees, where most die. In some cases, there are public hearings on bills at which members of the public can express their views. After considering a bill, a committee may take no

FIGURE 5.B

Basic Steps in the Legislative Process

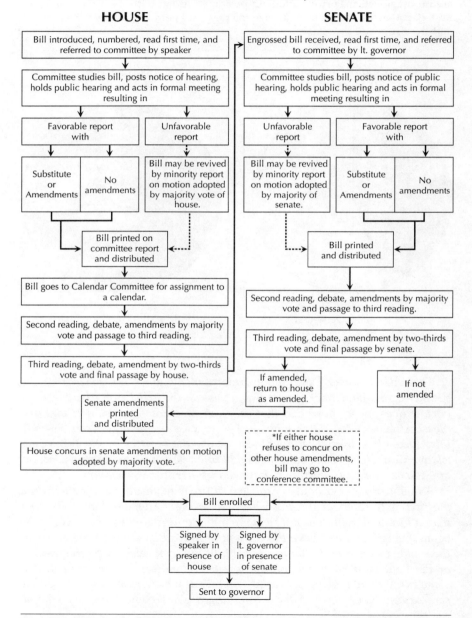

Source: Texas Legislative Handbook: 1993–1994, Legislative Roster With Committees.

action on a bill or may issue a report that expresses the committee's recommendation on the bill. Depending on the nature of the bill, if a house committee reports on it, the bill is placed on one of the house calendars. Bills are taken from the calendars and voted upon by the full house. Bills reported out of senate committees are also placed on a calendar. Often, however, for a bill to avoid being killed in the senate, it must be brought up out of its regular calendar vote: this requires a two-thirds vote. Thus, although in a technical sense, legislation might only require majority support in the senate, bills must often have two-thirds support just to be considered.

Bills must pass both houses in exactly the same language. If separate versions of a bill have passed, a conference committee may be appointed by the speaker and the lieutenant governor to resolve the differences. If the conference committee version of the bill is approved by both houses, it is sent to the governor for approval or veto.

The legislative process is a complex one involving detailed rules and procedures. The process is designed to make it difficult to pass legislation, the idea being that there should be a strong consensus in favor of a bill before it becomes law. The vast power of the speaker and lieutenant governor may provide more centralized control over each house than in other legislative bodies. Their support of a particular piece of legislation may only be a necessary, but not sufficient, condition for final passage.

This chapter details the immense power of the presiding officer, the speaker, of the Texas house of representatives. It shows that, although it looks like many other state legislative bodies in the nation, the Texas Legislature operates quite differently. Finally, it explores the emerging partisanship and speculates as to the impact it will have on the future power structure of the Texas Legislature.

In examining legislatures, scholars tend to look at how effective they are at making laws and how they are organized or structured. Studies of the legislative leaders and the committee systems have been the most common. Although it is rarely discussed, there is a relationship between leadership and committee systems in that more powerful committee systems are generally associated with weaker speakers and less powerful committee systems are associated with stronger speakers. This is the case in the entire history of the U.S. Congress and in most state legislatures. It is not, however, the case in Texas. In Texas, the speaker has allowed and fostered the creation of an extensive and powerful committee system, but has remained one of the most powerful legislative leaders in the nation. One of the primary reasons that the leadership has remained so strong in Texas has been the nature of the state's party system.

For all practical purposes, Republicans were merely an afterthought in Texas politics until the election of John Tower to the U.S. Senate in a 1961 special election. Eventually, the Republican delegation in Austin grew, but this growth was far from dramatic. Even as the numbers grew over time, partisanship was kept to a minimum. This was due in part to the fact that even as the numbers of Republicans grew, they were still in the minority. Under that scenario, continuing nonpartisan traditions served them well. In short, if they refused to support the Democratic leadership and issued partisan challenges to the leader's power they would most assuredly be squeezed out of all leadership positions and thus lose what power they had. By continuing to support moderate to conservative Democratic leaders, they assured themselves of continued access to power. As Figure 5.A shows, in 1996 the Republicans took control of the senate for the first time since Reconstruction, and already the politics of the institution are changing.

The senate, of course, is headed by the lieutenant governor, who is elected by a statewide popular vote. Under the rules of the institution, this leader has tremendous power over the agenda and appointments to committees. In previous sessions, Lieutenant Governor Bullock had been characterized as being a highly partisan figure by Republicans in the senate. Amazingly, in 1997, the legislative session began with calls for renewed bipartisanship and an increasing importance for members of the G.O.P. in the chamber. In fact, the Republicans have majorities on some committees and Bullock has shown flexibility in his control of the agenda. This change is dramatic. Consider that in 1989 when the members were asked about the overall amount of party influence in the legislature only 33.9 percent of the house members and zero percent of the senate members thought it was very significant. In contrast, 62 percent of the house members and 69 percent of the senate members thought that party influence was minimal or unimportant in the legislature.[1] By 1991, the early signs of partisanship were emerging. Among house Democrats, 69 percent thought that their party affiliation was an important factor in their voting, compared to 75 percent of Republicans. The real split was over the member's perception of partisan influences on the leadership. Forty-two percent of house Democrats thought party affiliation was important to the speaker, but 66 percent of house Republicans thought it was important.[2] The reality was that signs of partisanship becoming a factor were visible by 1991; it is only in 1997 that a Republican majority in the senate has forced changes in the leadership.

WHY COMPARE?

It is often the case that people who study a particular state's governmental institutions believe that the state's institutions are unique. This is not the case with legislative institutions. There are fifty state legislatures,

---

1. Gregory S. Thielemann, *Texas Legislative Survey*, The University of Texas at Dallas. Richardson, Texas. 1989.
2. Gregory S. Thielemann, *Texas Legislative Survey*, The University of Texas at Dallas. Richardson, Texas. 1991.

all of which, to varying degrees, are patterned after the U.S. Congress. Studies of legislative institutions tend to agree that none of the state legislatures match the U.S. Congress in sophistication or development, and scholars who have examined the Texas Legislature agree. Nevertheless, comparison between the two legislative institutions is useful in that the shortfalls of the Texas legislative system are obvious.

It can be useful to think of the Texas Legislature and the U.S. Congress as parts of a whole government. The task of each is essentially to make laws, but they must interact with the other branches of government in order to accomplish this task. At the federal and state level, the policy-making environment is constantly changing and thus forcing the legislative branches to adapt. For example, these changes may involve adapting to different styles of leadership in the executive branch or adapting to different restrictions on lawmaking by the courts. In many ways, this ability to adapt and "go with the flow" is critical to the ability of legislative branches to make laws. Although all legislative institutions share common traits, the external pressures they face will vary and, not surprisingly, so will their responses. The ability to adapt is, in fact, at the heart of the variation between the U.S. House and the Texas house of representatives. At the national level, the U.S. Congress is free to pursue lawmaking with few limitations. Its membership has evolved from citizen legislators to highly paid professional legislators with an abundance of skilled staff support. In Texas, this evolution has been much slower. The result is a unique arrangement in which the Texas house appears to be similar to the U.S. Congress on the surface, but is in reality very different. This chapter focuses on three such variations: (1) the constitutional framework that structures the legislative process, (2) differences in leadership, and (3) most important, the committee system. In examining the committee systems of the U.S. Congress and Texas house, we uncover great differences in degree of specialization, the ability of the leadership to coopt committee chairs, and the length of tenure of committee members.

The Constitutional Framework

The most obvious difference between legislative bodies is the structural restrictions placed upon them. Structural restrictions refer to the forces that are separate from the personality and skill of the members and yet help shape policy. Constitutional requirements for lawmaking are an example. At the national level, the Constitution gives Congress the ability to make laws and places virtually no constraints on the institution in pursuing that task. Although the U.S. House of Representatives has 435 members, these members have significant staff support and a highly developed and democratic committee structure that facilitates debate and lawmaking.

It is impossible to understand why the Texas house is the way it is without understanding the political environment in which it operates, particularly the state's constitutional framework for passing legislation. The Texas Constitution, ratified in 1876, was written at the close of Reconstruction by farmers who wanted to limit the power of government and thus reduce the abuse that was prevalent under the reconstruction regimes. In many ways it was simply a reaction to the corrupt administration of the Republican Reconstruction Governor E. J. Davis. Because the Davis administration was generally regarded as having behaved in a dictatorial fashion in the process of looting the state treasury, the Constitution of 1876 severely limited the power of the governor. The Texas governor operates without the traditional powers of a chief executive, such as having control of the state bureaucracy and its expertise. The governor is at a tremendous disadvantage vis-a-vis the legislature in making policy, and Texas house leaders have rarely felt threatened by the governor. This desire to weaken the executive branch left the policymaking aspects of state government by default to the legislative branch.

Of course, the authors of the Constitution of 1876 were concerned with limiting government in general and not simply the office of the governor. The overriding sentiment was that the less government there was, the better off Texans would be, and toward that end, the Constitution of 1876 also limited the ability of the legislature to make policy. The constitution did this primarily in two ways: by limiting the amount of time the legislature could meet and by insuring that the membership would remain citizen legislators. These constitutional restrictions on government activities that directly affect the Texas Legislature include limiting the time frame for legislative activity to 140 days every two years and by making the Texas house abnormally large (150 members). This limitation, to biennial 140-day sessions, places problem-solving and policymaking on a restricted timetable, and results in a high premium being placed on expeditious rather than thorough action. Committees respond by limiting debate usually to hours rather than days, even on complicated legislation. If the end benefit of legislative service is policymaking,[3] then achievement of this goal by the Texas Legislature is severely handicapped by the antiquated Constitution of 1876.

Beyond the obvious time problems, members' average tenures are reduced by the constitutional mandate for part-time wages—$7,200 per year.[4] This part-time salary, along with minimal funds for support staff,

---

3. Wayne L. Francis, "Costs and Benefits of Legislative Service in the American States." *American Journal of Political Science*, vol. 29, pp. 626–42.

4. See Malcolm E. Jewell and Samuel C. Patterson, *The Legislative Process in the United States*, 3rd ed. (New York: Random House, 1977) and Wayne L. Francis and J. R. Baker, "Why Do United States State Legislators Vacate Their Seats?" *Legislative Studies Quarterly*, vol. 11, pp. 119–26.

significantly increases the importance of fundraising and increases the importance of lobbyists, who have the time and funds to provide expert information that staff would provide in other legislative institutions.

LEGISLATIVE LEADERSHIP

One obvious difference between the U.S. House of Representatives and the Texas house is that the leaders are different, with different personalities and leadership styles. There are also variations in the rules that determine legislative leadership.

One important example is the variations in rules that bring the leader to power. In the U.S. Congress, the Speaker of the House is elected by a popular vote of the membership. In general these votes have been on strictly party lines, although dissent is possible. There is considerably more variation within the states. New Jersey's system of rotating leadership differs significantly from the intense competition in Ohio and Kansas. In Kentucky, the incumbent governor (if a Democrat) has selected the leadership, whereas in Alabama, Georgia, Louisiana, and Oklahoma, the executive has some influence over the leadership.[5] There are states in which the power of the office precludes real competition unless an incumbent speaker is retiring or is seen as unlikely to return. The level of party influence on the selection of the speaker can also vary in each state. Some states have high degrees of party loyalty, making speaker selection a function of the majority party caucus. Some other states usually elect their speaker in the majority party's caucus, but have occasional revolts. This was the case in 1979 in New Mexico[6] and Minnesota[7] when a minority of the majority caucus engaged in a coalition with the minority party to defeat the majority caucus's candidate. Other states operate without regard to party, making speaker elections and committee assignments virtually nonpartisan affairs.

Many structural factors, including a relative lack of partisanship, have resulted in making the speaker of the Texas house one of the most powerful in the country. In Texas, the speaker is elected by collecting pledge cards from any members, regardless of party affiliation, and because parties play no role in electing leaders or selecting committee assignments, they have no organizational role to play. Because speakers achieve power through personal rather than partisan relationships, they possess highly centralized power. This strong centralized leadership is in many ways a response to the lack of partisanship reflected initially in the speaker's election. Pledge cards are collected long before the session begins, and it is during this process that the speaker trades committee

5. Alan Rosenthal, *Legislative Life* (New York: Harper and Row, 1981).
6. Alan Rosenthal, *Legislative Life*.
7. Royce Hanson, *Tribune of the People: The Minnesota Legislature and Its Leadership* (Minneapolis, MN: University of Minnesota Press, 1990).

placement and chairmanships for votes. Because there is no formal caucus process to select nominees and bind members, the system tends to favor incumbents, as in other state systems.[8] The last two speakers, who have retired as of the time of this writing, have presided over ten sessions and have done so without serious or even frivolous opposition. Members are faced with the prospect of backing the winner or facing retribution; as a result, a bandwagon effect is common.

Without retirement or conviction, the reelection of the speaker is a foregone conclusion and the contest is in effect reduced to a ritual. Even a grand jury indictment of Speaker Gib Lewis in 1991 on two misdemeanor ethics charges did not shake his grip on the house. Only one member voted against his reelection, and in the ultimate act of cooptation, that member, along with every other freshman, was granted his first committee preference.

From the members' perspective, if they want the prestige of a committee chair, even with the strings attached, they must pledge to the speaker to gain power and vote with the speaker to keep it. Being appointed to a powerful committee or being named a chair affords members clear advantages. Committee chairs are valuable, providing additional staff and perks, including immediate access to the state's free-spending lobbyists.[9] Thus, members find themselves in a position of trading independence for access and seem to be satisfied with that arrangement.

COMMITTEE SYSTEMS

As the discussion of the election of Texas speakers suggests, another important factor in understanding variations in legislatures is found in the nature and power of their committee systems. In some ways, it is impossible to separate the nature of leadership from the committee system because the two are so closely interrelated. The evolution of strong committee systems in legislative institutions has in many ways been seen as a reaction to powerful speakers who use their power to dominate the lawmaking process in a dictatorial manner. In general, the development of strong committee systems was seen as a mechanism for decentralizing power, thus weakening speakers and making the lawmaking process more democratic. This link is undeniable, and is best reflected in the advice offered at the National Conference of State Legislatures in 1978, when they advised new leaders to "Get control of the committee system and you'll be able to manage the entire legislature."[10]

8. Malcolm E. Jewell and Samuel C. Patterson, *The Legislative Process in the United States*, 3rd ed. (New York: Random House, 1977).
9. Gregory S. Thielemann and Donald R. Dixon, "Rational Contributors: The Elections for the 71st Texas House." *Legislative Studies Quarterly*, vol. 19, pp. 495–506.
10. Alan Rosenthal, *Legislative Life*.

The relationship between leadership and committee systems is critical to understanding the strength of the leadership in a legislature. Because committees have developed as the primary policymaking unit in lawmaking, the leaders' control over them is important: by controlling the committee system, leaders can manage the activity of the legislature as a whole. Leaders influence the nature of the committee system by determining the number of committees, the rules that influence bill assignment, the membership and thus the orientations of committees, and the leadership of the committees.[11] The more control the speaker has over these actions, the more control the speaker will have over the entire legislative process.

Committees and Leadership in the U.S. Congress

In the U.S. Congress, some speakers have developed unique styles in order to cope with the committees. Perhaps the most powerful of all speakers, Joseph Cannon (who was speaker from 1903 to 1911), had absolute control over the committee system. His control over jurisdiction, appointments, and member advancement made him a monarch in a system that had only the trappings of democracy. Specialization was allowed so long as the members did not challenge the speaker. Changes in the electoral environment and the defection of Republicans who felt Cannon's wrath and desired more autonomy led to his overthrow. The expanded autonomy of the committees made Congress significantly more democratic. Sam Rayburn, Speaker of the House almost continuously from 1940 to 1961, achieved his success not by domination and coercion, but by building coalitions that were unique to each policy question. With both Cannon and Rayburn, the nature of the leadership's relation to the committee system determined its power relative to the speaker. Committees in the national legislature have become powerful forces: however, this powerful committee system did not appear instantaneously, but developed gradually.

Most scholars of Congress suggest that, in our time, Congress has become more and more specialized as it has divided its work among the committee system. Specialization occurred for a number of reasons, including the need for members to enhance their effectiveness, clarify their responsibilities vis-a-vis the leadership, and enhance the internal democracy within the legislative body by dispersing more power to the members. In each case specialization was both a method and a byproduct of achieving the goal. This trend toward specialization began in the mid-nineteenth century and has accelerated ever since.

The first stage of specialization occurred by the middle of the nineteenth century as standing committees became a norm. Barbara Hinckley

---

11. Alan Rosenthal, *Legislative Life*, p. 163.

wrote, "With increasing demands for specialization and division of labor, committees became the site of major legislative decisions by the middle of the nineteenth century."[12] The principal reason for developing standing committees was to encourage specialization and thus allow the legislative branch to foster the creation of its own experts. As problems became more numerous and complicated, the committee of the whole became obsolete. While members feared the prospect of placing policy expertise in the hands of a few rather than the whole, the decision to turn to standing committees was not at all surprising. At the time, experts already existed, only they were part of the executive branch. For the legislative branch to compete, it needed its own experts.

As time progressed, the number of standing committees grew and the different areas of specialization became more refined. Unfortunately, the workload was not evenly distributed; some members were overworked, while others remained relatively idle. Legislators were spending enormous amounts of time on private and local concerns as well as on nonlegislative duties. To cope with this problem, the La Follette–Monroney Committee was established in 1945 to study methods of increasing legislative efficiency.[13] Most of this committee's recommendations were embodied in the Legislative Reorganization Act of 1946, which was designed to protect expertise by encouraging specialization over specific policy areas. As George Galloway described the act, it did this by reducing the number of committees on the house side from 48 to 19 and on the senate side from 33 to 15, each with specific policy jurisdictions.[14] To equally distribute the workload, it limited the number of assignments to one or two per member and banned introduction of some types of private bills. In order to allow the members to cope with the changing policy problems, it allowed for the expansion of staff support.[15] The thrust behind this reorganization of the legislature was to allow the legislature to cope better with itself and the changing policy environment. By reducing the workload of the membership, it hoped to allow specialization by affording members the time and opportunity to develop or enhance their knowledge in the specialized policy areas the committee system offered. Galloway wrote that these reforms did not lighten the workload of the members, but the increase in staff allowed them to cope with it.[16] Staff alone could not solve the problems that emerged in the 1970s as the seniority system and Southern control of committee chairmanships led the body into a new crisis. In short, Southerners were using

12. Barbara Hinckley, *Stability and Change in Congress* (New York: Harper and Row, 1988), p. 9.
13. George B. Galloway, *History of the House of Representatives* (New York: Thomas Y. Crowell Co., 1961).
14. Ibid., p. 58.
15. Ibid., p. 125.
16. George B. Galloway, *History of the House of Representatives*.

their positions as committee chairs to block progressive legislation favored by a majority of the party, and to cope with this the committee system was altered.

The division of labor was refined in the subcommittee reforms of the 1970s, when specialization reached new heights. Subcommittees became the work units of Congress, as the institution created more specialized policymakers who were free of the control of committee chairs and thus free to use their own expertise in policy decisions. Although the growth of subcommittee government was in part attributed to the desire to increase accountability in Congress, one of the side effects of this action was to create a more specialized institution with narrow jurisdictions. Representative David Obey summed up the impact of these changes best when he told the New York Times that the replacement of the committee system with the subcommittee system gave every organized special interest group "a port of entry into Congress."[17]

It is important to keep in mind that throughout this period parties played a critical role in organizing the legislative institution. They shaped the election of the leaders and the power of the parties within the institution. This was true in the eras of committee power and subcommittee power. It is true that on rare occasions, such as the ouster of Cannon, partisanship would break down and bipartisan efforts would change the leadership, but these cases were exceptions and not the rule.

To summarize, the organization of the U.S. Congress consistently evolved through increased division and specialization of labor. While the motivations for changes came from very different sources, ranging from executive encroachment to internal democratization, the specialization of policymakers was the desirable goal. Several ways to compare committee systems emerge from the example of the U.S. Congress: (1) whether they share a pattern of evolution, which includes the division of labor and specialization; (2) whether the goals of the system are to foster policy expertise; and (3) whether the results are judged by how well they achieve these ends. The following section will show how the committee system of the Texas house of representatives differed from the developmental pattern of the U.S. Congress.

COMMITTEES IN THE TEXAS HOUSE

Over the years, the members of the Texas house of representatives have been characterized in unflattering terms by the popular press as well as scholars of legislative institutions. Although many of the criticisms have been justified, many have failed to fully consider the external influences that produce such an institution. These external pressures have resulted in the creation of a unique relationship between leadership

---

17. *New York Times*, 13 November 1978.

and committee systems. The Texas system has certainly evolved, although not to the extent that the U.S. Congress has, and yet it remains free of the levels of specialization scholars have come to associate with the evolution of committee systems. Important differences exist between the U.S. House and the Texas house that shape the nature of leadership and its ability to control the committee system. As with U.S. House speakers, control of the committee system is very important to state legislative leaders. In Texas, this power resembles the extremes of Cannon. In general, centralization of power influences the role of committees in the body as a whole.[18] In Texas, the committee system has undergone a process of evolution that on the surface resembles that of Congress and other state legislatures, but the driving forces behind the changes differ greatly. In general, the more extensive the committee system, the more powerful it is. In Texas, just the opposite is the case. Although committee reform is generally associated with enhancing specialization, committee reform in Texas is always linked to abuses of power by the leadership and is, to date, always short-lived as the leadership reasserts its control even in the face of scandal. In the Texas house, committees represent opportunities for cooptation, not opportunities for specialization. The more committees and thus leadership positions, the greater the powers of the leadership. In 1974, to reduce the power of the speaker, the number of standing committees was reduced to twenty-two, and thus chairs and vice-chairs were limited to forty-four. These reforms were presumably intended to limit the speaker's influence; the reduction of the number of committees was associated with increasing committee power.

In 1991, in spite of past corruption resulting from the extreme centralization of power, the leadership's influence recovered as the number of committees increased from twenty-two to thirty-six. This means that when the chairs and vice-chairs are added together, the speaker needs only three additional votes to obtain a majority of the entire legislature. In a survey of fifty-six members, the 1974 reforms were seen as designed to increase the power of committees.[19] The membership did not see these reforms as influencing the leadership, however, because the speaker remained in control. Thus, in Texas, the extensive committee system simply affords the speaker with the opportunity to coopt members rather than creating a more democratic institution.

This cooptation extends beyond party lines. At the heart of the extreme centralization of power in the hands of the speaker is the nonpartisan nature of the Texas house. The nonpartisan election of the speaker establishes a system in which the speaker is not required to treat members of his or her party any differently than members of the opposition.

18. Alan Rosenthal, *Legislative Performance in the States: Explorations of Committee Behavior* (New York: The Free Press, 1974).
19. Gary Moncrief and Malcolm Jewell, "Legislator's Perceptions of Reform in Three States," *American Politics Quarterly*, vol. 8, pp. 106–27.

In some legislative institutions, strong party influences have served to at least decentralize power to the level of the party. In a system where the leadership desires cooperation from all members, their numbers encourage the speaker to forge coalitions and leadership teams with members of both parties. This mutual interest helps to maintain the centralized leadership and reduces sharp partisan divisions in the house. Unlike states where the party system plays an important role in influencing and even eliminating the way a speaker uses power, in Texas, partisanship is effectively inconsequential.

Speaker domination of the committee systems is assured through the extensive jurisdictional overlap found in the Texas house committee system. Jurisdictional overlap refers to the situation in which more than one committee has jurisdiction over a certain policy area. In many ways, the Texas house is set up to prevent specialization by avoiding delineation of clear boundaries of committee jurisdiction. This is accomplished through establishing ambiguous and duplicative jurisdictions for the committees. The system has a "catch-all" committee, State Affairs. This committee receives the most legislation (482 in 1989), significantly more than the average substantive house committee (145). The State Affairs Committee is charged with "questions and matters of state policy, the administration of state government, the organization, powers, regulation and management of state departments . . . etc."[20] Traditionally, its broad mandate makes it the "speaker's committee," wherein he places allies and sends controversial pieces of legislation to ensure an outcome favorable to the chair. For example, in the 69th session, Gib Lewis gave State Affairs jurisdiction over the tax bill when his brand of tax legislation could not be created in Ways and Means.

By observing committee names, jurisdictions might seem obvious; however, looks are deceiving in most cases, because the rules are intentionally written to be vague and to allow the speaker great flexibility in assigning legislation. Although no clerk suggested that the bills were incorrectly routed, they all pointed out bills that could have been placed under their jurisdiction but were not. In spite of the convenience of having a generalized State Affairs Committee to which the speaker can assign sensitive bills, the jurisdictional boundaries of the remaining committees have not been clarified.

In addition to the "catch-all" State Affairs Committee, there are so many committees with similar subject matter that the expertise is spread thin. Duplicative jurisdictions abound in the house rules. Two judicial committees, Judiciary and Judicial Affairs, have nearly identical jurisdictions, according to the house rules. The sole difference is that Judicial Affairs has jurisdiction over the state courts and judicial agencies. Although Texas has never been known as an environmentalist state, the

---

20. House Rules 1989 (Austin: Texas House of Representatives), pp. 25–6.

house has granted the three committees of Natural Resources, Agriculture, and Environmental Affairs power over regulation of land and water. Two committees, Business and Commerce and Labor and Employment Relations, are charged in the rules with jurisdiction over "hours, wages, collective bargaining and the relationship between employers and employees."[21] Even where specific committees exist, there is no guarantee that they will be assigned the legislation because of the expansive jurisdiction of State Affairs. The lack of committee boundaries gives the speaker considerable leeway in routing bills and thus centralizes power with the speaker in spite of the extensive committee system. Because the committees are tools of the speaker, increasing the number of committees actually increases the speaker's power.

FURTHER EVIDENCE OF TEXAS'S UNIQUENESS

This description of the committee system of the Texas house indicates that leadership is in total control of the legislative process. In order to further examine the extent of this control, data were collected on the committee system and membership of the Texas house of representatives between 1975 and 1991 (sixty-fourth through seventy-second sessions). This historical period corresponds to the tenure of two of Texas's most prolific speakers, Billy Clayton and Gib Lewis. These historical data were supplemented with surveys of the Seventy-first and Seventy-second house membership.[22] In the Seventy-first session, the members were asked questions covering a wide range of topics, including a battery of more than twenty about the committee system. As the surveys and other evidence were analyzed, it became apparent that the leadership was more important than committees in the Texas house. To develop a better sense of the way the system actually worked, thirty-four of the thirty-six chief clerks of the house committees were interviewed in depth about the relationship between the speaker and the committee as well as the actual workings of the committee. Taken together, the evidence suggests that the Texas committee system is not designed to facilitate specialization, and demonstrates that within the organizational framework of the Texas house of representatives, extensive committee systems are used to foster centralization of authority in the hands of the leader rather than to help in the dispersion of power. Thus, although on the surface the organization of the Texas house might appear to be decentralized, in fact it has created one of the strongest speakers in the country.

---

21. Ibid., pp. 16, 22.
22. These surveys were conducted by the author and involved 87 of 148 members in the Seventy-first session and 92 of 150 members in the Seventy-second session.

Committee Tenure

Although it is true that the Texas house committee system makes specialization difficult by virtue of its jurisdictional problems, the system also seems to encourage members to move frequently among committees. The leeway granted the speaker in referral of legislation means that members who want to serve on a committee relating to their specialty have no sure way to tell if a committee with the right-sounding title will get the legislation related to the member's interest. Of course, if all the members served twenty years, the body would have a great many experts. In the Texas house, however, tenure is low, and in the past eighteen years tenure on specific committees has been much lower. This works against developing expertise and specialization in the body, because members seldom acquire much experience in a policy area. Table 5.1 compares the experience levels of the members of the house with the experience level of the members on the four "influence" committees from 1975 to 1991.[23] As expected, the members of the influence committees tend to be more experienced than the average house member. This is generally true over time, although State Affairs and Ways and Means occasionally had less-experienced members than the house as a whole. Of more importance is the fact that, in every case, committee tenure is significantly lower than the average house member's tenure who serves on that committee. This suggests that even when members have tenure in the house, there is virtually no experience on the committees. In this system the leaders are either not encouraging or not allowing members to develop expertise in the jurisdictional areas of the influence committees.

The argument could be made that these influence committees will naturally have lower tenure because new members would need to prove their value or loyalty before being assigned to them. Table 5.2 shows the same comparison for six selected "non-influence" committees during the same period.[24] As with the influence committees, even when a member builds up tenure in the body, it does not translate into committee tenure and thus experience. In other words, the committee system does not benefit from increases in the average tenure of the house members.

Further evidence of the power of the speaker in a legislature with an extensive committee system is found in the views of the members. Members of the seventy-second session were asked to assess the overall policy influence of the speaker, the parties, the committees, the lobbyists, and the press, by ranking the most influential "1" to the least influential "5"; the speaker's average rank was 1.54 compared to the committees' 2.97,

---

23. All tenure is calculated in years. Each session in this study includes members who entered office in mid-session.
24. These six committees are selected because they represent diverse policy areas. Note that these results mirror those in the remaining substantive committees.

TABLE 5.1

Committee and House Tenure of Members of "Influence" Committees
in the Texas House of Representatives, 1975–1991

Session (Avg. Tenure)	Appropriations Committee	House	Calendars Committee	House	Ways and Means[1] Committee	House	State Affairs Committee	House
Speaker Clayton								
64th 1975–76 (3.5)	0.9	8.8	0.0	3.4	0.9	3.6	0.7	1.5
65th 1977–78 (3.9)	1.9	8.8	0.9	6.9	0.2	2.6	0.8	3.1
66th 1979–80 (4.2)	2.2	8.8	0.7	5.8	1.2	3.2	1.6	3.6
67th 1981–82 (4.6)	1.7	7.2	1.8	5.6	1.5	3.8	1.5	4.6
Speaker Lewis								
68th 1983–84 (4.3)	1.7	5.8	0.4	5.1	1.5	4.1	0.8	4.0
69th 1985–86 (4.8)	2.3	7.0	0.7	7.4	0.9	3.5	1.1	4.3
70th 1987–88 (5.3)	2.8	7.6	0.4	6.7	0.9	7.2	1.4	6.2
71st 1989–90 (6.1)	3.3	8.3	1.5	8.6	2.2	9.8	1.8	4.8
72nd 1991–92 (6.0)	1.7	5.9	1.3	10.4	1.5	8.8	2.5	7.2

1. Was Revenue & Taxation until 65th Session.

TABLE 5.2

Committee and House Tenure of the Membership on Selected "Non-Influence" Committees with Tenure in Years, 1975–1991

Session (Avg. Tenure)	Business & Industry[1] Committee	Business & Industry[1] House	Energy Committee	Energy House	Higher Education Committee	Higher Education House	Public Education Committee	Public Education House	Environmental Affairs Committee	Environmental Affairs House	Judicial Affairs Committee	Judicial Affairs House
Speaker Clayton												
64th 1975–76 (3.5)	0.0	2.4	0.0	5.3	0.0	3.1	0.0	3.5	0.9	4.0	0.0	4.9
65th 1977–78 (3.9)	0.9	1.8	1.0	3.1	1.1	3.6	1.0	4.5	1.5	3.1	0.4	2.5
66th 1979–80 (4.2)	1.1	3.3	1.3	7.1	0.7	3.1	0.9	3.6	1.6	4.4	0.5	6.9
67th 1981–82 (4.6)	2.4	3.8	1.8	5.8	0.9	3.4	2.2	5.5	0.7	4.0	0.4	5.8
Speaker Lewis												
68th 1983–84 (4.3)	0.9	5.3	2.0	7.8	0.7	3.8	2.7	5.1	0.7	3.8	0.2	2.7
69th 1985–86 (4.8)	1.1	4.7	1.8	6.2	1.6	7.4	3.3	5.3	1.3	4.9	1.3	5.6
70th 1987–88 (5.3)	0.7	6.0	2.4	6.2	2.2	8.3	2.7	3.3	1.8	6.4	0.9	6.4
71st 1989–90 (6.1)	1.1	6.0	2.8	6.4	3.1	8.5	2.9	6.2	2.0	5.3	1.6	6.3
72nd 1991–92 (6.0)	1.7	6.8	3.5	6.4	3.5	9.8	3.7	7.3	2.6	6.2	1.1	6.6

1. Becomes Business and Commerce

and the lobbyists' 2.98.[25] These results are not surprising, given that the speaker controls the committee organization and has wide discretion over the assignment of legislation (due to the ambiguous and overlapping jurisdictions). In addition, of thirty-four committee clerks interviewed, twenty-two recalled at least one instance when the speaker requested action on a bill, and every clerk emphasized the need to accommodate the speaker.

These powers of the speaker to appoint committee members are used to foster low levels of expertise within committees. The result is a highly centralized power system in the Texas house. If an institution's leadership views centralization of power as essential to achieving institutional and policy objectives, then the very purpose of the committee system must be viewed in a different light. Before 1974, the speaker had absolute control of all appointments. Since the 1983 reforms, the speaker has appointed all chairs and vice-chairs, the entire membership of all six procedural committees and the appropriations committee, and a minimum of one-half of the remaining membership on the substantive committees. The end result of these "reforms" did not change speaker domination, because the speaker still appoints a majority of each committee's members.[26]

To facilitate power, the speaker fosters a lack of specialization through the appointment process. Whether one considers those committees under complete speaker appointment control or those with the partial seniority system, the tenure on committees is low, and few have a membership with an average tenure of greater than one term (two years). Of course, this assumes that tenure on a committee enhances expertise in a policy area. Although membership does not guarantee expertise, it seems plausible to suggest that serving on a committee advances the opportunity for political gain. Tables 5.3 and 5.4 show that turnover is extensive, and that much of it results from reassignment rather than retirement.[27]

Conclusions

In summary, the organization of the Texas house of representatives is unique. The most obvious deviation the Texas house makes from the traditional committee systems model is that committees divide the workload without appearing to foster the sense of specialization and dispersion of power that usually accompany such a division of labor. A high

25. This survey was conducted by the author during the Seventy-second Legislature's special session of August 1991. A total of 101 members participated.
26. A seniority system accounts for the remaining members on substantive committees. Members list, by seniority, their top three choices and receive the committee of their highest preference on which their remains a vacant seniority slot.
27. The Sixty-fourth session is deleted because of significant changes in the prescribed number of members on each committee. After the Sixty-fourth session, the numbers remain relatively constant.

TABLE 5.3

Turnover on Selected Texas House "Influence" Committees
1975–1991 Accounting for Retirement

Total Committee Turnover %
% of Turnover From Reassignment

SESSION	Appropriations	Calendars	State Affairs	Ways & Means
Speaker Clayton				
65th	38.1 / 37.5	42.8(e) / 33.3	76.5(f) / 46.1	66.6(b) / 50.0
66th	47.6 / 30.0	77.7 / 28.6	60.0 / 77.7	38.5 / 40.0
67th	47.6 / 50.0	44.4 / 25.0	60.0 / 66.6	53.8 / 71.4
Speaker Lewis				
68th	47.6(a) / 50.0	77.7 / 28.5	80.0 / 75.0	61.5(b) / 50.0
69th	41.3 / 50.0	77.7 / 100.0	66.6(c) / 90.0	80.0(c) / 60.0
70th	41.3 / 91.6	77.7 / 57.1	46.1 / 33.3	84.6 / 63.6
71st	37.9(d) / 17.4	25.0 / 50.0	46.1 / 50.0	46.1 / 66.8
72nd	73.9 / 70.5	55.5 / 40.0	53.8 / 57.1	46.1 / 66.6

(a) 21 to 29 members (b) 13 to 15 members (c) 15 to 13 members (d) 29 to 27 members
(e) 7 to 9 members   (f) 17 to 15 members

degree of centralized power still exists in the Texas house. Centralization of power has been shown to affect the role of committees in the body as a whole. If leaders view centralization of power as essential, as in the Texas house, the purpose of the committee system is different. Committees designed to specialize do not work the same way as committees designed to centralize authority. Without this distinction, cross-state studies of committee systems have little purpose. In the Texas house, the organizational purpose of the committees relative to the body as a whole is to enhance the centralized authority of the speaker, rather than to encourage specialization in policymaking. The use of committees to facilitate the speaker's power is demonstrated by the organization of the committees, the ambiguity of their jurisdictions, and the lack of members' opportunities to be policymakers and advance legislation.

In Texas, power remains centralized with the speaker through control of the committee system. The speaker controls the organization of the

Table 5.4

Turnover on Selected Texas House "Non-influence" Committees
1975–1991 Accounting for Retirement

Total Committee Turnover %
% of Turnover From Reassignment

Session	Business & Industry	Energy	Environmental Affairs	Higher Education	Judicial Affairs	Public Education
Speaker Clayton						
65th	54.5 / 66.6	54.5 / 50.0	61.5(d) / 87.5	36.3 / 75.0	81.8 / 77.7	72.7(d) / 62.5
66th	63.6 / 85.7	63.6 / 85.7	54.5 / 83.3	81.8 / 77.7	72.7 / 87.5	54.5 / 66.6
67th	54.5(a) / 83.3	63.6 / 42.9	72.7 / 75.0	63.6(c) / 57.1	81.8 / 55.5	27.2 / 100.0
Speaker Lewis						
68th	77.7 / 71.4	63.6(a) / 85.7	81.8 / 44.4	84.6(b) / 45.4	90.9(a) / 50.0	54.6(a) / 66.6
69th	77.7 / 57.1	66.6 / 50.0	55.5 / 80.0	55.5 / 80.0	44.4 / 75.0	33.3 / 66.6
70th	66.6 / 83.3	77.7 / 57.1	55.5 / 100.0	44.4 / 75.0	66.6 / 33.3	44.4 / 50.0
71st	55.5 / 80.0	55.0 / 40.0	66.6 / 0.0	44.4 / 20.0	55.5 / 100.0	44.4 / 40.0
72nd	55.5 / 60.0	55.5 / 60.0	44.4 / 50.0	44.4 / 100.0	66.6 / 66.6	22.2 / 50.0

(a) 11 to 9 members   (b) 13 to 9 members   (c) 11 to 13 members   (d) 13 to 11 members

committees, has wide discretion over the assignment of legislation (due to unclear committee jurisdictions), and can use the appointment system to foster low levels of expertise by keeping tenure among the members low. Because every bill can be steered to at least two different committees, membership on a particular substantive committee does not guarantee that the member will see the legislation he or she desired when assignment bids were made. As a result, the members' dependence on the leadership is reinforced, because they must maintain good relations with the speaker to gain access to desired legislation. The extent of the problem is reflected by the fact that all thirty-four committee clerks interviewed felt that legislation went to other committees that could have been placed in their own. The members appear to be satisfied with the current centralization of power, and exhibit a willingness to play by the speaker's rules to achieve desired positions. Representatives have shown little inclination to challenge the speaker and change the rules. In spite of the tremendous centralization of power in the Texas house, in a survey of the seventy-first session membership, members overwhelmingly opposed committee reforms that would have reduced the speaker's power over the chairs. The survey found significant opposition (two to one) to having committee chairs elected. In addition, most members reported satisfaction with their committee assignments, which confirms results from other states.[28] One possible explanation for this satisfaction is that the members have been appeased. The extensive committee system affords the speaker the ability to accommodate members in the assignment process, even if the reality of overlapping jurisdictions reduces the members' influence in any given area.

Because of the nature and organization of the Texas committee system, the speaker remains the centralized power figure in spite of the extensive division of labor, and the committees are not fully developed as specialized policymakers. In Texas, it is an organizational reality that the committee system enhances rather than diminishes the power of the speaker by providing endless opportunities for formal cooptation. Hedlund suggested that this provides evidence that appointments are accommodation based.[29] This certainly is the case in Texas, where members are accommodated whenever possible, provided that they are willing to pass legislation for the leader later. Political accommodation in Texas is an outgrowth of a system under extreme external pressures to produce legislation.

The Texas committee system differs from the national model because its problems are different. Organizationally, the primary concern is to expedite legislation rather than compete with the executive branch over policy questions. In other legislative institutions, the forces of partisanship would reduce the control of the leadership over the committee system. It seems plausible to suggest that if the G.O.P. assumes control of the legislature, this change will be expedited. The Republicans' emergence from permanent second class status has certainly created a renewed enthusiasm for party labels in the electorate and in the institutions. With this emergence comes an accompanying obligation to change, and institutional change in the legislature is an easy place to begin.

28. Wayne L. Francis, "Costs and Benefits of Legislative Service in the American States," *American Journal of Political Science*, vol. 29, pp. 626–42.
29. Ronald D. Hedlund, "Organizational Attributes of Legislatures: Structure, Rules, Norms, Resources," *Legislative Studies Quarterly*, vol. 9, pp. 51–121.

6
Judicial Selection in Texas: Democracy's Deadlock

ANTHONY CHAMPAGNE
UNIVERSITY OF TEXAS AT DALLAS

As Figure 6.A indicates, Texas has a large number of judges and a complex court structure. In all, the state has 3014 judges. In Texas, all appellate judges and all trial judges are elected, except for some municipal judges. These are partisan elections in which the judges run for office with a party label.

Most Texans' experience with the judicial system probably involves either municipal courts or justice of the peace courts, because they deal mostly with traffic offenses. However, controversies involving the Texas judicial system have mostly centered on the district courts, which are the major trial courts in Texas, and the appellate courts: these courts deal with the high-dollar lawsuits and with major criminal cases.

Texas is unusual in that it has two supreme courts, the Texas Supreme Court, which deals with civil appeals, and the Texas Court of Criminal Appeals, which deals with criminal appeals. Only one other state, Oklahoma, has this type of court structure. Of the two courts, most political battles are over seats on the Texas Supreme Court because their decisions set the tone for tort law in the state. Although the Texas Court of Criminal Appeals deals with questions of liberty, and even with questions of life and death, that court generates less political conflict, because monetary issues are not involved.

The Texas system is a hodgepodge of courts. Not all county-level courts, for example, have the same jurisdiction. Some county court at law judges have roughly the same powers as district judges; other county court at law judges deal mostly with drunken driving cases. Although there have been efforts to restructure the Texas court system to create more uniform jurisdiction and reduce the number of courts, these efforts have failed and have produced limited controversies. One rarely hears, for example, of the efforts to combine the Texas Supreme Court with the Texas Court of Criminal Appeals or to make the jurisdiction of county courts uniform. Nor does one hear of the widespread use of visiting judges—often retired or defeated judges—who hear cases in parts of the state where there are major case overloads. The Texas justice system would collapse due to insufficient numbers of judges if retired and defeated judges were not appointed to hear cases.

What one does hear about—indeed, what has for years been the leading

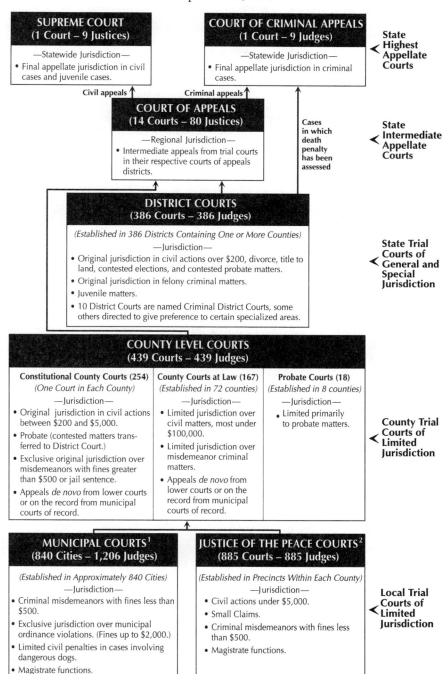

FIGURE 6.A

Court Structure of Texas
September 1, 1994

Source: Texas Judicial Council and Office of Court Administration, Austin, Texas.

judicial controversy in the state—is judicial selection. This chapter explores the controversy surrounding the selection of judges in Texas.

Texas elects all its appellate and trial judges, with the exception of some municipal judges. These elections are partisan, and the judges campaign for office with the backing of a political party. For fifty years the system of selecting judges in Texas has been criticized by reform groups, and for fifty years not much has changed. For the past decade, efforts to change the system of selecting judges have increased substantially. Chief Justice John Hill resigned from the Texas Supreme Court on January 1, 1988, in order to promote changes in the state's judicial selection system. Almost all the effort to change the way judges are selected in Texas has concentrated on the judges of the appellate and district courts, which are the major trial courts. It is in these courts, of course, where the stakes are the highest in terms of possible criminal penalties and civil damages. However, the increased pressure for changes in the way Texas selects its judges comes from many sources.

As Texas elections have become more competitive with the rapid increase in Republican Party strength, judicial elections have been increasingly determined by the party affiliation of judges. In Dallas County, for example, regardless of the experience and qualifications of the candidates, Republican judicial candidates win and Democratic judicial candidates lose. In Harris County, where there is more flux in party preferences from year to year, the popularity of presidential candidates has been an important factor in determining the outcome of trial court elections. Notably incompetent or unqualified people have been elected to judicial office simply because they had the right party affiliation for a particular election year. In 1994, in a race for the Texas Court of Criminal Appeals, Texas's highest criminal court, a highly regarded Democratic judge with significant judicial experience was defeated in his campaign for reelection by a Republican candidate with no judicial experience and almost no litigation experience, even though that candidate misled the press about his experience and even his place of birth.[1] However, 1994 was a very good year to run for judicial office in Texas as a Republican.

It has been argued that voters generally know little about judicial candidates,[2] leaving their voting decisions solely to the party label of the candidate. As a result, judges are elected on the basis of party affiliation rather than on the basis of their experience or qualifications.[3]

In addition, as judicial elections become more competitive, they be-

---

1. See Wayne Slater, "Law board drops inquiry of Appeals Judge Mansfield," *Dallas Morning News*, 28 June 1995, pp. 1A, 12A.
2. Anthony Champagne and Greg Thielemann, "Awareness of Trial Court Judges," *Judicature*, vol. 74, (1991), p. 271.
3. However, party affiliation may provide a cue to the underlying ideology of the judge. See Philip DuBois, *Judicial Elections and the Quest for Accountability* (Austin, University of Texas Press, 1980).

come more costly because judicial candidates must spend money to encourage voters to vote for them. These judicial races, especially races for the Texas Supreme Court, can be very expensive. It is likely that a competitive race for the Texas Supreme Court will now cost each candidate in the general election around $3,000,000.[4] Even races for the intermediate appellate courts and for some of the state's trial courts can cost hundreds of thousands of dollars. The problem with the costs of judicial elections is that the money does not come from a broad base of Texans; instead, the money comes from interests with economic concerns about the outcomes of court cases. For example, the funding of judicial races in Texas often becomes a battle of interest groups in which plaintiffs lawyers provide funding for one judicial candidate, and civil defense lawyers, business political action committees, and medical groups fund the other candidate.[5] Many reformers are concerned about the propriety of judges being so dependent upon funds from groups that are involved with the outcomes of their decisions.

The 1996 elections for the Texas Supreme Court suggest, however, a new development in reference to the role of money and interest groups in Texas judicial politics. Democratic candidates for the Texas Supreme Court could not raise money, even from plaintiffs lawyers who would usually fund a Democratic candidate against conservative Republicans. The only candidates who were able to raise substantial sums were the Republican incumbents. Although it may be too early to assert this point with much certainty, it may be that the increasing growth of the Republican Party state-wide has so discouraged plaintiffs lawyers that the funding battle between plaintiffs and civil defense interests is coming to an end. It may also be that Democrats are recognizing that they face an increasingly hopeless task in running for the Supreme Court. One incumbent Republican, Greg Abbott, did not even face a Democratic opponent in his reelection campaign. If this new development continues, it will cause a major shift in the extent to which business interests can continue to support changes in the judicial selection system and a shift in the traditional opposition to changes by the Democratic Party and by plaintiffs lawyers.

For the past decade civil rights groups have argued that the current system for selecting judges in Texas makes it difficult for minorities to be elected to the bench.[6] They argue that because appellate and major

---

4. For a discussion of the role of money in Texas judicial races, see *Judicial Reform in the States*, Anthony Champagne and Judith Haydel, eds. (Lanham, MD: University Press of America, 1993), pp. 104–10.
5. A discussion of the way competing interest groups fund judicial campaigns is in Anthony Champagne, "Campaign Contributions in Texas Supreme Court Races," *Crime, Law & Social Change*, Vol. 17 (1992), p. 91.
6. A superb discussion of the issue of minorities, judicial representation, and judicial selection is in Ronald W. Chapman, "Judicial Roulette: Alternatives to Single-Member Districts as a Legal and Political Solution to Voting-Rights Challenges to At-Large Judicial Elections," *SMU Law Review*, (1995), p. 457.

trial court judges are elected on either a county or multicounty basis, minority candidates must run in districts that are dominated by whites, and racial prejudices make it very difficult for minorities to win judgeships in white districts. There are 18 judges elected state-wide; only 2 are minorities. There are 80 appeals court judges in Texas; only 8 are minorities. There are 396 district court judges; only 11 percent are black or Hispanic.[7]

The major arguments against the current system of judicial selection are the following: (1) The system is too political, emphasizing party over qualifications. (2) The system is overly dependent upon money from interests with stakes in the outcomes of court cases. (3) The system places minority judicial candidates at a disadvantage. Given these charges against the current judicial selection system, it is necessary to explain why the current partisan election system remains in place. First, however, it is important to get an overview of the variety of ways in which judges in the United States are selected.

The Primary Ways of Selecting Judges

In the United States, judges are usually chosen by some method of election or appointment. Federal judges, for example, are appointed. They are nominated by the president, confirmed by the Senate, and serve until they die, retire, or resign from the bench. Some states use an appointive system in which the governor appoints state court judges. A couple of states have a system in which the legislature selects judges without nomination by the governor. In addition to appointive systems, the election of judges is popular. Judges are elected in partisan elections, such as in the Texas system, or in nonpartisan elections.

Over the past fifty years, a system that combines elective and appointive systems has become common. That system is known as merit selection, or the "Missouri Plan" system. Under merit selection, a commission, usually including members of the bar and lay people and usually chosen by the bar and political officials within the state, solicits prospective nominees for judgeships and screens the applicants. The commission then creates a list of three to five prospective nominees for a judicial vacancy and submits those names to the governor. The governor usually must appoint one of the persons listed by the commission. After a time, that judicial appointee runs for office in what is called a retention election. In such an election, the judge faces no opponent, but voters are asked to vote on whether the judge should be retained in office. This method has aspects of an appointive system, with gubernatorial appointment from the commission's list. It also has aspects of an elective system in that the judge runs in a retention election.

---

7. Sam Attlesey, "Standoff between Judicial Reformers Stalls Legislation," *Dallas Morning News*, 20 April 1997, p. 48A.

Judicial Selection in Texas 93

TABLE 6.1

Systems of Selection in the States

Merit System	Appointment	Partisan Election	Nonpartisan Election	Mixed System*
Alaska	California (G)**	Alabama	Georgia	Arizona
Colorado	Maine (G)	Arkansas	Idaho	Florida
Connecticut	New Hampshire (G)	Illinois	Kentucky	Indiana
Delaware	New Jersey (G)	Louisiana	Michigan	Kansas
D.C.	Rhode Island (Mixed)	Mississippi	Minnesota	Missouri
Hawaii	South Carolina (L)	N. Carolina	Montana	New York
Iowa	Virginia (L)	Pennsylvania	Nevada	Oklahoma
Maryland		Texas	N. Dakota	South Dakota
Massachusetts		W. Virginia	Ohio	Tennessee
Nebraska			Oregon	
N. Mexico			Washington	
Utah			Wisconsin	
Vermont				
Wyoming				

* Usually, in mixed systems all or some appellate judges are chosen with a merit selection system and some trial judges are elected.
** (G) indicates gubernatorial appointment; (L) indicates legislative appointment; (mixed) indicates some judges are appointed by the governor and some by the legislature.
Source: American Judicature Society, June 2, 1993.

In many states there is a mixture of selection systems, in which some levels of courts or some judicial districts are chosen under one system and other levels of courts and other judicial districts have judges chosen under another system. As Table 6.1 illustrates, there is no agreement among the states as to which system of selection is the most appropriate. The multiple selection systems of the U.S. state judiciaries reflect the cultures and political values of those states.

All systems of selection have been criticized. As noted elsewhere in this chapter, there are concerns that too much political maneuvering enters into elective judicial politics, that too much money is involved in judicial races, and that voters are often unaware of the candidates. The latter criticism is made of both partisan and nonpartisan systems. Appointive systems, whether gubernatorial or legislative, it is argued, reek of cronyism, wherein judgeships are used as political rewards for friends and supporters of the appointing officer. Merit selection has also been criticized because cronyism has occurred in the selection of judges by commissions and the appointment of judges from the commission's list by the governor.[8]

None of these systems of selection has a consistently good record when it comes to the selection of minority judges, although in some cases impressive numbers of minorities have been selected. For example, President Jimmy Carter was very concerned with diversity on the federal bench, and his judicial appointments are remarkable in their representation of minorities. That pattern is not consistent in any system of selection, however. President Carter's successor, Ronald Reagan, was much less interested in diversity on the bench and he made relatively few minority judicial appointments.

Because of the failure of any system of selection to consistently lead to substantial appointments of minorities, civil rights groups have tended to look for other ways of increasing minority representation. They have commonly borrowed from litigation over school boards and city councils, and have argued that in states with elective judiciaries, the judicial districts for those judges should be small and should be drawn in such a way that they lead to the election of substantial numbers of minority judges. In states with appointive judiciaries, minorities must seek other measures, such as political pressure on governors, to gain substantial minority appointments.

Texas could select its judges in any of the ways discussed above. However, Texas owes it current system of selecting judges to a Republican who ruled Texas during Reconstruction, Governor E. J. Davis.

The Texas Experience

The Texas Constitution of 1876 created an elective system for judges in Texas. While it does not require partisan election of judges, that was a natural result of an elective system in Texas. As mentioned in the earlier chapter on the Texas Constitution, the framers of the 1876 Constitution feared a powerful governor, such as the Reconstruction Governor E. J. Davis. As a result, they created a very decentralized government with numerous officials holding offices independent from the office of the governor. Judicial offices were also removed from gubernatorial jurisdiction by making them independently elected officials.

In the aftermath of Reconstruction, serious candidates for office in Texas were Democrats and ran on the Democratic Party ballot. It was rare for any Democratic nominee in Texas to even have Republican opposition, much less to be threatened by a Republican opponent. In effect

---

8. Richard Watson and Robert Downing, *The Politics of the Bench and the Bar* (New York, Wiley, 1969).

Texas had a kind of nonpartisan system for elections—everyone ran as a Democrat, and so party label was unimportant. That began to change in judicial races in the early 1980s. Governor William Clements, the first Republican governor in Texas since Reconstruction, was elected in 1978 and began appointing Republicans to new and vacant judicial offices. These judges had to run for elective office in the first election after their appointment, and they ran as Republicans. More important, Texas was being transformed into a competitive two-party state. With the presidential candidacy of Ronald Reagan in 1980 and again in 1984, Republican candidates for judgeships could capitalize on increasing numbers of Republican voters and Reagan's popularity and be elected to office.

As a result of the appearance of a more vigorous two-party system, judicial elections in Texas became partisan contests and, as those elections became more heated, it was necessary for candidates to raise more money to get elected to office. At roughly the same time, special interest groups became more involved in judicial politics. This was a natural development, because as judicial elections became competitive, interest groups had more choices of candidates they could support or oppose. Even at the state level, judges were seen as being increasingly involved in public policymaking, and the interest groups, wanting a voice in all aspects of policymaking, thus became more involved in judicial elections.

It is rare to find someone who will speak favorably about the Texas system for selecting judges. It is a very political system in which unqualified persons are chosen for important offices. In addition, enormous amounts of money are spent in judicial races, raising questions about judicial integrity and impartiality, and voters often do not know the qualifications of the candidates for whom they are voting. Civil rights groups add that it is a system wherein very few minorities hold judicial office. Given this, one may reasonably ask why Texas still chooses judges through partisan elections.

Why Texas Still Has Partisan Elections

It is important to understand that there are many factions involved in the debate over judicial selection. One has to examine the key special interest groups in order to determine the selection system each believes is in their best interests.

The Political Parties

The Democratic and Republican parties in Texas need to maintain their numbers and power. In part, that is done by having a large number of partisan offices that can be political rewards for the party faithful, which in turn encourage people to get involved and to work on behalf of the party and its candidates. A large number of partisan offices can also be a source of pride and prestige for a political party successful enough to capture many of those offices.

Judgeships in Texas are not only numerous, they are also prestigious and pay fairly well. If the partisan election of judges was abandoned in favor of another system of selection, such as nonpartisan election or an appointive system, it would be contrary to the interests of the political parties. As a result, both the Democrats and Republicans can be expected to resist change.

The Plaintiffs Bar

Texas is, in general, a conservative state with a pro-business environment. There is a tendency to elect conservative, pro-business governors who appoint conservative, pro-business judges. As a result, plaintiffs lawyers, those who sue on behalf of injured parties, often against businesses, have until recently strongly supported partisan election of judges. Their fear has been that Texas would move toward an appointive system, such as merit selection, for selecting judges.

From the perspective of a plaintiffs lawyer in a conservative pro-business state, there is a great likelihood that a conservative pro-business judge will be appointed to office. Given that concern, it seems preferable to maintain the partisan election system, wherein the plaintiffs lawyers might exert some influence over the selection of judges by contributing generously to judicial campaigns. However, this traditional support for partisan elections is lessening among plaintiffs lawyers for one major reason: the Republican Party's ascendance to power. In the aftermath of the 1994 elections, it has become clear that Texas as a whole is moving in a conservative direction and that Republicans, who tend to be more conservative than Democrats, are able to win elections both at the top (gubernatorial) and bottom (judicial) of the ballot. Republicans are now a majority on the Texas Supreme Court. It is clear that plaintiffs lawyer contributions to judicial races are no longer enough to elect judges sympathetic to the plaintiffs bar. Thus, the obdurate opposition to judicial selection changes by plaintiffs lawyers has lessened. It may be that plaintiffs will now be better off with a nonpartisan system for electing judges. In a nonpartisan system, the Republican Party label would not be a tool for electing large numbers of conservative, pro-business, anti-plaintiff judges. Nor would it be in the best interests of the plaintiffs bar to favor an appointive or merit selection system because, in an era of increasing Republican strength, Republican governors would likely try to appoint conservative, pro-business Republican judges to the bench.

Civil Defense Lawyers, Business Interests, and Medical Interests

Businesses and professional groups, especially physicians, are likely to be sued and are represented by civil defense lawyers. These defense interests have long worried about the influence of plaintiffs lawyer contributions in judicial races. Not only have they contributed great amounts of money in judicial races to counter the contributions of the plaintiffs bar, but they believe that they have suffered in the courts at the hands of plaintiffs-oriented judges who were chosen under a partisan election system. As a result, these defense interests have traditionally supported merit selection as the appropriate system of selection for judges. Not only is it likely that the appointing governor will have a conservative, pro-business perspective, but because no one runs against a judge in a retention election, these elections are usually inexpensive, and the importance of plaintiffs lawyer contributions is minimal.

However, this traditional support for merit selection of judges among defense interests may be declining as those defense interests, especially in the aftermath of the 1994 elections, see more conservative, pro-business Republicans being elected to office.

Minorities

Minority groups want to elect more African-American and Hispanic judges to the bench. However, the current system of partisan elections has led to the election of small numbers of minorities to the bench, and in 1994, eight of the ten minority judges in Harris County were defeated. As a result, minority interest groups concerned about judicial selection do not like the system, in which the districts are county-wide or larger.

Some have argued that minorities would be better off with a nonpartisan election system. Because minorities in Texas are overwhelmingly Democratic voters, and because large numbers of minority judicial candidates who have been defeated have been Democrats, it may be that in a nonpartisan system, the recent tendency in Texas to vote Republican would not affect judicial races, and more minorities would win judgeships. However, the counterargument is that minorities tend to vote straight Democratic tickets and the elimination of the party label in judicial races would vastly reduce minority voting in those races.[9]

Minority groups involved in judicial selection in Texas dislike appointive systems because of a concern that governors would not appoint many minorities to the bench.[10] Because Texas is increasingly Republican and minorities provide little of the electoral base of the Republican Party in Texas, it seems unlikely that minorities could expect many appointments from Republican governors.

Minorities do not trust the current elective system, have concerns about a nonpartisan system, and are hostile toward an appointive system; therefore, minorities have tended to support the partisan election of judges from small districts. Civil rights groups have argued that district court judges (the major trial court judges in Texas) should be elected from districts about the size of the state representative districts. In a

9. Chapman reports that more than 90 percent of African-American voters and between 60 and 70 percent of Hispanic voters vote Democratic. See Ronald W. Chapman, "Judicial Roulette," p. 482.
10. Of the seventy-nine judicial appointments made by Republican Governor William Clements, only six were either African-American or Hispanic. In contrast, one-third of the judicial appointments of Democratic Governor Ann Richards were minorities. See Michael Totty, "Is This Any Way to Choose a Judge?, *Wall Street Journal* 3 August 1994, pp. T1, T4.

county such as Dallas, the county would elect its thirty-seven district judges from eighteen districts, instead of the current system of electing those judges county-wide. Because several state representative districts have large minority populations, minorities believe that African-American and Hispanic judges can be elected from those districts. Texas minority groups have been unsuccessful in enlisting the federal courts in supporting their position that these minority districts should be created because the current system violates federal law, but the Department of Justice under President Clinton has shown sympathy for these efforts.

Judges

Judges have a key interest in the battle over judicial selection. Their main concern is political security. In addition, sitting judges have a considerable amount of power. Within the legal community and within county politics, judges are often well connected and influential figures. Thus, if there was an appointive system such as merit selection, judges would want to be "grandfathered" into the system so that they would reap the benefits of retention elections. With retention elections they would run for office and have no opponents, and probably no need for significant fund-raising efforts. Because only about 1.6 percent of judges are defeated in retention elections,[11] some sort of system that includes retention elections would be very attractive to judges. However, judges would also want to avoid the risk of being screened out by the merit selection commission or not being appointed by the governor.

There might be some judicial support for nonpartisan elections. Incumbent judges would have a political advantage in a nonpartisan election, and would not be subject to the partisan sweeps that have occurred in some counties such as Harris, where judges have been voted out of office simply because they had the wrong party label for that particular election year.

Most judges, who are in office because they have been elected from a large district, will not support the formation of smaller districts. If they suddenly have to campaign in a much smaller district, they are in danger of losing.

THE AMALGAM OF COMPETING INTERESTS

The problem that has occurred from the amalgam of competing interest groups is that the key interests in judicial selection politics are very different. The political parties have no doubts: they want partisan election of judges. The Democratic Party would, because of its strong minority constituency, be more tolerant of smaller districts than would the Republican Party. The Republican Party would oppose smaller districts because such a system would provide Democrats with the means to

11. Susan Carbon and Larry Berkson, *Judicial Retention Elections in the United States* (Chicago, IL: American Judicature Society, 1980), p. 21.

break the Republican stronghold on large counties such as Dallas County and Tarrant County. Republicans are currently winning with larger districts, and would prefer the status quo. An appointive system is risky. In spite of the state's increasing Republican representation, a Democrat could be elected governor. Therefore, Republicans might see the current system as providing them the most benefit in terms of controlling the state's judiciary.[12]

Plaintiffs lawyers have no major problems with the smaller districts promoted by minorities. They have increasingly mixed feelings about the value of partisan elections in general, a system they have strongly supported in the past. However, plaintiffs lawyers oppose an appointive system such as merit selection, because conservative, pro-business judges would be selected.

Defense interests have traditionally supported merit selection, although with increasing Republican strength in Texas, they are more satisfied with the current system of selection. Defense interests do not want significantly smaller judicial districts in Texas. In at least some urban counties, the most notable being Dallas County, smaller districts would break conservative Republican control of the courthouse. It is more important, however, that, as theories of politics from the days of James Madison have suggested, the smaller the constituency, the more sensitive the elected official must be to that constituency. An elected official in a small district cannot play one interest against another simply because, unlike in a larger district, the constituents are more likely to be homogeneous. Thus, business interests fear what lawyers call "home cooking"; judges who are very responsive to the demands of constituents.

Judges don't want any change in the system which will endanger their jobs. If there is a change, their ideal would be a system that made their jobs more secure. Thus, for judges, retention elections are especially attractive and significantly smaller districts are threatening to their careers.

THE LIEUTENANT GOVERNOR'S COMMITTEE

Lieutenant Governor Bob Bullock, concerned about the role of money in judicial elections and the possibility that the Department of Justice would refuse to approve the creation of any more courts in Texas (on

---

12. Conservative columnist William Murchison expressed a widespread Republican view of judicial reform when he wrote, "The Democratic-inspired idea behind judicial reapportionment is to unhorse Republican judges, replacing them with black or brown Democrats grateful to the party establishment." See William Murchison, "Why Morales Deserved to Lose," *Texas Lawyer*, 6 September 1993, p. 8. Although former Republican Governor William Clements and Republican Texas Chief Justice Tom Phillips supported judicial reform in a jointly written newspaper opinion piece, they recognized that many Republicans felt otherwise, and wrote, "After 31 Democratic state judges lost in November's election, many Republicans are reluctant to reform Texas' judicial election process. They see a basic unfairness in changing the judicial system just when it seemingly begins to favor them." See Bill Clements and Tom Phillips, "GOP sweep shouldn't obscure need for Texas court reform," *Dallas Morning News*, 27 January 1995, p. 29A.

the grounds that the current system discriminates against minorities), created a committee in 1994 to explore the possibilities of developing a judicial reform proposal. The composition of the committee was such as to give key interests a voice in developing the proposal. Three Democratic state senators and three Republican senators were appointed. One of the Democratic state senators was an African-American who had close ties to civil rights groups in Houston that advocated greater representation of African-Americans on the bench. One of the Democratic state senators was Hispanic, and had close ties to civil rights groups in San Antonio that advocated greater representation of Hispanics on the bench. Four members of the committee were judges: one Republican and three Democrats. Three of the judges were Texas Supreme Court justices, and one was the presiding judge of the Court of Criminal Appeals. All were well respected in the legal community.

The president of the Texas Trial Lawyers Association, the major plaintiffs attorney organization in the state, was a regular attender of the meetings; another was a public relations specialist who represented business in political and legislative matters. Although there were complaints that the meetings were closed to the public, that there were no public or consumer representatives on the committee, that there were no lower court judges on the committee, and that no members of the Texas House of Representatives were there, important interests in judicial politics were represented.[13]

It soon became clear to the committee that there were no easy solutions to the politics of judicial selection wherein all competing interests could be readily accommodated. Some sort of compromise would have to be reached. Minorities were willing to support modifications of the appellate courts in exchange for greater representation of minorities on trial courts. While minorities believed that it would be possible to draw smaller districts within counties to increase minority representation, they knew that the size of appellate court districts were so vast that small districts for appellate courts would generally still be so large that minorities would benefit little. Business interests saw an opportunity. They would support greater minority representation on the trial court bench in exchange for an appointive system such as merit selection. Plaintiffs lawyers saw their grip on appellate courts weakening. It would not make much difference whether Republican governors appointed conservatives to the appellate bench or voters elected conservative Republicans to the bench. Smaller trial courts, however, opened up the possibility that at least some pro-plaintiff trial judges could continue to be elected.

One problem with judicial selection was that, among minorities and

---

13. An example of these complaints that additional interests should be represented on the committee is in Robert Elder, Jr., and Walter Borges, "A Bullock in a China Closet? Group Tackles Judge Selection," *Texas Lawyer*, 15 August 1994, p. 1.

plaintiffs lawyers who had long fought merit selection, the system was perceived as so evil that it could not be supported. Republicans had fought very small judicial districts and judges were uncomfortable with the idea of small districts as well. As a result, creating a compromise was difficult. However, the committee agreed on a compromise wherein appellate judges would be appointed by the governor. Trial judges in urban areas would be elected from county commissioners precincts. After serving for a time they would run county-wide in retention elections. They would later have to be reelected from county commissioners precincts. In order to depoliticize the judiciary, judges were to be elected in nonpartisan elections, which would protect judges from the party sweeps of recent elections.

The compromise seemed to have something for everyone. Business was given an appointive system. Because the governor would appoint appellate judges, they would have greater career security and no worries about campaign funding. In addition, an appointive system enhanced the power of incoming Governor Bush. Minorities and plaintiffs lawyers got smaller trial court districts, which would allow for the election of more minorities and some plaintiffs-oriented judges. Judges were protected from party sweeps. All of these interests seemed to be accommodated without resorting to merit selection or the formation of very small electoral districts.

However, not everyone was happy with the accommodations. Although African-Americans were very supportive of the compromise, Hispanics were not. The two largest counties in Texas—Harris and Dallas counties—elect a total of 96 of the 386 district court judges in Texas. Thus, those counties are the most important in any plan that would increase minority representation on the bench. Each county in Texas is divided into four county commissioners precincts. Under the compromise, one-fourth of Harris County and Dallas County judges would be elected from each county commissioners precinct in that county. Harris and Dallas counties currently each have three white county commissioners precincts and one African-American precinct: Hispanics believe that this indicated that the compromise would not promote the election of more Hispanic judges. To achieve their objective, they felt that considerably smaller districts would be needed.

The political parties also opposed the compromise. Nonpartisan elections might protect the interests of judges, but nonpartisan elections weakened the political parties. In addition, an appointive system for appellate judges reduced the number of elective offices and thus reduced the role of the parties. Governor Bush, although his powers would benefit from an appointed appellate judiciary, opposed the compromise, probably because he did not want to oppose the Republican Party.

The compromise sailed through the Texas senate, because it had the support of the committee's creator, the influential Lieutenant Governor

Bob Bullock. Bullock, the state's most effective political leader, has such influence over the state senate that any legislation he backs has a high probability of success. In the Texas house, however, the plan had opposition. Unlike Bullock, Speaker of the House Pete Laney did not give judicial selection reform priority. Party opposition, especially that of the Republican Party and Governor Bush, emboldened dissenters. Hispanic house members also opposed the compromise, but offered an alternative, which was to elect district judges from state representative districts rather than from county commissioner precincts. That proved unacceptable: business and Republicans could not approve of such a small constituency for judges. The chance to change the way judges are selected in Texas was gone.

THE 1996–1997 EFFORT

Buoyed by the passage of judicial reform legislation in the senate as a result of Lieutenant Governor Bullock's initiative, the Texas Supreme Court appointed task forces to develop proposals for improving the Texas judiciary. One of those task forces examined judicial selection, but its effort was doomed to failure. The task force expressed its concerns about the current system for selecting judges, but its members were unable to agree upon an alternative judicial selection system.[14]

Chief Justice Tom Phillips, long an advocate of judicial selection reforms in Texas, again tried to push the issue in his State of the Judiciary address, in which he severely criticized the partisanship of the current system, the role of money in judicial races, and lack of minority representation on the bench.[15]

As the 1997 legislative session entered the home stretch, however, the prospects for reform remained slim. In the senate, one proposal provided for the appointment of appellate judges and the election of district judges in nonpartisan elections. Both appellate and trial judges would then run in retention elections, although trial judges would run in regular nonpartisan elections after two retention elections. In counties of more than one million, district judges would be elected from county commissioners precincts. The other major senate proposal provided for the appointment, election, and retention of appellate judges and eliminated straight party voting for appellate and district judges. Appellate judges would have to run in partisan elections following the expiration of their appointed terms and then would be subject to retention elections.[16]

Of these two proposals, the first bill was sponsored by state senator

14. Texas Commission on Judicial Efficiency, *Governance of the Texas Judiciary: Independence and Accountability*, Volume 1 (1996), pp. 23–24.
15. Thomas R. Phillips, "State of the Judiciary Address," 24 February 1997 (mimeographed).
16. Texas Senate Research Center, "Comparison of Selected Judicial Selection Legislation," 24 February 1997 (mimeographed).

Rodney Ellis, an African-American Democrat from Houston, but he admitted that it did not have enough support from non-minority legislators to pass. The second proposal was by a white Republican from Lubbock, state senator Robert Duncan. Minorities threatened to oppose the Duncan plan on the grounds that it did not provide increased chances for minority representation on the bench. Senator Ellis, for example, threatened to filibuster the Duncan bill and the chairman of the Mexican-American Legislative Caucus, Representative Hugo Berlanga, a Democrat from Corpus Christi, claimed the plan "is going to meet very stiff resistance."[17] Minority leaders were especially adamant that any judicial selection change include both trial and appellate judges. Their hope was that some compromise would develop to allow them to get smaller trial judge districts, and therefore more minority judges, in exchange for an appointed appellate judiciary, which would be favored by business interests. If the Duncan bill passed, minorities feared business interests would gain their objective of changing the way appellate judges were selected and then would never support the minority group objective of smaller trial court districts.[18]

Minority lawmakers tried to kill Duncan's plan because they did not believe minorities would benefit from the plan, pointing out that if appellate judges were appointed, diversity on the bench would not necessarily follow. Governor Bush, for example, has appointed sixty-seven judges to vacant positions since January 1995. Only five have been black and only five Hispanic.

After a considerable amount of posturing, senators Ellis and Duncan agreed to a compromise bill by which appellate judges would be appointed. District judges would also be appointed, but the districts would be county commissioners precincts. The appointed judges would then run against opponents in the next primary elections. However, all candidates would run in all primaries, creating a nonpartisan primary election. If a candidate did not receive fifty percent of the vote, there would be a run-off in the general election. The winner would serve four years and would then run in a nonpartisan retention election.[19]

The compromise plan, however, still did not resolve the concerns of Hispanics, and many incumbent judges were uncomfortable about the plan as well.

Conclusion: It Is Hopeless

The problem with judicial reform has been two-fold: (1) with the exception of Lieutenant Governor Bullock, political leaders in Texas have not chosen to make judicial reform part of their agenda, and (2) there

17. Attlesey, *supra* note 7.
18. Ibid.
19. "Texas Judges," *Dallas Morning News*, 2 May 1997, p. 32A.

are so many competing interest groups with divergent concerns in the debate over reform that change in the way judges are selected has been unlikely.

What does the future hold? The problem remains in accommodating the various interest groups involved in this issue. The interest group struggle has created a policymaking deadlock concerning reform. The result of this deadlock is that the existing system, despite its many flaws, will continue for want of an acceptable alternative.

PART III

Politics

7
Party Identification and Public Opinion in Texas, 1984–1994: Establishing a Competitive Two-Party System

JAMES A. DYER, JAN E. LEIGHLEY,
AND ARNOLD VEDLITZ
TEXAS A&M UNIVERSITY

As shown in this chapter, one of the most remarkable developments in modern Texas politics has been the expansion of the Republican Party. Until 1978 no Republican since Reconstruction had been able to capture the governorship. In 1978, William Clements, a Republican, was elected governor. Clements was defeated in 1982, but recaptured the governorship in 1986. In 1994, another Republican, George Bush, became governor. Republicans were winning other statewide offices. By 1994, there were Republicans elected to the Texas Railroad Commission, the State Board of Education, the Texas Court of Criminal Appeals, the Texas Supreme Court, and the Office of Agriculture Commissioner. In addition, both U.S. senators from Texas are now Republicans.

While two key offices, the office of lieutenant governor and the office of speaker of the Texas house, have eluded the Republicans, Republicans have been a growing force in the state legislature. It is unlikely that a Republican speaker will be elected until there is a majority of Republicans in the house, and the election of a Republican lieutenant governor must await the retirement of the enormously popular and powerful incumbent, Bob Bullock. However, Republicans can now seriously consider the capture of these offices, something unimaginable a decade ago.

The dominance of the Democratic Party in Texas politics, a dominance that existed for over a century, has clearly disappeared. There are several implications of this change in party identification. African-Americans and, to a somewhat lesser extent, Hispanics continue to have strong Democratic loyalties. As the Democratic Party weakens, the political power of minorities in Texas may also be lessened. At the same time, power is flowing to the Republican Party, a party with few ties to African-Americans and Hispanics. It seems unlikely that a heavily white Republican Party will be very responsive to the needs and political demands of minorities: this could lead to an expansion of racial and ethnic tensions in the state.

Many of the funds for Democratic Party activities now come from trial lawyers, whereas funding for Republican Party activities tends to come from medical doctors, other professionals, and from the business community. In the first six months of the Bush administration, it became clear that trial lawyers and the individual and consumer interests they often promote have suffered at the hands of an increasingly conservative and pro-business legislature.

It may be that as the Democratic Party is increasingly funded by trial lawyers and its core voters are increasingly minorities, the party will represent more liberal interests. That will make the Democratic Party less the "umbrella" party that it once was. In an earlier era, the Democratic Party was a home for liberals, conservatives, reactionaries, union members, minorities, business people, and trial lawyers. It was a party that brought together enough diverse interests that it was dominant. The major challenge for the Democratic Party is that it not limit its appeal to interest groups that are too small to win elections. The Republican Party will have to adjust to being a party in power, and must learn to adjust to the competing pressures of varying interests within the party. It has already had difficulty in dealing with the competition between pro-business, economic conservatives and the religious right. As the party increases its power over the government, more such difficulty can be expected.

As in the rest of the South, the dominance of the Democratic Party in Texas during the twentieth century has its roots in the Civil War and its aftermath. During Reconstruction, the Republican Party controlled the state; after Reconstruction, the Republican Party was not only voted out but was rendered meaningless as a viable contender in elections. With the resounding defeat of Republican Reconstruction Governor E. J. Davis in 1873, Republicans were not able to win statewide office in Texas again until 1961, when John Tower was elected to fill the vacant senate seat of Democrat Lyndon Johnson (who had just won election as vice president).

Hence, for many decades, through the early 1970s, electoral competition in Texas occurred exclusively within the Democratic primary. Throughout this period, the Democratic Party in Texas had two distinct factions, one consisting of conservatives, the other liberals. Candidates from each of these factions would fight it out in the primaries, with the winner—usually the candidate from the conservative faction—sailing to victory in the general election.

Observers of Texas politics have noted the potential for a competitive two-party system in the state for decades. In *Southern Politics*, for example, V. O. Key observed that the New Deal had strained the coalition of conservatives and liberals within the Democratic Party, "possibly in portent of the rise of a bipartisan system."[1] Decades later, the increasing

1. V. O. Key, Jr., *Southern Politics in State and Nation* (New York: Vintage, 1949), p. 255.

presence of the Republican Party in the state suggests that Texas *is* a competitive two-party state. The successful election of Republicans to the governorship and other statewide offices, as well as the particularly strong party organizations in urban centers such as Dallas and Houston, are signs of a more competitive party system in the state.[2]

Whether the Republican Party will consolidate, increase, or even lose these gains in the state over the next decade is open to question. If the increasing success of the Republican Party in the state during the 1980s was simply a short-term, personalized response to a very popular President Reagan, then we might see no further gains, and perhaps even a decline, in Republican Party success in the post-Reagan era. However, if the Republican successes of the 1980s reflected a long-term shift of the partisan loyalties of a large proportion of Texans, then we might be witnessing the establishment of a two-party system in the state of Texas for the first time since Reconstruction.

This chapter focuses on changes in Texans' party identification between 1984 and 1994. Our primary interest is in describing trends in party identification, in an effort to document the nature and sources of changes in the party system in Texas over this period. A secondary focus is to determine the extent to which party identification structures Texans' positions on policy issues and their voting choices. We find that more Texans identify themselves as Republicans today than in 1984, nearly eliminating the historical predominance of Democrats in the state, and that party identification continues to influence Texans' voting choices.

At the same time, the ideology of the Texas electorate in 1994 is almost exactly the same as it was in 1984. As many Texans report being conservative today as they did a decade ago. We conclude that the 1984–1994 period was one of both dealignment and realignment in Texas politics. On the basis of these changes in party identification and continuity in political ideology, we expect that the realignment will continue to favor the Republican Party in the coming years, due to the conservative ideology of a majority of Texans. That is, because Texans are now more likely to identify with a political party that is consistent with their personal political ideology, we expect these changes in party identification to be sustained, and that the Republicans will, at minimum, maintain their new level of support in Texas. To put these observations in a broader context, we begin with a brief discussion of the scholarly research on party identification and party realignment.

Party Identification and Realignment

One of the central concepts emerging from scholarship on mass political behavior in the United States is that of party identification—a psy-

---

2. Kim Quaile Hill and Kenneth R. Mladenka, *Texas Government: Politics and Economics*, 3rd ed. (Belmont, CA: Wadsworth, 1993).

chological attachment individuals have toward a political party.[3] Party identification is critical in understanding several important aspects of voters' political behavior, most notably which candidate the voter chooses, and positions on other political issues.[4] Although party identification was initially conceptualized as highly stable and immune to change, many have challenged this assumption.[5]

Some scholars, for example, argue that party realignments like that in the 1930s—in which large, enduring shifts in voting coalitions supporting major parties create new dominant parties—result from supporters of one party changing their loyalty from the old majority party to a new party. Other scholars disagree, arguing that realignments result from new voters being mobilized to vote for the new party.[6] With this debate unresolved, some scholars have begun to study state electorates that seem to be undergoing shifts in the party loyalties of their citizens.

Dyer, Vedlitz and Hill, for example, report that in Texas, between 1984 and 1987, the proportion of self-identified Republicans in the state increased from about 23 percent to nearly 30 percent, while the proportion of self-identified Democrats in the state decreased from around 39 percent to about 33 percent. The sources of these changes include the mobilization of new voters and new residents of the state, as well as some conversion of middle class and upper-middle class Democrats to the Republican Party. As of 1987, however, whether the gains in party identification made by the Republican Party in Texas would be sustained in the long-term was unclear.[7] This period in Texas may actually have been one of dealignment (Democrats and new voters becoming independents) rather than realignment (Democrats and new voters becoming Republican).[8] In the next section, we use more recent data on the party identification of Texans to show that the 1984–1994 period was one of *both* dealignment and realignment.

We also consider the sources of changing party identification; that is, which demographic and ideological groups have changed their political party affiliations. The party realignment literature suggests that age

---

3. For the classic statement, see Angus Campbell, Phillp E. Converse, Warren E. Miller, and Donald E. Stokes, *The American Voter* (New York: John Wiley, 1960).
4. Norman R. Luttbeg and Michael M. Gant, *American Electoral Behavior 1952–1992* (Itasca, IL: Peacock, 1995).
5. See, for example, Charles H. Franklin and John E. Jackson, "The Dynamics of Party Identification," *American Political Science Review* (1983), vol. 77, pp. 957–73; Michael B. MacKuen, Robert S. Erikson, and James A. Stimson, "Macropartisanship," *American Political Science Review* (1989), vol. 83, pp. 1125–42; Benjamin I. Page and Calvin C. Jones, "Reciprocal Effects of Policy Preferences, Party Loyalties, and the Vote," *American Political Science Review* (1979), vol. 73, pp. 1071–90.
6. See, for example, James Sundquist, *Dynamics of the Party System* (Washington, D.C.: Brookings, 1983).
7. James Dyer and Don Haynes, "Modeling Change from Survey Data," *in* Frederick Williams, *Measuring the Information Society* (Beverly Hills, CA: Sage, 1988).
8. James A. Dyer, Arnold Vedlitz, and David B. Hill, "New Voters, Switchers and Political Party Realignment in Texas," *Western Political Quarterly* (1988), vol. 41, pp. 155–67.

should be associated with changes in party identification: specifically, younger Texans should be more likely to change their partisan affiliation. The literature also suggests that individuals whose interests are represented better by the new party will be more likely to change their partisan affiliation. Hence, we also expect that conservatives and high socio-economic status individuals should be more likely to change their affiliation to the Republican Party. Alternatively, a dealignment argument would predict that the groups we just identified—the young, conservatives, and high socio-economic status individuals—would not switch from the Democratic Party to the Republican Party, but would be more likely to identify themselves as independents.

PARTY IDENTIFICATION IN TEXAS, 1984–1994

The past thirty years have marked a period of significant change in the partisanship of Texans. In the 1950s, the Democratic Party clearly commanded the loyalties of the majority of Texans: more than 60 percent identified with the Democratic Party. At the same time, less than 10 percent of the electorate identified themselves as Republicans and the remaining 25 percent to 30 percent reported being independents. The particular strength of the Democratic Party—and weakness of the Republican Party—is underscored by comparing the pattern of party identification in Texas during this period with the pattern of party identification in the entire nation. The most striking difference between the state and national electorates is that, nationally, about 30 percent of voters were identified as Republicans—a 20 point difference from the Texas electorate! Only about 50 percent of the national sample identified with the Democratic Party, while about 20 percent identified as independents. Thus, in the 1950s, Texans clearly identified much less with the Republican Party—and much more with the Democratic Party—than did the national electorate.[9]

In the 1960s Texans' party loyalties slowly began to change. The percentage of people identifying as Republican went from below 10 percent in the 1950s to somewhat above 10 percent throughout most of the 1960s. There was little change in Democratic strength over this period: most of the increase in Republicans resulted from a decrease in the proportion of independents. Change accelerated in the 1970s with an increase in the

9. The survey estimates for Texas are based on survey data collected as part of the Belden Poll, a statewide public opinion survey of adults in Texas which was conducted between 1954 and 1972. More recent data reported below were collected as part of the Texas Poll, a quarterly statewide public opinion survey conducted by the Public Policy Research Institute at Texas A&M University. In both surveys, individuals were asked the following question: Generally speaking, do you usually think of yourself as a Republican, a Democrat, and Independent or what? Individuals who claimed to be strong Republicans (Democrats) or Republicans (Democrats) were categorized as Republicans (Democrats), individuals who claimed to be independents, or independents leaning toward either the Republican or Democratic party were categorized as independents.

FIGURE 7.1
Partisanship in Texas, 1984–1994

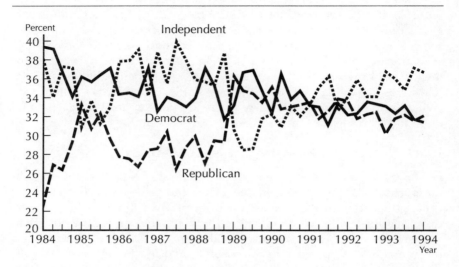

Source: Texas Poll supported in part by Harte-Hanks Communications Inc. and conducted by the Public Policy Research Institute, Texas A&M University. Surveys conducted in winter, spring, summer, and fall of each year. Sample size of at least 1,000 before removing missing data.

proportion of Republicans and a decline in the proportion of Democrats. By 1984, about 25 percent of Texans identified themselves as Republicans and the proportion of Democrats had dropped below 40 percent.

In the decade following 1984, the Republican Party continued to gain identifiers, while the Democratic Party lost them. By 1994, the statewide electorate was about equally divided among Democrats, Republicans, and independents: 33 percent identified as Democrats, 31 percent as Republicans, and 36 percent as independents[10] (see Figure 7.1). With Texas becoming considerably more Republican, by 1990 the partisan divisions in the nation and in Texas were similar: nationally, 36 percent identified as Democrats, 32 percent as Republicans, and 32 percent as independents (see Figure 7.2).[11]

The partisanship trends in both Figures 7.1 and 7.2 suggest that de-

---

10. These numbers are the average of self-reported party identification from the first two Texas Polls in 1994. Thus, they do not coincide precisely with the data presented in Figure 7.1.
11. In all of the partisanship analyses reported here, people reporting they didn't know, were apolitical, or identifying with other parties are omitted. The percentage in these categories is less than 10 percent. National data are between 1954 and 1986 are from the National Election Study surveys during election years. National studies between 1987 and 1993 are from the annual General Social Survey surveys with the exception of 1992.

FIGURE 7.2

Partisanship in the US, 1984–1994

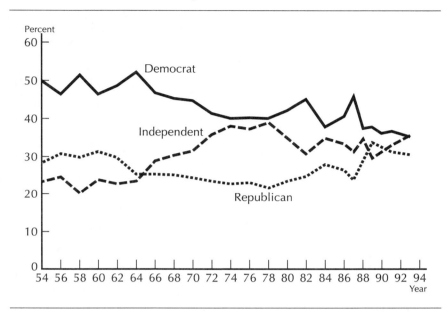

Source: NES surveys 1972–1986, GSS surveys 1987–1993

alignment may precede realignment. During the 1970s there was a national decline in Democratic and Republican identification and a growth in the number of independents (i.e., dealignment); in Texas, similar patterns occurred prior to 1987. During the 1980s, the national proportion of independents declined as Republican identification increased (i.e., realignment); a similar pattern occurred in Texas after 1987. While the increase in Republican identification at the national level is smaller than that associated with past party realignments, it suggests that some individuals may have shifted from being independents to being Republicans, or that younger voters initially entering the electorate were identifying with the Republican Party. The much larger increase in Republican identification in Texas over several decades—from about 10 percent in the 1950s to more than 30 percent in the 1990s—is indicative of a long-term shift in partisan identification.

THE CHANGING DEMOGRAPHIC BASES OF PARTISANSHIP

Analyses of the social groups that identify with the Democratic and Republican parties nationally suggest that the poor, the less educated, ethnic minorities, and women are more likely to associate with the Dem-

TABLE 7.1
Party Identification by Ideological, Ethnic, and Educational Groups

84–85	Liberal	Conservative	Anglo	Black	Hispanic	Not HS	High School	College
Republican	19%	42%	36%	6%	15%	19%	31%	39%
Independent	31%	30%	32%	24%	30%	27%	32%	33%
Democrat	51%	28%	32%	70%	55%	54%	37%	28%
93–94	Liberal	Conservative	Anglo	Black	Hispanic	Not HS	High School	College
Republican	13%	47%	38%	5%	16%	17%	29%	42%
Independent	36%	33%	36%	25%	34%	33%	36%	34%
Democrat	51%	20%	26%	70%	50%	50%	34%	24%
Change	Liberal	Conservative	Anglo	Black	Hispanic	Not HS	High School	College
Republican	–6%	5%	2%	–1%	1%	–2%	–1%	4%
Independent	5%	2%	4%	1%	4%	6%	4%	1%
Democrat	0%	–8%	–6%	0%	–6%	–4%	–3%	–5%

ocratic Party. Conversely, the wealthy, the well educated, whites, and males are more likely to associate with the Republican Party. Texas in the 1950s was an exception to this, given the extraordinary strength of the Democratic Party. That is, the Democratic Party was strong because it attracted the support of many different social groups. Alternatively, in competitive two-party systems, social groups will tend to support the party that most closely represents their interests. Thus, we would expect that the increased strength of the Republican Party in Texas has been accompanied by greater distinctions in the social groups supporting each party.

To verify these expectations, we examined differences in party identification among four social groups and the changes in these distributions between 1984 and 1994. These data are presented in Table 7.1. The top half of the table shows the distribution of party by ideology, ethnicity, and education; the bottom half of the table shows the same distributions in the 1990s.

In both periods in Texas, the relationships between these various demographic groups and party identification are typically what we expected, based on national data, although some of these relationships are stronger than others. Liberals, for example, are likely to be Democrats, while conservatives tend to be Republicans. African-Americans are likely to be Democrats, as are Hispanics, while Anglos are more likely to be Republicans. Although the differences are smaller, women are more likely to be Democrats than are men, and those with more education are more likely to be Republican than those with less education.

To identify the sources of partisan change in Texas, it is useful to look at two other individual characteristics that are associated with changes

TABLE 7.2

Party Identification by Age Cohorts and Length of Residence

84–85	Age 18–29	Age 30–44	Age 45–61	Age 62+	0–10 years	Over 10	Life
Republican	39%	29%	29%	26%	39%	33%	27%
Independent	31%	37%	31%	22%	35%	32%	30%
Democrat	30%	35%	40%	52%	27%	34%	43%
93–94	Age 18–29	Age 30–44	Age 45–61	Age 62+	0–10 years	Over 10	Life
Republican	34%	35%	28%	26%	38%	34%	28%
Independent	38%	34%	39%	30%	34%	36%	34%
Democrat	29%	31%	33%	44%	27%	29%	38%
Change	Age 18–29	Age 30–44	Age 45–61	Age 62+	0–10 years	Over 10	Life
Republican	−5%	6%	−1%	0%	0%	1%	1%
Independent	7%	−3%	7%	8%	0%	4%	4%
Democrat	−2%	−3%	−7%	−8%	1%	−5%	−6%

in party identification: age and length of residence. These data are presented in Table 7.2. Looking across the age cohorts (i.e., columns), it is clear that younger people in Texas are more likely to be Republicans than are older people; this is true for both the 1980s and 1990s. Looking across the columns for length of residence, newcomers to Texas are more likely to be Republicans than those born here. It is likely, then, that the increasing Republican strength in the state results from younger Texans entering the electorate and adopting a Republican Party identification, and from newcomers to the state, who are more likely to identify with the Republican Party.

These data on the relationship between age and partisanship suggest that the changes in partisanship we have observed will likely endure over the next several decades, in the absence of any dramatic political or social crises in the state. As the younger Republican voters age, they will likely continue to be Republican, and thus replace older, Democratic voters.

The most notable change in the partisanship of demographic groups concerns political ideology. As expected, changes in party identification in the 1980s were associated with more distinctive party identifications adopted by liberals and conservatives. Between 1984–85 and 1993–94, Republican strength among liberals declined by 6 percent. While in 1984–85, 19 percent of liberals identified with the Republican Party, in 1993–94, only 13 percent of liberals identified with the Republican Party. At the same time, Democratic strength among conservatives declined by 8 percentage points (28 percent in 1984–85, compared to 20 percent in 1993–94). Hence, a "sorting out" occurred, as individuals became more likely to identify with the party that represented their ideological beliefs. Smaller, though nonetheless significant, changes occurred for well-educated individuals, who became more likely to identify with the Republican Party over the period. These patterns, along with those discussed above regarding age and partisanship, suggest that by 1994, many Texans had realigned their loyalties to the Republican Party.

Concluding that Texans had realigned their partisan loyalties by 1994 presumes that the observed changes in partisanship will endure; that is, that the "new" Republicans will not revert to their old Democratic loyalties. Although only time will provide definitive evidence on this point, our belief that this realignment is an enduring change is based on three factors. First, the changes in party identification have resulted, probably for the first time since Reconstruction, in most conservatives identifying with the Republican Party and most liberals identifying with the Democratic Party. Second, the partisan shift also results in demographic groups being aligned more closely with the parties that have traditionally represented their political interests on a national basis. Third, this shift is evidenced in the younger cohorts of the electorate who will replace older Democratic members of the electorate over the next several decades. For these reasons, we expect that the new Republicans will remain loyal to their party, even in the face of short-term, election-specific (i.e., candidates or issues) factors that might weaken or challenge their new party attachment.

That political ideology is a more enduring aspect of public opinion than is party identification is evidenced in the contrast between the relatively dynamic change in partisanship in Texas over the 1984–1994 period and the fairly stable distribution of political ideology in Texas. To measure political ideology, survey respondents between 1984 and 1994 were asked the following: How would you describe your views on most political matters? Generally do you think of yourself as liberal, moderate, or conservative?

The responses to this question are presented graphically in Figure 7.3. The fairly straight lines across the graph indicate that there has been little variation over time in Texans' responses to this question. About 40 percent of Texans described themselves as conservative, another 40 percent described themselves as moderate, and about 20 percent described themselves as liberal throughout this period. Beyond its consequences for party identification, one of the practical implications of the underlying stability of political ideology in Texas politics is the fact that the slow but steady partisan change we have observed above has not resulted in any major policy shifts.

Thus, party change in the state does not appear to be driven by a broader change in the ideological orientation of Texans. Instead, Texans are moving to better align their long-standing ideological positions with the party or independent position that seems to represent their beliefs better. Because Texans' ideological beliefs have been stable over the past

Party Identification and Public Opinion in Texas, 1984–1994 117

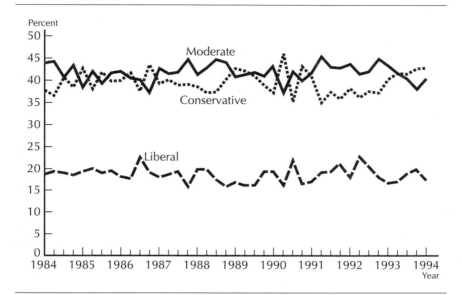

FIGURE 7.3

Ideology in Texas, 1984–1994

Source: Texas Poll supported in part by Harte-Hanks Communications Inc. and conducted by the Public Policy Research Institute, Texas A&M University. Surveys conducted in winter, spring, summer, and fall of each year. Sample size of at least 1,000 before removing missing data.

several decades, we suspect that this change in party identification will be sustained over the coming years.

TAXING AND SPENDING POLICY SUPPORT: DOES PARTY MAKE A DIFFERENCE?

Historically, the Republican and Democratic parties and their followers have taken fairly distinct positions on a number of political issues. In contemporary U.S. politics, the issue that seems to attract the most attention from candidates and voters alike is that of government spending. Ronald Reagan, for example, came into office in 1980 portraying the Democratic Party as the party of big spenders and promising to cut government spending. Many other conservative politicians make similar claims. The question we ask is whether this caricature of Democrats as big spenders, and Republicans as budget cutters, reflects different policy positions of party supporters. That is, do Republican and Democratic identifiers in Texas have distinct positions on issues relating to government spending and taxing policies?

We might expect one of two different answers to this question. The first relies on the stereotypical portrayal of Texans as conservative, and suggests that differences between the parties on spending preferences would be muted, with both sets of partisans preferring less spending to more. The second possible answer relates to a major finding from the previous section of this chapter: that conservatives in Texas are now more likely to identify with the Republican Party, while liberals are more likely to identify with the Democratic Party, than they were in earlier decades. Because individuals with different beliefs about the role of government are now more likely to identify with different parties in Texas, we should find differences in spending preferences between Democrats and Republicans in the 1990s. If the caricature of Democrats as big spenders is correct, then Democrats should consistently prefer to spend more than Republicans.

In a 1989 Texas Poll survey, respondents were asked if spending should be increased, decreased, or kept the same on a variety of issues. On almost every issue significantly higher proportions of Democrats than Republicans favored increasing spending for that state program. For example, while the majority of both Democrats and Republicans wanted to increase spending for the elderly, only 60 percent of Republicans favored such increases, compared to 78 percent of Democrats.

This same pattern was true for spending on the public schools (48 percent of Republicans preferring increases, compared to 64 percent of Democrats) and on colleges and universities (41 percent of Republicans, 53 percent of Democrats favoring increases). The greatest differences between members of the two parties was seen in wanting increases in spending on the poor (36 percent of Republicans prefer increasing spending, compared to 61 percent of Democrats) and health (46 percent Republicans, 71 percent Democrats). While Democrats seeking greater spending on these traditional Democratic issues seems understandable, it is perhaps surprising that the same pattern emerges for Republicans on issues such as fighting crime (66 percent of Republicans prefer increasing spending, compared to 77 percent of Democrats) and prisons (41 percent Republicans, 59 percent Democrats). Thus, it appears that Texans from both parties support increased state spending, but there are differences between the two parties on which programs to spend more.

Another policy area in which Republicans and Democrats in Texas may differ is in preferences on how to solve state budget problems. In three surveys from 1985 to 1987, Texans were asked if, in order to handle state budget problems, they preferred cutting spending, raising taxes, or some combination of cuts and tax increases. About half of the respondents in each survey favored cutting spending, and the other half supported cuts in combination with tax increases or tax increases alone.

To test for partisan differences on preferences for dealing with budget problems, we analyzed the 1986 survey data. We find a modest difference between support for either option and party status, with Republicans slightly more in favor of cutting spending (48 percent to 43 percent) and Democrats somewhat more willing to raise taxes (10 percent to 16 percent). These differences are in the predicted directions, given our description of party orientations among the Texas electorate, but they are relatively small, indicating that Democrats and Republicans do not differ drastically in their preferences on this specific budget and taxing issue.

Even weaker partisan differences emerge on the policy question of how to raise state revenue. Most Texans, regardless of partisanship, have a relatively conservative idea of where any new revenues should come from. In numerous surveys over the past ten years, Texans have tended to oppose increased property taxes or the adoption of a personal income tax, and have tended to be somewhat more supportive of sales and corporate taxes. In a 1986 Texas Poll survey, for example, respondents were asked which type of tax they would prefer if additional revenues had to be raised. Only 3 percent said they preferred increased property taxes and less than 4 percent wanted a personal income tax. About 10 percent suggested a corporate income tax, while 24 percent preferred an increase in the state sales tax.

Partisan differences on this issue appear both in the degree to which party members support a particular tax and the extent to which they oppose one. For example, Democrats and Republicans scored equally low in preferring an income tax (3 percent and 4 percent respectively), but more than 41 percent of Republicans were strongly opposed to the income tax compared to only 28 percent of Democrats. Republicans were more in favor of the sales tax (30 percent to 21 percent) while Democrats were slightly more opposed to it (9 percent to 12 percent). Few Democrats (2 percent) or Republicans (3 percent) preferred the property tax, while fewer Democrats were in favor of the property tax than were Republicans (30 percent compared to 22 percent).

In general, Republicans and Democrats in Texas differ slightly in their views on taxing and spending. Democrats are more likely to prefer increased spending and raising revenue through increased taxes, while Republicans are less likely to prefer increased spending and more likely to prefer program cuts to raising revenue. The magnitude of these differences, however, should be understood within the context of fairly widespread support for increased spending within both parties.

PARTY IDENTIFICATION AND VOTE CHOICE

Despite the growth of candidate-centered campaigning and professional campaign consultants in national as well as statewide campaigns, scholars have consistently found that party identification is still an important factor determining vote choice in elections.[12] Our previous discussion of the importance of party divisions within the Texas electorate

---

12. Norman R. Luttbeg and Michael M. Gant, *American Electoral Behavior 1952–1992*.

lead us to expect that, in Texas, party identification would be a very important influence in electoral choices. Examination of Texas Poll data from 1986 to 1990 confirms this expectation.

Table 7.3 compares party identification and candidate choice for major statewide offices in 1990. These data demonstrate a consistent and significant level of party voting among Texas citizens. Those who profess a party identification tend to vote consistently for those candidates with whom they share a party affiliation, and this holds for each office. For example, in the 1990 gubernatorial race, 90.5 percent of Republicans voted for Clayton Williams, the Republican candidate, while 82.8 percent of Democrats voted for Ann Richards, the Democratic candidate.

In 1986 respondents were also asked whether they voted a straight ticket or for candidates from different parties in (nongubernatorial) state and local elections. Using these reports, we again see the high level of party-based voting among the Texas electorate: more than 73 percent of Republicans and more than 82 percent of Democrats reported voting for their party all or most of the time. These reports, as well as those on actual vote choices, suggest that party identification among Texans is strong, and plays an important role in Texans' choice of political candidates.

Conclusions

Our analyses underscore the fundamental importance of partisanship in structuring the political behavior of Texans.[13] Partisanship in Texas reflects major social divisions in the state and largely determines an individual's vote in elections. The largest policy differences between Republicans and Democrats in Texas, however, are on which programs to spend more—not on whether spending should be increased or decreased.

Partisanship trends in Texas between 1984 and 1994 were marked first by a growth in the proportion of independents in the state, and second by a growth in Republican partisanship. The growth in Republican identification is associated with several factors. New voters, who began their electoral experience in a different political environment than did their parents, and newcomers to the state disproportionately identify with the Republican Party in Texas. Another factor associated with increasing Republican strength is the greater likelihood of individuals who consider themselves to be conservatives to identify with the Republican Party rather than the Democratic Party. Furthermore, demographic groups that have typically identified with the Republican Party (i.e., individuals with high socio-economic status) also shifted toward the Republican Party.

The ideological and demographic shifting of voters to more "appro-

---

13. Angus Campbell, Philip E. Converse, Warren E. Miller, and Donald E. Stokes, *The American Voter*.

TABLE 7.3

Party Identification and Vote Choice[a]

Vote Choice	Republican	Independent	Democrat
Governor 1990			
Democrat	9.5	43.5	82.8
Republican	90.5	56.6	17.2
Lieutenant Governor 1990			
Democrat	27.0	55.4	89.6
Republican	73.0	44.6	10.4
Attorney General 1990			
Democrat	17.2	53.1	89.6
Republican	82.8	44.6	11.8
Supreme Court 1990			
Democrat	9.3	31.0	67.4
Republican*	90.7	69.0	32.6

* Indicates incumbent
[a] Table entries indicate proportion of each partisan group reporting to vote for either the Democrat or Republican candidate in each race.
Source: Texas Polls, Summer 1986; Fall 1990; n>900.

priate" (in terms of the ideological positions of the Republican and Democratic parties) usually results in more homogeneous parties, which should create a party system that more accurately represents the distinctive ideological positions of conservatives and liberals and class interests of various demographic groups. In turn, the electoral choice between the candidates of the Republican and Democratic parties is likely to be a more meaningful one.

The electoral consequences of increasing Republican strength, however, must be considered in light of the concomitant increase in the proportion of Texans who identify themselves as independents. Texas does have a more competitive party system, as noted above. However, consistent with national trends in party identification, Texas also has a party system composed of almost equal proportions of Democrats, Republicans, and independents. This suggests that with the increasing strength of the Republican Party comes a volatility in the electoral system. The large proportion of independents in the electorate suggests that election-specific factors such as campaign spending, candidate characteristics, and the issues raised in campaigns (whether political or personal) may be particularly important in determining who wins elections.

An interesting question is what the future of partisanship in Texas will be. The data suggest that, other things being equal, Republican partisanship will continue to grow, although undoubtedly as part of a long-term process. Assuming that younger voters continue to tend to be Republican, they will increasingly replace older Democrats. At the same time, the relatively large number of independents could be mobilized by either party. The latter, of course, will be dependent on the strategies of elected officials as well as party leaders.

What are the limits to Republican growth? An increasingly large proportion of minorities in Texas, who historically have been more likely to identify with the Democratic Party, could sustain the electoral base of the Democratic Party. At a broader level, the larger proportion of independents in the electorate and the greater ideological homogeneity of the two parties probably make it unlikely that the Republican Party would ever reach the dominance in percentage of voters that was held by the Democrats prior to the 1970s. What seems more likely is that the electorate will provide support for a viable and competitive two-party system, which will have significant consequences for how government in Texas is organized (e.g., the state legislature), how interests are represented, and thus the nature of public policy in Texas.

8
Texas Elections

JAMES CARTER
SAM HOUSTON STATE UNIVERSITY

Campaigning for office in Texas has become an exhausting job. Gone is the relaxed pace of an earlier era. When Sam Rayburn campaigned for his first political office, the Texas House of Representatives, in 1906, he rode from town to town with his opponent. They gave speeches together and then took off to the next town. When his opponent became ill, Rayburn stopped campaigning until his opponent was well enough to travel with him again. That type of campaign is unimaginable in modern Texas politics.

Now campaigns are expensive and time consuming. Candidates must rush from meeting to meeting, often by plane. They must hold press conferences, do interviews, raise money, and run television ads. The pace is a frenzied one, and at the end of the day more than one candidate has forgotten the name of the town in which he or she was speaking.

One reason for the change in Texas politics is that elections are more competitive. Texas is, after all, a two-party state. Another reason is the huge growth of Texas. No longer are campaigns among the friends and neighbors of a rural community where one is known to all. Campaigns are now in urban areas, big cities where residents often do not know their own next-door neighbor.

Most important, however, is that the mass media has changed Texas politics. It is no longer enough to walk around a town square shaking hands and then visit the local newspaper editor to buy a few political advertisements and hope for an editorial endorsement. One needs to reach the anonymous urban voter, and that means one needs money for huge urban daily papers, for radio, and, most important, for television. Those ads take money, and plenty of it. Even relatively obscure races like those for the Texas Supreme Court can cost $3 million or more. Races for the governorship can cost the two major candidates $30–$50 million.

Elections are also increasingly complicated. A number of plans, such as early voting, have an effect upon political strategy. With early voting, for example, it is risky to "bunch" television ads right before election day, because early voting creates numerous possible election days. When should ads be clustered: at the beginning, end, or middle of early voting?

Other efforts to expand the electorate create potential fraud problems. How, for example, are elections in nursing homes to be monitored? One recently retired Texas congressman was once accused by his opponent of having his supporters vote on behalf of ill and possibly senile nursing home residents. Efforts to expand the numbers of registered voters create problems in policing the behavior of one's opponents. Efforts to increase voter rolls may also be biased in favor of one party. Registering voters in welfare offices, for example, would likely benefit Democrats. If elections were held in a Nieman-Marcus store, on the other hand, Republicans would benefit.

As this chapter points out, there have been numerous efforts to expand the franchise, and numerous problems posed by that expansion. What becomes clear is that the old-fashioned, inexpensive, friendly campaigns of the Rayburn era are gone, replaced by a hectic, money-grubbing pace of electioneering coupled with greater efforts to expand voting of an increasingly apathetic electorate.

Elections in Texas today are significantly more complicated and burdensome than at any point in recent history. This is true for the candidate running for office as well as the voter trying to make a choice.

Most people involved in public life today will say that politics is not as much fun as it used to be.[1] Pushed to explain why, they will point to, among other things, the continuous and grueling effort currently required to get elected to and remain in a public office. This chapter explores some of the reasons for the increased demands for getting elected to office, some of the recent burdens added to the traditional problem of staying in office, and the ways in which they are played out among a variety of political participants.

The reasons for the increased demands in political life fall into two categories: (1) informal responses made piecemeal over time by various candidates to an increasingly competitive climate, and (2) the formal procedural changes (laws and public policies) instituted by the state government to increase voter turnout. Whatever the rationale and the explanation for the new election realities, the results are that campaigns for office last much longer, the monetary costs of elections remain enormous, and the grimness and hostility of contemporary politics seem to be breeding an increasing cynicism throughout the political system.[2]

TIME AND MONEY

Elections are no longer episodic contests, but are now a tapestry of political activity that extends from one election day to another. There is no off-season, and actual governance can only with great difficulty be separated from campaigning. Political life has always demanded an intense commitment on the part of participants, but the recent levels of

1. Mary Lou Cooper, "Leaving the Legislature." *States West* (May 1996), pp. 3–5.
2. Ruy A. Teixeira, *The Disappearing American Voter* (Washington, D.C.: The Brookings Institute, 1992).

personal, organizational, and financial demands have dramatically transformed our political system.

The current marathon nature of campaigning and the fatigue that sets in by election day were well expressed by Republican Clayton Williams, when in 1994 he reflected on his state of mind at the end of his bid for the Texas governorship in 1990: "It was all a blur by then . . . I had run for twenty-two months. I was real sick of it." Of course, the memory of that arduous campaign may have been better had he won the governorship.[3]

The large amounts of money that must be raised today for a candidate to be competitive in a political race are illustrated by the last two contests for governor. Clayton Williams and Ann Richards spent $50 million in 1990. In 1994, Ann Richards and George W. Bush spent at least $30 million. The financial burden of running for office does not stop at the highest offices, however. The cost of campaigning has become a major hurdle for public service at all levels. It is not unusual for mayoral contests in Texas's largest cities to approach $1 million, for congressional races to cost several hundreds of thousands of dollars, and for judicial races to run well into six figures.[4]

Even for those who have it, spending this kind of money on something as unpredictable as politics is difficult. For those who do not have it, finding the necessary financial support to run for political office requires particular interpersonal and political skills, and has long been a significant obstacle for those who have political aspirations. The organizational and personal time required for campaign financing is an irritating factor to candidates and campaigns and threatens some of the democratic features of our elections. Time devoted to fundraising reduces the time that candidates can spend communicating their ideas and positions on issues to the general public. The cost of campaigns also raises the personal stakes for winning and losing, contributes to the intensity and hostility of current political discourse, and serves as a further obstacle to entering public service.

POLITICS IS NOT JUST LOCAL ANYMORE, IT'S ALSO PERSONAL

Former U.S. House Speaker Tip O'Neill once said "All politics is local." We find today that politics is not just local: it is also personal. Perhaps one of the most telling examples in Texas of the personal toll that politics can take is seen in the hard feelings between former Governor Ann Richards and former Texas Attorney General Jim Mattox, which resulted from their contest over the Democratic nomination for

---

3. Victoria Loe, "Richards, Bush Finish with a Flurry." *Dallas Morning News*, 8 Nov. 1994, p. 13A.
4. David B. Magleby and Candice J. Nelson, *The Money Chase: Congressional Campaign Finance Reform* (Washington, D.C.: The Brookings Institute, 1990).

Texas governor in 1990. The bitterness remained so deep after that contest that some believe Ann Richards allowed her own political career and the interests of the Texas Democratic Party to be adversely affected by the dispute.

The Richards camp felt that in the 1990 primary contest Mattox breached every rule of political etiquette, especially with regard to a member of his own party, when he raised questions about Ann Richards's past drug use. The Mattox campaign's justification of the attack was one that is commonly heard among partisans and political activists. In brief, the argument is that if a candidate cannot answer questions among friends, then how will he or she be able to withstand the onslaught when the other party raises the issue in the general election; in addition, because it is naive to believe that a potentially explosive issue will not be raised in the general election, it is better to air such issues as early as possible and to put them to rest in the primary if possible.

The fact that Jim Mattox had a reputation as a hardball politician and a rough and tumble fighter did not help. The Richards camp felt, however, that Mattox's attack revealed him to be more than a tough competitor: to them he was someone who would stop at nothing to win. Mattox and his supporters seemed surprised by the intensity of Richards's response. As subsequent events illustrate, the incident led to political infighting that brought with it dire consequences for the success of the Texas Democratic Party as well as for Ann Richards.

In 1992, U.S. Senator Lloyd Bentsen resigned his senate seat to become secretary of the treasury under President Clinton. As governor, Ann Richards was responsible for appointing someone to fill the senate vacancy. Numerous Democrats scrambled for the appointment and Governor Richards, apparently remembering the Mattox attack two years earlier, refused to consider Jim Mattox. Because of his long record of public service and high name recognition, Mattox was thought by many to be the Democrat with the best chance of holding onto the senate seat, since a special election would occur rather quickly after the appointment.

As a result of Governor Richards's refusal to appoint Mattox, the contest for a Democratic replacement for Bentsen turned into a free-for-all. Numerous candidates emerged, none of whom had the name recognition, toughness, or electoral experience of Jim Mattox. Ann Richards ultimately appointed, and the Texas Democratic Party was forced to accept, the likable, intellectual, but relatively apolitical Bob Kreuger as Bentsen's replacement. After taking office, Senator Krueger immediately alienated his Democratic Party base by opposing President Clinton's economic plan, one of the few Democrats in the U.S. Senate to do so. Kreuger then proceeded to run a lackluster campaign against State Treasurer Kay Bailey Hutchinson to defend his newly acquired senate seat.

When polls showed Kay Bailey Hutchinson well ahead prior to the election, Senator Krueger's limpid campaign resorted, in desperation, to putting him in dark glasses and a leather jacket in an imitation of actor Arnold Swarzenegger saying "Hasta la vista, baby" in the movie "The Terminator." The ad was a desperate, last-minute attempt to invigorate Kreuger's campaign and to try to overcome the somnolent campaign style of Kreuger. Instead, the ad underscored Kreuger's lack of vigor and subjected him to further ridicule for political ineptness. The successful challenge by Kay Bailey Hutchinson resulted in Texas having two Republican U.S. senators for the first time since Reconstruction.

Subsequent events proved that this Democratic debacle was still not enough to assuage the hurt feelings that continued to motivate the Richards camp. In 1994, the Democrats had an opportunity to reclaim Bentsen's U.S. Senate seat. The second time around Governor Richards had no official role to play in the selection of the Democratic nominee. As a governor up for reelection and as nominal head of the Texas Democratic Party, however, Ann Richards was a major player even if she was confined to an informal role. Once again Jim Mattox sought the party's nomination. In the beginning Democratic prospects looked good as Senator Hutchinson struggled with allegations of misconduct in her State Treasury Office. Unfortunately for Democrats, the charges were subsequently dropped and ultimately played almost no role in the campaign.

During the 1994 Democratic primary, the silence of Ann Richards was in startling contrast to what some thought should have been self-interested glee at the possibility of a Democratic Party "Dream Team" with Ann Richards and Jim Mattox at the top of the same ticket. This would be the kind of ballot that Texas progressives had fought for years to achieve. Instead, rumors emerged of backstage support by Governor Richards for Richard Fisher, a political novice, ex–Ross Perot supporter, and Democratic Party newcomer. Some observers believe that Governor Richards's silence in the primary, if not her active support behind the scenes for Fisher, allowed him to take the party's nomination in a relatively tight contest with Mattox. Fisher then went down to an ignominious defeat, similar to that of the previous Richards nominee Bob Kreuger. Ann Richards lost the governorship in the same election.

Many Texas political operatives believe that with Mattox on the ticket, and a potentially higher Democratic turnout, Ann Richards might have found the additional help she needed to hold on to the governor's mansion, even if Mattox had ultimately failed to win the Senate seat. Politics in this case had certainly been local and personal.

Should Politics Be Fun?

Politics is not much fun anymore, except perhaps for an aggressive person who thrives on a diet of constant controversy. Of course, Texans in general are not fond of politics, politicians, or government, and most

Texans feel that politics should be hard work like every other job.[5] If politics were fun, public life might attract the wrong kind of people with the wrong incentive. Enjoying politics might encourage politicians to stay on longer than is healthy for the proper conduct of public business. Some observers point out that the monetary rewards (except in the state legislature) and the perquisites of political office seem to be more than adequate to make up for any distress that has crept into the game in recent years. If politics is as fearful and threatening as some portray it to be, why is it so rare to have a contest for a public office in which no one submits their name for the job?

There are others, however, who worry that if current trends continue, the best and the brightest of our population may not want the bother of running for office and of defending their private life along with their public record on a daily basis.[6] Should we worry about the attractiveness of political life at the end of the twentieth century?

Political scientists have long identified certain social and economic traits that make a career in politics more or less likely.[7] Personal characteristics like income level, family history, social status, and occupation act as informal screening devices to eliminate some people from the potential officeholder class. It is possible that the current hostile and invasive tenor of political life has added another filter for those seeking public office.

Politics is an all-consuming, extravagantly expensive, harsh process that in the last decade of the twentieth century can exact a severe personal toll on those who participate. David Dean may have made this point as well as anyone when he said just before the 1994 election, "It (politics) is a very passionate process. . . . The victories are incredibly high and the defeats are incredibly low. It's hard to overstate either extreme."[8]

Changes in the Practice of Elections

Over the past several years, many formal and informal changes have occurred with regard to elections. Some of these changes we might applaud. Other changes are doubtful contributions to the success of the political process or to the practice of democracy.

In Texas, there have been significant formal changes in the practice of elections as well as highly visible and widely commented upon informal changes in campaign tactics. Informal but significant developments in-

---

5. Molly Ivins, *Molly Ivins Can't Say That, Can She?* (New York: Random House, 1991).
6. John G. Tower, *Consequences: A Personal and Political Memoir* (New York: Little, Brown, 1991).
7. Shirley Williams and Edward L. Lascher, Jr., eds., *The Career Paths of American Politicians* (Berkeley: Institute of Governmental Studies Press, University of California, 1993).
8. Victoria Loe, "Richards, Bush Finish with a Flurry." *Dallas Morning News*, 8 November 1994.

clude negative campaigning, attack ads, and the rise of the never-ending campaign. Procedural changes include motor voter registration, mobile voting, retail voting, and early voting. The procedural changes are not as obvious to the public as the jousting that goes on between candidates before an election, and they have not penetrated the public's consciousness to a great degree. However, rules and procedures are never neutral. Someone or some group is always advantaged or disadvantaged by the structure of the game, and these formal procedural changes have effects not only on voting behavior, but also on the conduct and expense of campaigns, and thus on the kinds of individuals who seek and succeed in winning public office.

THE NEVER-ENDING CAMPAIGN

Perhaps the biggest informal change in elections, and one that has been evolving over some time, is the never-ending campaign for public office. Just a few years ago, an early start in seeking a public office was hailed as a major innovation. Jimmy Carter is widely credited with having triggered this development when he began his 1976 presidential campaign long before the first of the primaries and before any potential opposition was mobilized. Many observers attributed Jimmy Carter's victory to his fast start and the degree to which it kept his opponents off-balance. The formal announcement of Senator Phil Gramm and others for the presidency almost two years before the 1996 election now seems to be business as usual. When Phil Gramm made his announcement, the opposition was already present and many of them had been touring the country seeking support. An early start no longer places a candidate ahead of the field but is considered a requirement for any serious office-seeker. The next campaign begins the day after an election, as is illustrated by the challenges made to the campaign finance activities of Vice President Al Gore in the days following the 1996 election. The media were already discussing how the revelations would affect the vice president's chances in the next election. In contrast, the relative quiet in the Texas Democratic Party as late as the summer of 1997 with regard to the next gubernatorial race indicates that George Bush, Jr. may be reelected easily.

Texas politicians say that politics has always been all-consuming and never-ending. A public official has many events to attend: high-school football banquets, Lions Club meetings, school openings, Chamber of Commerce luncheons, and dedication ceremonies for every new park and commemorative plaque. Any officeholder or candidate who fails to stay in touch with these grassroots is courting electoral disaster. However, this is still much easier for an incumbent than a challenger, and one of the reasons that not so long ago incumbency was thought to be a distinct advantage.

A challenger might step forward and begin fundraising and meeting and greeting voters at some relatively early stage, but the intensity, the public awareness, and the massive coordination and organization required for a bid for public office came only at a later date, closer to election time and in the "political season." Voters were thought to be disinterested in politics in non-election years and, at best, only partially attentive in election years. Candidates felt that it was a waste of money to try to reach voters too early, and attempted to have their campaigns peak on election day. Consequently, most of their resources were focused on the period of time closest to the election, a time when voters were thought to finally be interested in the contest.

Voters may not have changed substantially, as low turnout rates indicate, but the available forums for political messages have multiplied, and a loosening of requirements in the fairness and equal time doctrines imposed by the Federal Communications Commission have led to a now-constant stream of political information emanating from television, radio, computer networks, and direct mailings.[9] Political life has become a seamless tapestry rather than a period of relatively obscure work punctuated by a series of episodic and sporadic events known as elections.

When one election cycle is ended, nothing is finished. Where there used to be a "honeymoon" period for elected officials, now there is likely to be an immediate feeling of performance anxiety. The day after an election the officeholder, with the possible exception of United States senators who enjoy the luxury of six-year terms, is required to step forward and start campaigning all over again, because it must be assumed that a challenger has already begun the process of seeking his or her office. If the officeholder is not prepared to define him or herself, a challenger is always more than happy to tell people how the incumbent has failed. The media contributes to this by being even more voracious than in the past and apparently ready to contribute to any ongoing dialogue, whatever the quality of substance or level of incivility represented.[10]

Elections may not actually be won or lost a year or two before the actual vote, but the momentum that is built up early can provide an almost insurmountable obstacle even for an incumbent to overcome, and the impetus can propel someone into office. The actual time left over for governance by those who do take office is reduced dramatically since every public decision can be and often is attacked almost immediately.

Portraying yourself in a favorable light, fending off attacks to your character, getting the word out about your accomplishments, all become

---

9. *Talk Back Live.* "Talk Radio Shows: Do They Influence the Voters?" National Public Radio, 2 November 1994, Program 145. (Journal Graphics Transcripts 1-800-talk-sho).
10. Dave Denison, "Prime-Time Politics: Why TV News Doesn't Get the Picture," *The Texas Observer*, 21 December 1990, pp. 4–8.

part of the governing process.¹¹ Programs are held hostage to the daily political conflicts. Votes in the legislature and decisions made by the governor and other executive officials are influenced by the political use that will be made of them by challengers.

Some observers argue that this is exactly the way that democracy is supposed to work. Elected officials are supposed to be constantly looking over their shoulders to determine whether they are properly representing the people who elected them. Others point out that such immediate concern about potential voter reaction and reelection can be as debilitating as it is democratic, and that the paranoia that current conditions generate can restrict possibilities for leadership, innovation, and the inclination to cast unpopular votes. In addition, intensely committed and well-funded interest groups seem to be capable of dictating the public agenda and skewing the public debate, rather than contributing to an open-ended discussion about the common good.¹²

As a result, officeholders and politicians are required to get on the correct side of an issue as quickly as possible, the correct side being the one reflected by the majority in the most recent poll. Many debates, such as the debate in Texas over capital punishment and the use of law enforcement and prisons to address crime, are foreshortened. They devolve into contests among politicians over who can appear tougher on crime, and even who will execute the most criminals, rather than an enlightened and informed discussion of the full range of social, economic, and cultural factors that contribute to the crime problem.

An example of the influence of public sentiment came in recent years when Governor Ann Richards, supposedly a Texas progressive if not a liberal, was asked in a televised interview what recent massive expenditures on prison construction told people in other states about Texas. She answered, "It tells them that in Texas, we are hard on criminals." There seemed to be no room for concern to be expressed about root causes of crime such as inadequate educational opportunities and underfunded social assistance programs.

Campaign Work

The kind of daily effort, organization, expense, attention to current events, and internal communication that is currently necessary to campaign for statewide office in Texas is illustrated in the following essay by Travis Lucas, a travel aide for Land Commissioner Garry Mauro in the 1994 campaign.

---

11. Timothy E. Cook, *Making Laws and Making News: Media Strategies in the U.S. House of Representatives* (Washington, D.C.: The Brookings Institute, 1989).
12. Thomas E. Mann and Gary R. Orren, eds., *Media Polls in American Politics* (Washington, D.C.: The Brookings Institute, 1992).

THE NEVER ENDING DAY
Travis Lucas

Campaign days begin early.

As Texas Land Commissioner Garry Mauro's travel aide during the 1994 elections, most days began for me at 5:00 a.m. After eating breakfast and getting dressed, I would drive to the nearby convenience store to buy all of the major daily Texas papers. My first task was to search through the papers for any stories on our contest, for any articles that even remotely seemed to affect our race, and then for public opinion polls and editorials.

Soon afterward, I would arrive at the airport at least forty-five minutes before our departure. I would pack our private plane (the only efficient way for a statewide candidate to travel effectively in all of Texas's 254 counties) with the press release packets we would use for that day, and call into campaign headquarters to check on the latest directives and information. When the commissioner arrived we would board the plane and I would brief him on the newspaper stories, headquarter's information, and the coming day's events.

On a typical day, we would fly first to a mid-sized town, perhaps Tyler in east Texas, for a press conference. The press conference could cover any possible number of subjects. As an aside, I must say that our campaign thoroughly prepared for these events. Commissioner Mauro's presentations were persuasive and well prepared to get the media's attention, especially television.

Next, the commissioner and I would be driven by a local supporter to a smaller, nearby town where another press conference would be held. Perhaps at a meeting of a local board of realtors, a veterans group, or a civic group. While en route, I would call headquarters on one of our mobile phones to check on the latest news out of Austin. I called in as frequently as every thirty minutes during a day since the need for the latest news is crucial in a campaign.

After the second press conference, the commissioner would move on to other locales, not only giving press conferences but also "working the courthouses." Although campaigning via television is a necessity for a statewide candidate in Texas "pressing the flesh" and shaking hands the old-fashioned way is just as important.

Most of the small towns that we campaigned in have courthouse squares where retail shops and professional businesses are located. Many of the local citizenry frequent these areas. A candidate's dream is to be able to meet so many people in one place! As my candidate "worked the crowd" shaking hands, I would write down each person's name (discretely) so I could write them letters, acknowledging the candidate having met them and asking for their support. Of all of the campaign techniques we used, I found this approach to be the most effective for the candidate. The voter was able to ask questions and voice comments to the candidate. This offered the citizen accessibility to the officeholder, reinforced the accountability of the candidate to his constituency, and allowed the candidate to use his charm to win over undecided voters.

During the day, we would drive or fly from town to town meeting and greeting people until around five or six o'clock in the evening. At that point we would usually fly into a nearby big city for a scheduled fundraiser. Those events could last sometimes up to three hours (as most did) until all the speeches were made, handshakes exchanged, and goodbyes said. It would be somewhere around midnight by the time we landed back in Austin. The commissioner and I would feel exhausted after the eighteen hour day. As the long day came to an end, I might drive the Commissioner home or drop by the campaign headquarters to re-stock my travel bag (loaded with items such as cellular phone batteries, a sewing kit, makeup for doing live interviews at television stations and "push cards" or small handouts stating the candidate's positions). There was little time for sleep, but that was one of the sacrifices I was willing to make to participate in a statewide campaign! Of course, we won our race over a relatively well-known opponent, which made all of the work and the long days worthwhile.

Early Voting

Early voting is perhaps the most widespread and fundamental change in formal voting procedures in Texas in recent years. Prior to early voting reforms, Texans had the opportunity to request an absentee ballot if they were willing to assert a legitimate reason why they would not be able to go to their normal polling place on the day of an election. In general, few questions were asked of those who requested absentee ballots, but there were certain aspects to the practice that made it difficult for most voters to use. Absentee ballots had to be requested and received within certain restricted time periods prior to election day, and because absentee voting was the exception for most voters rather than the rule, only the more sophisticated voters were aware of the appropriate time period for requesting and casting absentee ballots. In addition, the paperwork was somewhat daunting for less-educated voters.

Early voting is substantially different from absentee voting in two ways. First, it is no longer necessary to give a reason for voting early. The early voting period lasts for sixteen days prior to the election: with certain exceptions made for holidays and other potential calendar conflicts, the actual early voting period begins twenty days before and ends four days before election day. Second, the consistency of this practice from election to election, and the requirement for the same simple sign-in procedure as is required on election day, makes the act of early voting little different from an election-day vote. Early voting makes casting a ballot in Texas a much more convenient activity for most citizens.

The effect of early voting on Texas elections has not been confined to ease of voting. Candidates, campaigns, and political parties have all been drastically affected by early voting. Although total voter turnout may have increased only slightly, significant numbers of people cast their votes early now, and the early voting block often represents the largest number of citizens voting in any single block in most counties. Candidates must devote substantial time and resources to an organized effort to turn out voters during this period.

As a consequence, the task of getting elected to office is more burdensome and requires an even greater level of organization to be competitive. Prior to the implementation of early voting, well-organized campaigns paid relatively little attention to absentee voters, although they did try to identify citizens who were likely to be out of town on election day and assist them in obtaining absentee ballots. Today, the candidate who is not prepared to make use of every hour of the sixteen-day early voting period stands a good chance of being swamped by the early voting efforts of their opponent. Consequently, the expenses in both monetary terms and in human effort are much greater. The traditional final push of radio and television spots, newspaper advertisements, phone banks, and block walking to get out the vote must now be sustained for a sixteen-day period.[13]

Both major political parties seem to have something to gain from early voting, although Democrats were the principal architects of the practice. Because low voter turnout is traditionally thought to work against Democratic candidates, the lengthened voting period should give the Democratic Party a greater opportunity to get their reluctant voters to the polls. The profile of voters who are most likely to vote early, however (well-educated, suburban, and higher incomes), seems to favor Republican candidates. For this reason, and in practice, the early vote frequently tends to be a more conservative vote.

Regardless of which candidates or parties benefit from the practice of early voting, a few doubts have been raised about its ultimate contribution to good government. One is the possibility that voters will vote before all of the necessary information is available to them. Indeed, a voter who votes early may subsequently find that their opinion of the candidates has changed due to information that surfaces late in the campaign. In addition, some observers see the early vote as being by definition a relatively uninformed vote, even though the profile of the early voter is in some contradiction to this. In fact, those who vote early are likely to be more active in and knowledgeable about politics and candidates, and thus more likely to have collected information sufficient to cast an informed ballot. This is in part because early voters also tend to be the most committed political participants. For example, it is not unusual for campaign workers and party activists to vote early so that they can be free to concentrate their efforts on turning out other voters on

---

13. Delbert Taebel, Nirmal Goswami, and Laurence Jones, "The Politics of Early Voting in Texas: Perspectives of County Chairs." *Texas Journal of Political Studies* (Spring/Summer 1994), vol. 16, p. 22.

election day. Some have justified their early vote by saying that, even if they die between the time of casting their ballot and the actual election day, their vote will still count!

The significance of the early vote is attested to in the evaluations of campaigns after an election as well as in current campaign practices. Following an election, political discourse among campaign workers makes it appear as if there are actually two elections, the early vote and the election-day vote.

Motor-Voter

Motor-voter is an innovation that was debated at some length at the national and state level before it was finally adopted. The idea behind motor-voter, or tying voter registration to obtaining or renewing a driver's license, is appealing to most citizens because the first and seemingly simplest hurdle to overcome with regard to participating in politics is to register to vote. As simple as that sounds, there are large numbers of people who for one reason or another fail to become registered voters. As a result, both political parties have spent some part of their resources in the past on registration drives prior to elections. Of course, registration drives by Democrats and Republicans differ in their approach and in the groups that they target. It is safe to say that Democrats have spent more time and effort registering their potential voters than have Republicans, because the profile of the average Democratic voter is that of a person somewhat less likely to be registered without assistance.[14]

Democrats who championed the motor-voter cause were not content to limit registration assistance to obtaining a driver's license. The driver's license provision would reach young people, because there is hardly any rite of passage to adulthood more important in American society than obtaining a driver's license. In the course of the legislative history of the motor-voter bill, however, voter registration assistance was expanded to include other kinds of state and federal agencies, including those that provided hunting and fishing licenses, welfare payments, and other forms of public assistance.

Republicans opposed the original concept and were particularly against expanding it to numerous government agencies. They argued that such extensive registration activity could subject the registration process to fraud, that illegal immigrants and legal aliens might be inadvertently registered to vote, and that recipients of public assistance would feel coerced to register. A more overtly political argument was that Democrats were attempting to conduct massive inner-city registration drives at taxpayers' expense. Other arguments specifically attacked the idea of having welfare agencies perform voter registration duties. It

---

14. Daniel M. Shea and John C. Green, *The State of the Parties: The Changing Role of Contemporary American Parties* (Lanham, Maryland: University Press of America, 1994).

was argued that the sudden influx of voters with a direct interest in government assistance could distort the political system in favor of the "have-nots," who would certainly vote in their own interests and thus use their vote to raid the state or federal treasury to increase their benefits. This argument overlooked the fact that the middle class, as well as the wealthy, are just as likely to vote in their own interests as are the lower classes. However, because the middle class and the wealthy consider that they are the ones principally paying taxes, they feel they have more right to have a say over the dispensation of public funds.

While the proponents of motor-voter, mostly Democrats, advocated it as simply a more convenient, effective, and efficient way of promoting good citizenship, opponents argued that someone who is mandated, or strongly assisted, to register to vote is not as good a candidate for the practice of good citizenship as someone who seeks the franchise through their own sense of civic obligation. It is argued that assisted voters are probably not registered to vote in the first place because they are not very attentive to public issues. Consequently, they may bring a more volatile and random element to the election process.

If motor-voter is ultimately successful, however, and if the program is continued, this change in election procedures should lighten the burden for voters, for candidates, and for the political parties. While there may still be a need to register some new residents to the state before a particular election, the traditional registration drives should be less important. In addition, if every citizen in Texas who possesses a driver's license is a registered voter, the demographic composition of the voter pool should change substantially. The ultimate effect on voter turnout is still in doubt, however, because potential voters fail to vote for many reasons, only one of which is not being registered.[15]

Mobile Voting

Mobile voting is one of the forms of what is officially designated in Texas as branch voting, and is a less-sweeping reform in practice than motor-voter or early voting. Branch voting is mandated for counties and other significant electoral subdivisions with large populations (100,000 or more). It is optional in rural areas with lower populations. Branch voting allows for both temporary and permanent branch voting sites separated from traditional voting locations such as courthouses.

The temporary version of branch voting is often referred to as mobile voting. This practice allows a ballot box to be carried to different locations within a county during the early voting period. This is in stark contrast to the traditional practice of requiring all voters to travel to a central location to vote. The proponents of mobile voting argued that

---

15. Jerry L. Yeric and John R. Todd, *Public Opinion: The Visible Politics* (Itasca, IL: F. E. Peacock Publishers, Inc., 1993).

courthouses and other public office buildings are rarely visited by most people, are rather far removed from most daily routines, and are often geographically inconvenient.

Because of horror stories and legends of ballot-box tampering in Texas, eyebrows were raised when suggestions were made for changing the traditional location for ballot boxes. The law designates certain legitimate authorities (county commissioners) to decide when and where the ballot box shall be made available, but there is still substantial room for discretion. Even the seemingly charitable and innocuous practice of taking the ballot box to retirement homes, where the voting population faces real obstacles in traveling to another location to cast their ballots, has been called into question. There are those who fear that senior citizens are likely to be easy prey for unscrupulous election officials who may attempt to influence their vote, and that election officials may simply mark the ballot in favor of their own preference, independent of the wishes of a senior citizen who may suffer from bad eyesight or have other cognitive difficulties.

Retail Voting

Retail voting is the label attached to the permanent form of branch voting and carries with it some of the same baggage that caused doubts about mobile voting. Retail voting is the practice of locating ballot boxes in retail sites such as the local discount store or grocery store during the early voting period. The idea is to overcome the reluctance that people have to enter a government building to vote. For most people, a trip to government offices is not a regular occurrence, and because some government offices represent such things as tax collection and police work, some citizens have negative associations with them. The local grocery store, however, is a place many people visit on a daily basis, a place where they see their friends and neighbors; for this reason, retail voting should make voting substantially more convenient for most citizens.

Opponents argue that making voting more convenient may increase voter turnout but could also have a detrimental effect on the quality of voting. Voting could become something akin to impulse buying, placing the act of voting in the same category as the purchase of magazines and candies surrounding check-out counters. It is argued that retail voters may have given little or no thought to the election, the issues, or the candidates, and may be encouraged to vote on the spur of the moment only because the ballot box is available. Opponents of retail voting argue that voting should be a more thoughtful activity. Partisan bickering also enters the debate when retail locations for voting are discussed. While Democrats may prefer large discount stores and bait shops as voting locations, Republicans would probably prefer boutiques and upscale department stores.

Conclusion

Procedural changes made in elections and voting practices have been justified by arguing that voting should be made as simple and easy as possible. The legal changes aimed at increasing voter turnout by making it more convenient to be registered and to actually cast a ballot are as close to a practical endorsement of democracy as we as a society have been willing to come. But not everyone is certain that the direct rule of the people is desirable.

Indeed, we can no longer avoid facing up to any antidemocratic sentiments we might harbor. Traditional arguments that the size of modern societies, either geographically or demographically, is an insurmountable barrier to giving each citizen an opportunity to register an opinion on each issue are no longer credible. What was once science fiction is, in fact, now feasible. We are no longer forced to practice representative democracy. We could have public-access television channels that provide detailed information on all public issues and an immediate opportunity for an individual to register support or disagreement.

The question that we must now confront is not how could we do it, but why don't we? Citizen access cards could allow individuals to tap into the decision-making process simply by pressing a button on their remote control, or their computer, to directly register a "yes" or "no" to proposed policies, or even to offer judgments on the appropriate or inappropriate administration of policies.

The way in which one answers the question of whether to provide direct voter decision making hinges first and foremost on one's conception of human nature. Those who believe that human beings are capable of considering another person's interests to be almost as important as their own might answer that the direct rule of the people is both possible and desirable. If someone raises doubts or expresses skepticism about that possibility, the optimistic response is that even if humans are not quite ready for that level of public responsibility, they soon will be.

On the other hand, those who are skeptical about human nature generally show very little faith in the ability of citizens to see past their own needs. Even when these skeptics concede such a moral possibility, they argue that the demands of public issues on time and expertise in the modern world are simply beyond the capacity of most citizens. Consequently, they say, public decisions should necessarily remain the province of specialists, or at least of full-time participants.

It is probably safe to say that the skeptics are currently in ascendence in Texas. Whatever idealistic faith in the people we might hear expressed in party platforms, by academicians and theoreticians, by politicians in the heat of a campaign, or even by ourselves in our optimistic moments, we would probably all suffer severe anxiety about any real attempt to provide direct power to the people. Do we really want the average citizen to make decisions about health care, foreign policy, civil rights, education, or law enforcement?

There are substantive and important roles for citizens to play in Texas government short of direct rule and, as we noted at the beginning of this chapter, the role of citizen has become both more convenient and more burdensome. Citizens can, however, be attentive to the substantive conditions of the society around them, diligent in overseeing the decisions and actions of public officials, and can be vocal participants in public debates over public issues. Citizens can be regular voters, campaign workers, and perhaps with greater difficulty than in the past, even candidates for office. However, until citizens are assured the necessary leisure time to study public problems, an adequate flow of thorough and objective information, and the personal experience and expertise necessary to make public decisions in the modern world, they must rely on elected officials to be their principal link to the public realm. Consequently, the legal, cultural, economic, and social environment within which those elections take place are of essential concern to us all.

9
Gender and the Campaign for Governor

JEANIE R. STANLEY
POLITICAL CONSULTANT AND COAUTHOR OF *CLAYTIE AND THE LADY*, THE WOODLANDS

The game of Texas politics has long been played primarily by white males, although that tradition is being increasingly challenged by women and minorities. Minorities, in particular, have gained politically as a result of the Voting Rights Act, which provided the legal impetus for the change from at-large elections to single-member districts. Because those districts have been drawn with an eye toward maximizing minority representation, Texans are electing significantly increasing numbers of African-Americans and Hispanics to city councils, school boards, and the state legislature.

Women do not benefit from the Voting Rights Act, however. They are not a protected class under the law, and, even if they were, districting mechanisms such as single-member districts would not work for them. Nevertheless, women have made vast inroads in Texas politics since earlier in this century, when Miriam Ferguson was elected governor as a proxy for her husband, whose impeachment prevented him from serving again as governor. In those days, Ferguson supporters claimed that by voting for "Ma" Ferguson they were getting two governors for the price of one, because everyone knew that "Pa" Ferguson would be the major power broker in the administration. Another famous female Texas politician in the first decades of this century was Sarah Hughes. Today it is unlikely that a woman running for the Texas Legislature would be criticized for not being home washing dishes, as Sarah Hughes was in the years when she was serving in and campaigning for the state legislature, long before she became one of Texas's best-known federal judges.

Despite the changes in Texas politics and the much-increased role of women in politics, gender remains a political issue in Texas. Sometimes the issue is subtle, but it is important to understand it. As the next chapter explains, women often have political values different from those of men. In addition, when a woman runs for office, the campaign strategies required are different from those used by a man running for the same office.

As is pointed out in this chapter, one of the most amazing illustrations of gender politics occurred in the 1990 gubernatorial race, in which Republican candidate Clayton Williams faced Democrat Ann Richards. It was Clayton Williams's race to lose, and he did because of a series of campaign errors *that failed to recognize the importance of gender in elections and the retribution that could follow from women who in ordinary circumstances would have voted Republican. In terms of gender, the Williams campaign was a crude throwback to an earlier era in that he showed no sensitivity to the gender issue. In the 1994 gubernatorial election, George Bush did not repeat that mistake.*

In analyzing the 1994 elections, newspaper accounts frequently referred to the "angry white male" vote. Political pundits called 1992 the "Year of the Woman" and attributed the 1990 victory of Governor Ann Richards to the "woman's vote." "Gender gaps" in voter turnout, candidate preference, and issue perceptions have been widely reported in Texas elections since 1980. It is not surprising, therefore, that gender is an important consideration in developing campaign strategy. In fact, gender pervades every aspect of campaign politics, from donor and voter appeals to candidate image and issue communication or "spin." Gender is only one of many factors that affect election campaign strategies and voter behavior, but it is a significant one.

As most Texans do not (or prefer not to) believe that gender has much effect on their attitudes, political strategists rarely make direct appeals on this basis. Rather, they use subtle imagery and inference. Ironically, strategists succeed when gender is not perceived consciously by the voters as an issue in the campaign.

Another common misconception is that gender only becomes significant when a woman candidate is involved or when the abortion issue is prominent. Gender strategies have a much higher profile in statewide contests between male and female candidates, but gender is a factor in all races. Candidates and the electorate are divided on the abortion issue, but this issue is not necessarily associated with greater gender differences in voting.

The 1990 and 1994 governor's races in Texas provided examples of how gender becomes a pervasive but subtle element in campaign strategy. Ann Richards's win over Clayton Williams in 1990 and her subsequent loss to George W. Bush in 1994 illustrate the challenges of running as a woman, running against a woman, and appealing to an electorate carrying mixed notions about appropriate gender roles. These races also reflect the historical and cultural context in which Texas gender politics unfolds.

CULTURAL CONTEXT

The way in which gender becomes a factor in the political arena depends, in part, on the cultural context or environment in which the political contest takes place. For example, Texas history has given mixed messages with regard to the appropriate role of women. The "Old

South" image of the Southern belle and the "little lady" is juxtaposed beside the stronger role of the frontier woman and cowgirl. The tendency for Texans to appreciate independence and individualism can translate into a high regard for women who are willing to take risks and enter into politics. Many Texans, however, are uncomfortable with women assuming nontraditional roles, including that of assertive political leader.

Women in Texas, as in the rest of the country, are relative newcomers to politics. Texas was the first Southern state to ratify the 19th Amendment to the U.S. Constitution, which gave women the right to vote in 1920. Texas women were active in seeking support for women's suffrage and continued to advocate for other issues of particular concern to them. Often called the "Petticoat Lobby," these early women activists were caught off guard by the 1924 Democratic gubernatorial nomination of Miriam Ferguson, wife of Governor Jim Ferguson, who had opposed women's right to vote. When it was learned that her opponent was a proponent of the Ku Klux Klan, however, women activists and other Texans chose a "bonnet" rather than a "hood." Texans elected Miriam Ferguson as governor in 1924 and reelected her for an additional term in 1932. Although "Ma" Ferguson was one of the first women governors in the country, she was in reality elected as a surrogate for her husband. A few other women have run for governor since that time, but Ann Richards was the second woman elected as governor of Texas, and one of only fourteen women elected governor in the history of the United States.

Texans have been more willing to elect women to represent them in legislative bodies than to "run things" as executives, particularly at the state level. In 1993, Kay Bailey Hutchison was the first woman elected to represent Texas in the U.S. Senate, but only three Texas women, all African-American, have served in the U.S. House of Representatives: Barbara Jordan (1972–1978), Eddie Bernice Johnson (since 1992), and Sheila Jackson Lee (since 1994). Women have served in the Texas Legislature since 1924. Although their numbers increased dramatically after single-member districts were introduced in the 1970s, women compose less than 20 percent of the current legislative membership.

Women have served in greater numbers at the local level, particularly on city councils and school boards. In 1995, according to the Texas Municipal League, 17 women served as mayors. During the past decade, women were elected as mayors of major Texas cities, including Dallas, Ft. Worth, Houston, San Antonio, El Paso, Galveston, and Corpus Christi. The number of women seeking judicial, county, and statewide positions has steadily increased. There are many positions at the state and local levels, however, that have never been filled by a woman. Many continue to see political leadership as more appropriate for a man.

According to historical traditions, Texans expect a man and their political leader to be a hero, to be "tough," to be a man's man. The image

Gender and the Campaign for Governor   143

of the cowboy hero who will save the day is an appealing package for political candidates and officeholders. That most of the challenges facing Texas have little in common with the frontier past does not seem to matter. Even if candidates are more comfortable in a suit, they likely will don western clothes and talk about the glorious Texas heritage in their campaigns. No intellectuals, Yankees, or wimps need apply. Yet not all Texas voters are "Bubbas" or cowboys. Many voters have moved to Texas from other states or have lived in major metropolitan areas all their lives. These voters look for sophisticated, cosmopolitan leaders who can help the state achieve economic viability in an increasingly technical and international market. These voters do not have confidence in politicians who "talk Texan." Advertisers refer to the Texas market as being bipolar, simultaneously reflecting a "new" and an "old" Texas. Political candidates must appeal to both.

These often contradictory expectations of those who seek political office present a formidable challenge to candidates and campaign strategists as they develop a candidate's image.

CANDIDATE IMAGE

Most political leaders are male. The characteristics we associate with political leadership, therefore, tend to be male characteristics. Voters want to see a show of strength and decisiveness in the demeanor and body language of officeholders, and want to be sure that a candidate is "tough enough" for the job. Some voters also have an image of what a woman should be like and how she should behave. If a woman wants to be elected to office, she must exhibit the "male" characteristics needed for political leadership without behaving "inappropriately" as a woman.[1] As we follow a campaign between male and female candidates, we evaluate their ability to lead or to be "tough," but we expect the candidates to display acceptable behavior as ladies and gentlemen who disagree. A man running against a woman must be careful not to be "bested" by a lady. At the same time, he must behave as a gentleman and not be perceived as "beating up" on a woman. A woman must be tough without being strident or mean-spirited.[2]

The complexity of this gender dance in politics was evident in the 1990 and 1994 Texas gubernatorial elections. In 1990, Clayton Williams was chastised for not shaking Ann Richards's hand at a press conference and for using rough "cowhand" language when he said he would "head and hoof her and drag her through the dirt." In the 1990 gubernatorial

---

1. For a more extensive coverage of gender and candidate image, see Linda Witt, Karen M. Paget, and Glenna Matthews, *Running as a Woman: Gender and Power in American Politics* (New York: The Free Press, 1994) and Sue Tolleson-Rinehart and Jeanie R. Stanley, *Claytie and the Lady: Ann Richards, Gender and Politics in Texas.* (Austin, TX: The University of Texas Press, 1994).
2. See Witt et al., pp. 13–14.

elections, Ann Richards celebrated her tenth year of sobriety as a recovering alcoholic. Support for Richards dropped dramatically during the primary when she refused to answer a question concerning possible other drug abuse. She also was perceived by voters as running a highly negative campaign. Because voters generally hold women candidates to higher standards of morality and ethics than they do men, many observers did not think Richards could prevail. Over time, however, voters began to show grudging respect for her candor about her alcoholism. When Williams remarked that he "hoped she had not started drinking again," after she suggested their race was getting closer, public opinion shifted against him.

Voters also generally believe that women candidates will be more ethical and compassionate as elected officials than men. The 1990 Richards campaign worked hard to reinforce this perception. Her television spots pictured her with her father, as she assured Texans she would make insurance companies fulfill their responsibilities to "older folks" like her "daddy." She was often pictured with her children and grandchildren. Her strategy worked in 1990 but was not successful four years later. In 1994, the charge of negative campaigning against Richards surfaced again. Voters generally accepted Richards's "country" sense of humor and "one of the boys" demeanor, but they were uncomfortable with her calling George Bush a "jerk."[3] For his part, Bush learned a lesson from Williams's defeat and pointedly characterized his negative campaign comments as criticisms of Richards's job performance, not personal criticisms of his opponent. Bush repeatedly accused Richards of making personal attacks against him and his family, which would have been considered "unladylike" by the public. The exit poll results shown in Figure 9.1 indicate that more voters thought Richards made unfair attacks during the campaign.

In addition to accusing Richards of making personal attacks, Bush effectively neutralized a woman candidate's advantage of being perceived as more honest and caring by using media spots showing only his face talking directly to the viewers. Such spots convey a sense of candor and honesty.[4] Bush also ran as an outsider in 1994, which is an asset in today's cynical antigovernment atmosphere. Women candidates usually benefit from being perceived as outsiders, but Richards emphasized her experience as an incumbent, thus strengthening Bush's claim to being the outsider. Unlike her 1990 "New Texas" campaign theme, in which Richards promised to bring the people into government with her, Richards was now the political insider.[5] The 1994 Richards campaign did

---

3. For further discussion of gender and negative campaigning, see Tolleson-Rinehart and Stanley, pp. 74, 80–84.
4. Tolleson-Rinehart and Stanley, p. 80; Jeanie Stanley, "Bush, Richards both gear campaigns to women's vote," *Dallas Morning News*, 6 November 1994, p. 6J.
5. Witt et al., pp. 266–67; Tolleson-Rinehart and Stanley, p. 3.

Gender and the Campaign for Governor 145

FIGURE 9.1

Exit Poll on Unfair Campaign Charges by Gender

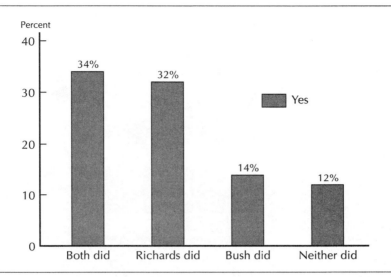

Source: *The Dallas Morning News* exit poll of voters casting ballots on the 1994 election day in Texas.

not maximize her gender advantages through either the general message or through specific issues.

Issues, Voter Attitudes, and Media Strategies

Voters make judgments about political issues much the same way they decide what to buy at the store or how to spend their leisure time. Their decisions reflect personal values, experiences, and beliefs. Frequently, their decisions reflect their gender. Most Texans get their information about politics from watching television. Only a few voters actually hear political candidates speak or work on their campaigns. It is no surprise, therefore, that political candidates spend much of their time raising money to produce and pay for television advertising. The way in which candidates and their issues are presented often determines election outcomes. As the public perceives issues and candidates through a gender prism, media and campaign strategists carefully consider ways to appeal to both men and women.

Studies over the years have consistently found gender patterns in voter attitudes about political issues. For example, women candidates, officeholders, and voters tend to be more concerned than men about

FIGURE 9.2

Gun Control by Gender

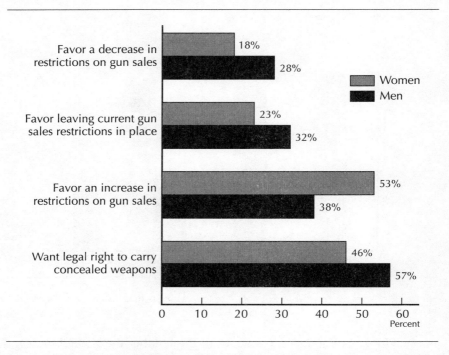

Source: The Texas Poll, conducted statewide by telephone Feb. 2–11, 1995, surveying 1,011 adults in a systematic random sampling of active telephone exchanges. Conducted for Harte-Hanks Communications Inc. and The Texas Poll News Syndicate by the Office of Survey Research at the University of Texas in Austin.

education, children's issues, and the welfare of children, the elderly, and the poor. Men have been more likely to favor the death penalty, less gun control, and expenditures for prisons (see Figure 9.2).

In some instances, men may have the same views as women, but the salience or importance of the issue may be greater for one gender. There are not significant gender differences on abortion, but the issue is of greater salience for women (see Figure 9.3). A 1992 poll in Texas indicated that women were far more likely to find out about a candidate's stand on abortion and to consider that issue as significant in determining their candidate preference. Women were not more or less likely than men to be pro-choice or pro-life.

Men and women may be similarly concerned about some issues, such as crime, juvenile delinquency, gun control, or teacher pay, but prefer different actions to address the problems. Women express greater fear about crime than do men, but they were less likely than men to rank it

Figure 9.3

Abortion as a Factor in Voting for a Candidate by Gender

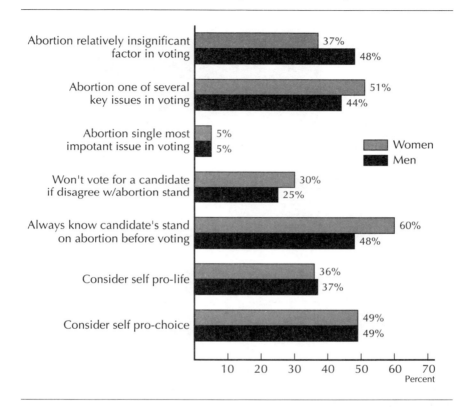

Source: The Texas Poll, conducted Statewide by telephone July 30–Aug. 7, 1992, surveying 1,004 adults in a systematic random sampling of active telephone exchanges. Conducted for Harte-Hanks Communications Inc. and The Texas Poll News Syndicate by Public Policy Resources Laboratory of Texas A & M University.

as the most important issue in the 1994 governor's race (see Figure 9.4 and Table 9.1). Women are not as likely as men to see personal access to guns as the answer to crime, but they are more likely than men to favor teen curfews and greater expenditures on education (see Figure 9.2).

Voters also perceive men and women candidates to be better able to handle certain issues. Because the public thinks women candidates are more compassionate, ethical, and caring, they trust women to address social welfare and education concerns.[6] Males are believed to be "tougher" on issues of crime and better able to handle financial matters.

6. Witt et al., pp. 10–11.

FIGURE 9.4

Fear and Personal Experience of Crime by Gender

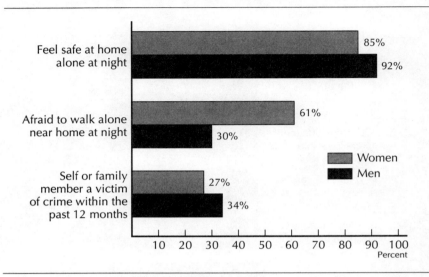

Source: The Texas Poll, conducted Statewide by telephone April 9–18, 1992, surveying 1,006 adults in a systematic random sampling of active telephone exchanges. Conducted for Harte-Hanks Communications Inc. and The Texas Poll News Syndicate by Public Policy Resources Laboratory of Texas A & M University.

In the 1990 governor's race, Richards and Williams promised actions consistent with the public's expectations of their respective genders. Ann Richards promised to end unfair treatment of the elderly by insurance companies and to make Texas government more responsive to the needs of average Texans. Emphasizing her experience as a mother and former

TABLE 9.1

Most Important Issue in 1994 Governor's Race
by Gender and by Candidate Preference

	men	women	Richards supporters	Bush supporters
crime/violence	23%	15%	18%	22%
education/schools	13%	23%	19%	18%
economy/jobs	7%	6%	8%	5%
taxes	5%	5%	4%	7%
prisons/judicial system	4%	3%	6%	2%

Source: The Texas Poll, conducted statewide by telephone Oct. 6–15, 1994, surveying 1,002 adults in a systematic random sampling of active telephone exchanges. Conducted for Harte-Hanks Communications Inc. and The Texas Poll News Syndicate by the Office of Survey Research at the University of Texas in Austin.

teacher, Richards also promised to improve education and secure a pay raise for teachers. Her opponent, Clayton Williams, promised to teach juvenile delinquents the "joys of busting rocks" and to apply his business expertise to better manage government. Williams stressed the need to get tough in education by returning to the basics and strong discipline. Richards was firmly pro-choice on abortion issues; Williams was anti-abortion. Whereas Richards described a new inclusive Texas, Williams talked of returning Texas to its previous greatness by restoring basic values and principles. The media campaigns of both candidates played to the strengths generally associated by the public with their gender. Richards was the compassionate outsider who would bring new people, including women, to the table. Williams was the tough cowboy businessman who would return common sense, business principles, and basic values to government.

In 1994, the Bush campaign worked to alter gender patterns in his favor. Hiring a consultant with a national reputation for advising Republican men running against female opponents, Bush took the initiative in defining the issues for his benefit. Education, usually a "good" issue for women candidates, was explained as a financial problem and a vehicle to fight crime, because voters usually think men handle business and crime matters better than women. Richards's anti-crime profile during her first administration appeared to neutralize the typical gender stereotype regarding crime, but the state's failure to address educational finance during her first term strengthened Bush's appeal as a businessman.

Bush (and Kay Bailey Hutchison) distanced themselves from the pro-life Christian Coalition during the state Republican convention, and generally portrayed themselves as moderates on social issues. Although Bush favored restrictions on abortion, including parental approval, he did not emphasize the issue during his campaign.[7] Bush made direct appeals to the professional, pro-choice Republican women who had crossed party lines to support Richards in 1990, and he placed women in key campaign positions.

Richards remained firm on her commitment to choice. This stance, as well as her reference to some religious radicals as "mongers of hate" during the Democratic State Convention, was used to mobilize the 63,000 Christian Coalition members against her. Unlike 1990, when a well-organized pro-choice coalition identified and turned out to vote large numbers of like-minded Texans, there was little pro-choice activity in 1994.

Labor Day brought media coverage of the candidates bird hunting. As a woman, Richards needed this opportunity to show her support for

---

7. Lori Stahl, "Suprisingly, abortion hasn't made election issue list," *Dallas Morning News*, 22 October 1994, p. 32A.

recreational gun use, as well as her ability to perform another "manly" function. When Bush accidentally and illegally shot an endangered bird, political analysts wondered if the mistake would be fatal by suggesting Bush did not have the "macho" traits expected of Texas political men. Bush's humor and candor, however, appeared to prevent any long-term damage. Voters who thought crime was the most important issue in the governor's race favored Bush, but Richards held her own on the crime issue (Table 9.1).

Campaign Organization and Funding

In the 1994 race, both campaign organizations had similar funds and resources. This was not the case in 1990, when Williams far exceeded Richards in available funds, particularly in regard to early fundraising, which permits more effective planning and spending. Part of Richards's difficulty in raising funds was attributed to her being a woman. Until the past few years, women candidates have not been able to raise as much money as their male counterparts, for several reasons. Most large donors are men who want to give their money to the candidate with the best chance of winning. Women are not as likely as men to be incumbents, and there often is a perception that women, as outsiders, are not as likely to win. In addition, women are less likely than men to donate to campaigns, and when they do, they give smaller amounts of money.

Efforts have been made to counteract this disadvantage for women. An early donor to the 1990 Richards campaign was Emily's (Early Money Is Like Yeast) List, a political action committee formed to encourage women donors and to provide early money to Democratic women candidates. Wish (the Republican counterpart to Emily's List: Women in the Senate and House), the Women's Campaign Fund, and the National Women's Political Caucus are other organizations that target women donors and candidates.[8] Since 1990, donations both from women and to women candidates have increased dramatically. Emily's List, for example, increased their donations from $1.5 million in 1990 to $6.4 million in 1992 and $8.2 million in 1994. Although women candidates still report greater difficulty in obtaining early money, their parity with male candidates has improved steadily. Ann Richards and Kay Bailey Hutchison matched or exceeded their opponents in 1994 fundraising.

As an incumbent in 1994, Richards was able to offset the usual disadvantage women have in the areas of fundraising and campaign organization. In contrast to most women candidates, Richards had paid

---

8. For additional information on groups organized to support women candidates, contact the Center for the American Woman and Politics (CAWP), Eagleton Institute, Rutgers University, New Brunswick, NJ 08901.

staff and did not have to depend as much on volunteers as she had in 1990. Both Richards and Bush were able to produce and purchase media spots in a timely fashion and otherwise develop and execute carefully planned campaign strategies. Although some observers noted that the 1994 Richards campaign organization lacked the fervor of the low-budget, volunteer-based, crisis-oriented campaign of 1990, few consultants would choose the latter. Observers also noted that the enthusiasm of interest groups supporting Richards was lower in 1994, as was voter support for the Democratic Party and Democratic candidates. Gender patterns in such support are discussed below.

POLITICAL PARTIES AND INTEREST GROUPS

Since 1980, Texas women have been more supportive of Democratic candidates than men. Women also have been more likely than men to identify with the Democratic Party (see Figure 9.5). Conversely, men have been more supportive of Republican candidates and the Republican Party. Gender differences vary with the election and candidates. In 1994, for example, women were more likely to support Democratic candidates for all statewide races except those for the U.S. Senate (see Table 9.2).

Gender patterns in political party support are issue and ideology based. Women identify themselves as more liberal and less conservative than men (see Figure 9.5). The Republican Party is considered more conservative than the Democratic Party, which has been associated with affirmative action and gender equity policies, as well as support for human services programs. Women are more supportive of such programs than are men.

Both political parties purport to recruit women candidates, but Democratic and Republican women complain that it is difficult for them to obtain their party's nomination. Their difficulty is attributed partially to the fundraising disadvantages discussed previously, as well as "old boy's networks," which sometimes dominate nominations within local and state political party organizations.

Interest groups often enjoy the support of one gender more than the other. The National Rifle Association, the Texas Fathers for Equal Rights, and the Texas Chamber of Commerce have more male than female members, but women compose the majority of the Texas State Teachers Association, the Parent-Teacher Association, and the Texas Women's Political Caucus. Similarly, interest groups may oppose or support issues about which there are gender differences among voters. The involvement of interest groups can serve as a catalyst for greater participation by men or women. Such was the case in the 1990 and 1994 Texas gubernatorial elections. The enthusiastic participation of a pro-choice coalition and

FIGURE 9.5

Political Ideology and Party Identification by Gender

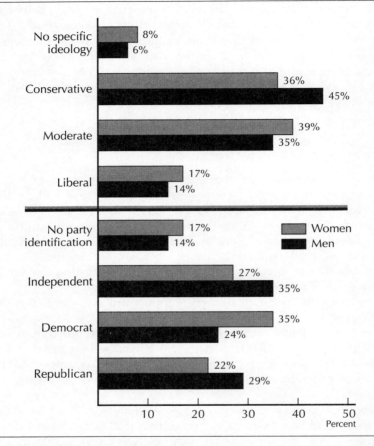

Source: The Texas Poll, conducted statewide by telephone Oct. 6–15, 1994, surveying 1,002 adults in a systematic random sampling of active telephone exchanges. Conducted for Harte-Hanks Communications Inc. and The Texas Poll News Syndicate by the Office of Survey Research at the University of Texas in Austin.

teachers organizations appeared to help Ann Richards in 1990, whereas the activities of the Christian Coalition and the National Rifle Association in 1994 helped George W. Bush.

Although candidates, campaign strategists, political parties, and interest groups assume that their efforts influence voters, the bottom line in politics is the vote. Men and women may report different attitudes and concerns, but what has been their voting behavior?

TABLE 9.2

Support for Major Statewide Races in the 1994 Election by Gender

If the election for [specific office] were held today, who would you vote for?

	All	Men	Women
For Governor			
(Dem) Ann Richards*	44%	37%	51%
(Rep) George Bush	45	51	39
For Senator			
(Rep) Kay Bailey Hutchison*	51	58	43
(Dem) Richard Fisher	32	28	37
For Lt. Governor			
(Dem) Bob Bullock*	54	50	57
(Rep) H. J. "Tex" Lezar	23	29	17
For Attorney General			
(Dem) Dan Morales*	41	39	43
(Rep) Don Wittig	29	35	22
For Comptroller			
(Dem) John Sharp*	43	45	40
(Rep) Teresa Doggett	26	29	23
For Land Commissioner			
(Dem) Garry Mauro*	37	33	40
(Rep) Marta Greytok	25	31	20
For Agriculture Commissioner			
(Dem) Marvin Gregory	25	20	30
(Rep) Rick Perry*	42	53	31

* indicates the incumbent

Source: The Texas Poll conducted Oct. 6–15, 1994 by the Office of Survey Research, University of Texas for Harte-Hanks Communications and The Texas Poll News Syndicate. Percentages given reflect responses of 675 Texans deemed to be likely voters in the 1994 Texas Governor's election. N=633. Margin of error ±4 overall, ±6 gender subsamples.

Voting by Gender

Since 1980, women have composed from 51 to 53 percent of the Texas electorate, according to exit polls.[9] The preponderance of women voters reflects their demographic majority—particularly among the older population, who are most likely to vote—as well as their slightly greater

9. As the percentage of voters casting their ballots prior to election day increased to almost 30 percent of the Texas vote in 1994, exit polls, which survey those voting on election day only, are not as accurate a measure of electoral behavior. In the 1994 election, for example, pre-election Texas polls found men expressing significantly greater intentions to vote than women. Although exit polls reported women to be 53 percent of those voting, more men than women may have voted early.

TABLE 9.3

Support for 1994 Gubernatorial Candidates by Gender

	Men	Women
(Dem) Richards	39%	47%
(Rep) Bush	47	36
still undecided	14	17

Source: The Texas Poll, conducted statewide by telephone Oct. 6–15, 1994, surveying 1,002 adults in a systematic random sampling of active telephone exchanges. Conducted for Harte-Hanks Communications Inc. and The Texas Poll News Syndicate by the Office of Survey Research at the University of Texas in Austin. Questions were straight "Who would you vote for if the election were today?" with candidates identified with party labels, just as they appear on the Texas ballot.

tendency to vote than men. As most highly contested races are won with margins of less than 3 percent, the higher proportion of women voters has resulted in special efforts to appeal to women, particularly when the gender gap first appeared in the early 1980s.

The 1990 and 1994 Texas gubernatorial races illustrate such targeted appeals. In 1990, the Richards campaign and the pro-choice coalition had extensive registration and early voting efforts directed toward pro-choice women. As mentioned previously, the Richards campaign appealed to these same women voters to support her reelection, but the level of pro-choice interest group activity (and public interest in the issue) was much lower in 1994. The Christian Coalition organized staff and volunteers to mobilize pro-life voters in both 1990 and 1994 for Williams and Bush, but their later effort was dramatically more extensive and successful. Contacts by the Christian Coalition often were made through churches, where women constitute the majority of active members.

Gender differences in support of gubernatorial candidates since 1986 illustrate changing patterns in the votes of men and women over time. Although women favored Mark White over Clements by 11 percent in 1982, gender differences became insignificant in 1986. Women were more likely to favor Richards than her opponents in both 1990 and 1994, but the gap was less marked in 1994 (see Table 9.3). In contrast, the percentage of men favoring Republican candidates increased in 1994. Gender patterns also fluctuate during campaigns, presumably reflecting gender differences in issues underlying candidate choice. During the 1990 campaign, for example, women were more likely than men to support Richards, and male Richards voters decided to support Richards later in the campaign.

Gender and Campaigns

Gender is a significant factor in explaining political behavior. Depending upon whether they are male or female, Texans have different experiences, role expectations, values, and attitudes. These differences are evident in politics, particularly because political participation and leadership, until recently, has been characterized as more appropriate for males than females. In addition, differences in the experiences, values, and priorities of women and men often result in different views on what political issues are important and what political actions should be taken.

Gender patterns in political belief and behavior have significant implications for campaign strategists. Although the most effective strategies may be subtle and therefore not noticed by the voters, targeted appeals are made to men and women by all candidates. In addition, women candidates and men running against women face particular challenges due to gender-role expectations for candidates, which may conflict with expectations of appropriate behavior for women and men running for office. The 1990 and 1994 Texas gubernatorial races illustrate the complex challenges facing candidates, campaign strategists, and voters as they address gender patterns in politics.

10
The Party System in Texas

Paul Lenchner
Texas A&M University—Commerce

From the end of Reconstruction until recently, Texas was a one-party Democratic state. Policy conflicts tended to occur within the party, and in the 1940s and 1950s there were major battles between the usually dominant conservative wing of the Democratic Party and its liberal wing. Republicans tended to be limited to wealthy businessmen, very conservative true believers, and "post office Republicans" who were affiliated with the Republican Party to gain patronage during the years when there was a Republican in the White House.

At times, conservative Democrats rebelled against their own party because the national Democratic Party tended to be far more liberal than the dominant faction of the state party. In the 1950s, this led to the unusual situation where all incumbent Democrats for statewide office except one ran for office on both the Democratic ticket and the Republican ticket. This development was an early effort by conservative Democrats in Texas to divorce themselves from the national Democratic Party. However, they could not completely shed their Democratic affiliations. Traditional loyalties to the Democratic Party in Texas were still strong and a complete switch to the Republican Party was still politically risky.

With the election of Republican John Tower to replace Lyndon Johnson in the U.S. Senate in 1961, the Republican Party began to become increasingly meaningful in Texas politics. It was not until 1978, however, that the Republican Party could claim control of state government. In that year, William Clements, a Republican, defeated the Democratic Attorney General John Hill in the race for governor. At the time, there were many who claimed that Hill's personality and ineptitude as a candidate lost the race, rather than Clements being the winner of the race. It mattered little, however, because with the governorship Republicans held tremendous patronage opportunities, and the Republicans were set to grow.

With the Reagan presidency, the opportunities for Republican growth in Texas continued. Ronald Reagan was incredibly popular in Texas, garnering nearly two-thirds of the general vote in 1984. His popularity and the momentum of Republican Party growth in Texas led to party switches by leading Democrats such as congressmen Kent Hance and Phil Gramm. At the same time, as Republicans were gaining ground in higher offices, they were winning lesser ones in many counties. By 1984, Dallas County had moved from being a one-party Democratic County to a one-party Republican County. Almost every countywide elected official in Dallas County was a Republican by then, either because they switched parties or because Republicans had been voted into office.

By the 1990s, the most interesting question involving the Texas political parties is whether the Democratic Party can survive or whether Texas will become as much a one-party Republican state as it once was a one-party Democratic state.

Political parties play a vital role in democratic politics. Through parties ordinary citizens can pool their greatest resource, their numbers, to become a force in electoral politics. By definition the rich have more money, but the nonrich have more votes. By coming together under the umbrella of a party, rank-and-file citizens can choose leaders responsive to their policy preferences. Moreover, through the party system voters can voice their displeasure with governmental performance by shifting their loyalty to the party out of power. Voters can hold officials accountable for their actions by the simple tactic of voting for the "out" party. If officials are smart, they will not let the "outs" claim popular causes, but will strive to keep in touch with the mass electorate.

The assumption underlying these observations is that there will be healthy *competition* between political parties. Without competition voters are denied clear choices, accountability is undermined (if there is no meaningful opposition from the "outs," who will keep the "ins" honest?), and the voice of ordinary citizens is muffled, if not silenced.

For nearly a century after the Civil War, Texas was denied the benefits of party competition. What competition there was occurred within the ranks of the dominant Democrats. Although some progressives were able to gain office, in general pro-business forces called the shots. Historian George Norris Green argued that this corporate establishment reached the zenith of its control between 1938 and 1957. This period saw "numerous and harsh antilabor laws, the suppression of academic freedom, a segregationist philosophy, elections marred by demagoguery and corruption, the devolution of the daily press, and a state government that offered its citizens, especially the minorities, very few services." Green added that by the late 1950s the establishment's style and tactics softened, but the substance of its control persisted for another quarter-century, if not longer.[1]

Of course, Texas politics has changed and is continuing to change. A state with a Republican governor, two Republican U.S. Senators, and Republican majorities on the State Board of Education and State Supreme

---

1. George Norris Green, *The Establishment in Texas Politics: The Primitive Years, 1938–1957* (Norman, OK: University of Oklahoma Press, 1984), pp. xi, 17, 192.

Court can hardly be called a Democratic stronghold. The story of Republican growth in Texas is an important one and has been told many times.[2] Closely related to that story, and also of great importance, is what has happened *within* each of the major parties. This second story is the focus of this chapter. We will see how Republican gains have promoted Democratic unity and how the rise in Republican strength has been accompanied by the development of fault lines within the Republican Party. Our conclusions will be based upon an analysis of state party conventions and an examination of voting records of members of the Texas house of representatives.

STATE PARTY CONVENTIONS IN FOUR DECADES

State party conventions mark the pinnacle of citizen involvement in party governance. To be selected as a delegate (or alternate) to one's party's convention, a person must first attend his or her precinct convention, then be selected to attend the county or senatorial convention in that area, and finally be chosen to attend the state convention. Only a minute percentage of voters are willing to make the commitment to attend the state convention; however, those who do provide the foundation for the party organizations. Among other tasks, the state conventions, which are now held in June of even-numbered years, are responsible for adopting the party's platform, choosing its officers, electing its members of the national party committee, and, in presidential election years, choosing its delegates to the national party convention.

In the one-party era Democratic state conventions were often rancorous affairs. Establishment conservatives battled with liberal "loyalists" (so called because of their loyalty to the national Democratic Party in the New Deal–Fair Deal period) and were generally successful in controlling the party machinery. Often the internal life of the Democratic Party was anything but democratic. "Parliamentary legerdemain was common, and disputes over rules and credentials could easily dissolve into fistfights."[3]

Even when the Republicans were a hopeless minority in Texas, the Republican Party's machinery, including its state conventions, also was frequently the scene of serious conflict. However, there was a fundamental difference between their conflicts and those of the Democrats. Republican divisions were rooted in personal and geographic rivalries, tensions between veteran leaders and newcomers, and squabbles over

---

2. For examples, see Roger M. Olien, *From Token to Triumph: The Texas Republicans Since 1920* (Dallas, TX: SMU Press, 1982); and Alexander P. Lamis, *The Two-Party South* (New York and Oxford: Oxford University Press, 1984), chap. 14.
3. Chandler Davidson, *Race and Class in Texas Politics* (Princeton, NJ: Princeton University Press, 1990), p. 161.

The Party System in Texas 159

patronage from Republican administrations in Washington. They were, however, not based upon policy differences. Philosophically the Republicans were united.[4] In contrast, the Democrats had the same splits as the Republicans (magnified by their much larger size), in addition to profound differences over ideology and policy.

1962

The year 1962 is a good place to begin a review of state conventions in the contemporary era of Texas politics. On the long road to a competitive party system, one of the most important mileposts was John Tower's election to the U.S. Senate in a special election in 1961, the first Republican victory in a statewide race since Reconstruction. It may be that the shock of this event prompted the Democrats to tone down their animosities when they gathered in El Paso the next year. The 1962 meeting did not see a repeat of "the bloodletting that had marred state conventions for so long."[5] But if the Democrats were behaving more civilly toward each other, there were still significant divisions at the convention. The dominant figure there was gubernatorial nominee John Connally, who had defeated the incumbent governor, Price Daniel, in the Democratic primary. Connally occupied a centrist position in the party with views that were, for the time, considered moderate to conservative.[6] He was definitely an establishment figure, but he embodied what Green viewed as a "more relaxed and mature" political style than many of his predecessors had shown.[7]

Two sizable groups of delegates had reservations about the direction in which Connally wished to lead the party. On one side was the Harris County (Houston) delegation, the convention's largest. This ultraconservative contingent drafted a platform repudiating the New Frontier programs of the Kennedy administration, a position clearly unacceptable to Connally, who had just come home after serving as Kennedy's Secretary of the Navy. According to one account, the Harris County proposals "read like something out of a John Birch society session."[8] (The John Birch Society is a secretive, fanatically anti-communist organization that sees a communist conspiracy as the source of virtually all of society's problems.) On the other side were the liberal loyalists, many of whom

---

4. Roger M. Olien, *From Token to Triumph: The Texas Republicans Since 1920*, chapters 2–6.
5. Chandler Davidson, *Race and Class in Texas Politics*, p. 166.
6. Dawson Duncan, "Democratic Platform Scrap Shaping Up." *Dallas Morning News*, 17 September, 1962, sec. 1, p. 14. At that time state party conventions were held in September in nonpresidential election years. In presidential election years, there were two conventions, one in June to choose delegates to the national party convention, and one in September (called the "governor's convention") with a state focus.
7. George Norris Green, *The Establishment in Texas Politics: The Primitive Years, 1938–1957*, p. xi.
8. Allen Duckworth, "Daniel Goes All-Out in Backing Connally," *Dallas Morning News*, 18 September, 1962, sec. 1, p. 6.

were affiliated with organized labor. Their most prominent spokesman was H. S. (Hank) Brown, president of the Texas State AFL-CIO. Brown said that labor did not expect to like the whole platform, but "we do expect a fair platform."[9] There were even threats that labor would withdraw its endorsement of Connally's candidacy if the platform were unsatisfactory.[10]

The Connally forces were able to maintain their control at the convention. A floor vote was not permitted on a minority platform written by Harris County delegates. Instead, the Connally-inspired platform, which attempted to provide some solace for all factions of the party, was overwhelmingly approved.[11] Thus the Democrats could reasonably claim to have achieved a measure of unity; however, it was unity of a relative sort. A grudging endorsement was all Connally could expect from the chairman of the Harris County delegation: "I generally take the position—as do others—that after the Democratic political organization chooses its nominees the least we can do is not actively support the opposition."[12] It hardly rated mention that former governor Coke Stevenson (1941–1947) and other old guard Democrats endorsed the Republican gubernatorial candidate, because this sort of thing had been going on for years.[13]

Journalists generally look for conflict or surprises in covering political events, and there was news for them at the 1962 Republican convention. As 3,200 delegates (easily the largest Republican conclave ever in Texas) gathered in Fort Worth, attention was focused on the race for party chair between incumbent Peter O'Donnell and Don Napier. There were two sources of contention between the opposing sides. It was partly a race between Dallas County (O'Donnell) and Harris County (Napier) favorites. There was also concern that O'Donnell was concentrating on his role as campaign manager for Republican gubernatorial candidate Jack Cox and not doing enough for other Republican nominees. But the race appeared friendly, and Napier refused to criticize O'Donnell. It is significant that there were no policy differences between the candidates, and both shared the Republican Party's staunch conservative philosophy.[14] At the last minute Napier withdrew from the race, and O'Donnell

9. Dawson Duncan, "Labor Not in Bag, Democrats Warned," *Dallas Morning News*, 18 September, 1962, sec. 1, p. 6.
10. See Allen Duckworth, "Democrats Anger Labor," *Dallas Morning News*, 19 September, 1962, sec. 1, p. 1; and Ed Johnson, "Democratic Unity in Double Trouble," *Fort Worth Star-Telegram*, 18 September, 1962, sec. 1, p. 3.
11. Dawson Duncan, "Connally's Forces Cut Down Opposition at Convention," *Dallas Morning News*, 19 September, 1962, sec. 1, p. 8.
12. Ed Johnson, "Divergent Democrats Talk Unity," *Fort Worth Star-Telegram*, 16 September, 1962, sec. 1, p. 1.
13. Johnson, "Democratic Unity in Double Trouble."
14. Mike Quinn, "Chairman's Race Holds GOP Stage," *Dallas Morning News*, 18 September, 1962, sec. 1, p. 5; Wick Fowler, "GOP Readies 'Triple Size' Convention," *Dallas Morning News*, 17 September, 1962, sec. 1, p. 1.

was elected by acclamation. In the words of one observer, "The move by Napier took away any tinge of disharmony for the GOP."[15]

1972

Nationally 1972 was an eventful year for the Democrats. Anti-Vietnam War leader George McGovern won the party's presidential nomination, defeating more centrist candidates Edmund Muskie and Hubert Humphrey. After running a strong third-party race in 1968, and despite being wounded by a would-be assassin in May, George Wallace brought his brand of conservative populism back to the Democratic race for the White House. In response to the civil rights, women's, and anti-war movements, the party adopted new rules requiring its national and state organizations to operate more openly, and mandated racial and gender diversity in choosing delegates to party bodies. These national developments had a noticeable impact on Texas Democrats.

By the time the Democrats gathered in June for the first of their two state conventions,[16] it appeared likely that George McGovern would be the party's presidential candidate. The Democratic nominee for governor was Dolph Briscoe, another in the party's long string of establishment conservative candidates. The challenge for Briscoe was to arrange an accommodation among the McGovern, Wallace, and traditional conservative forces. The most contentious issues were the election of convention and party leaders. It initially appeared that a battle would erupt over election of a chair for the convention. Conservatives favored state party chair Roy Orr, but he faced strong opposition from other factions. Briscoe tried to avert conflict by recommending his campaign manager, Calvin Guest, for chair and Orr for vice chair.[17]

The first part of Briscoe's plan succeeded, but the second did not. Following "a noisy, bitter battle for votes," Orr was defeated by Eddie Bernice Johnson, an African-American woman, 2,125 to 1,795 votes. After her election, Johnson was escorted to the platform by a group of black delegates and Frances (Sissy) Farenthold, a liberal whom Briscoe had defeated in the Democratic gubernatorial run-off. Johnson called her victory "the first step toward real Democratic justice in Texas."[18] Another step in that direction was taken at the party's second convention in September, when State Senator (and soon-to be elected U.S. Representative) Barbara Jordan, another African-American, was elected vice chair of the

---

15. Mike Quinn, "GOP Job Won by O'Donnell," *Dallas Morning News*, 19 September, 1962, sec. 1, p. 1.
16. See note 6.
17. Henry Holcomb, "Briscoe Action Could Avert Demo Disaster," *Houston Post*, 11 June, 1972, p. 23A.
18. Richard Morehead, "Democrats Drop Orr for Johnson," *Dallas Morning News*, 14 June, 1972, p. 1A. Johnson was elected to the Texas Legislature in 1972 and served there for two decades before winning a seat in the U.S. House in 1992.

party. Briscoe had favored another candidate but yielded to a unanimous recommendation from the convention's black caucus, and did not oppose Jordan. Her election as vice chair gave her an automatic seat on the Democratic National Committee, the first African-American in either of these posts.[19]

Liberals, women, and blacks did not fare so well in all the convention decisions, and there were times when the conservative forces asserted their traditional dominance.[20] However, on the whole, Briscoe's efforts to bring his party together can be judged a success. Houston liberal stalwart Billie Carr called the June convention open and fair. "I was pleasantly surprised," she said. "It's the best convention I ever attended."[21]

Democratic togetherness was still quite tentative. It was newsworthy that several of the party's candidates, including lieutenant governor nominee William Hobby, were bold enough to mention George McGovern while addressing the September convention and that they "received more cheers than boos" for doing so.[22] Still, it was unmistakable that Republican strength was building in Texas. John Tower was completing his second term in the U.S. Senate, and Republican gubernatorial candidates had polled 43 percent and 47 percent of the vote in the last two elections. Under the circumstances, the sensible strategy for Democrats was to build an inclusive party in which people with diverse views would feel comfortable. The corollary of the move toward inclusiveness was a shift toward the middle of the road. At times quickly, at times hesitantly, the Democrats were headed in that direction.

The Republican story in 1972 was similar to 1962. Once again there was controversy over the party's top officers, and once again the controversy was largely devoid of policy content. When the party convened in June, its gubernatorial nominee, Henry Grover, called for the resignation of state chair George Willeford and vice chair Beryl Milburn by the September convention. Their immediate sin was having backed another candidate in the primary. More fundamentally, they were charged with being part of a "little clique" headed by Peter O'Donnell. Grover accused the "clique of "run[ning] this party for years like a closed society and want[ing] to keep it that way."[23] The dispute was also rooted in friction between the Grover forces and the Tower forces. The senator's backers were believed to be more interested in keeping Tower's patronage pow-

19. Darrell Hancock and Henry Holcomb, "Compromise Prevents Democratic Splinter," *Houston Post*, 20 September, 1972, p. 1A.
20. Dave McNeely, "Liberals Lose Out," *Dallas Morning News*, 14 June, 1972, p. 5A.
21. Felton West, "Democrat Convention Pleases Both Liberals, Conservatives," *Houston Post*, 15 June, 1972, p. 1A.
22. Carolyn Barta, "Briscoe Asks Texas Democrats to Unite," *Dallas Morning News*, 20 September, 1972, p. 5A.
23. Art Wiese, "GOP Leaders Throw Down Gauntlet to Grover," *Houston Post*, 12 June, 1972, p. 3A.

ers than in electing a Republican governor and having to share their perquisites. Grover tried to force the issue, but was defeated on a resolution requiring the State Republican Executive Committee to meet within thirty days to replace the party's chair and vice chair.[24] By September a measure of intraparty unity had been achieved, and Willeford and Milburn were reelected to their posts without formal opposition. Some resentment remained, however; more than a third of the delegates were reported to have shouted "No" to the Willeford and Milburn nominations.[25]

1982

By 1982 it was unmistakable that Republicans were major players in Texas politics. John Tower had been elected to the senate four times, and the Republican contingent in the Texas house of representatives had grown from ten in 1972 to thirty-six in 1982. The greatest shock for Democrats was Bill Clements's upset victory in the 1978 governor's race. If there were any Democrats who had lingering doubts about the need to take Republicans seriously, the Clements win reconnected them with reality.[26]

In comparison to its predecessors, the Democratic state convention was remarkable for its harmony. State chair Bob Slagle and Billie Carr, who had had their differences in the past, joined in praising the platform, which Carr called the most liberal in party history. The platform supported the Equal Rights Amendment, was pro-choice on abortion, and had progressive planks on health care, education, the economy, and other issues.[27] Agriculture commissioner candidate Jim Hightower observed, "If we Democrats get any sweeter on each other, we're going to mold."[28] There was no mystery about the source of the unity. As one journalist remarked, "the *opposition party* [in regard to the governorship] decided it was time to start beating up on Republicans instead of each other."[29]

The evolution of Lloyd Bentsen's views and status among Democrats provides an additional illustration of the changing dynamics within the

---

24. Stewart Davis, "Grover Bid for Control Splits GOP," *Dallas Morning News*, 14 June, 1972, p. 1A; Jane Ely and Art Wiese, "GOP Axes Grover-led Ouster Bid," *Houston Post*, 14 June, 1972, p. 1A.
25. Art Wiese, "GOP Vote Takes Aim at Unity," *Houston Post*, 20 September, 1972, p. 1A.
26. See Glenn A. Robinson, "The Electorate in Texas," in Anthony Champagne and Edward J. Harpham, eds., *Texas at the Crossroads: People, Politics, and Policy* (College Station, TX: Texas A&M University Press, 1987), pp. 71–5.
27. Jane Ely, "SDEC Sets Tone of Unity for Convention Opening Today," *Houston Post*, 10 September, 1982, p. 7A; Jane Ely and Fred Bonavita, "Democrats Close State Convention United in Harmony," *Houston Post*, 12 September, 1982, p. 1A.
28. Jane Ely and Fred Bonavita, "Democrats Replay Unity Theme at Convention," *Houston Post*, 11 September, 1982, p. 19A.
29. Sam Attlesey, "Texas Democrats End Convention in Mood of Unity," *Dallas Morning News*, 12 September, 1982, p. 22A (emphasis added).

party. Bentsen won the Democratic nomination to the U.S. Senate in 1970 after a bitter primary race in which he defeated the incumbent, Ralph Yarborough, a liberal icon, by stressing "hot button" issues such as school prayer (for) and busing for school desegregation (against).[30] His tactics earned him the enmity of the party's progressive wing. After defeating George Bush in November in a campaign in which the candidates' "views were remarkably similar,"[31] once in office Bentsen moved toward the center. In the 1976 Democratic primary, he was not challenged from the left. His opposition came from an ambitious young Texas A&M professor who charged that Bentsen had been unfaithful to his 1970 campaign pledges. The challenger's name was Phil Gramm.[32] By 1982, Bentsen was an icon for virtually all Democrats. Democrats of diverse persuasions rallied behind him—and his proven vote-getting prowess—in his quest for a third term.

The Republican convention was a generally harmonious affair. Like all political conventions, it was marked by pep-rally-style rhetoric. Democrats were bashed, and Republican virtues were touted.[33] There was, however, one issue that divided delegates—abortion. In 1980 the party platform had a "no exceptions" abortion plank, and the 1982 platform and resolutions committee approved a similar plank by a fifteen to fourteen vote. However, the proposal was challenged on the convention floor, and after an emotional debate, the committee's recommendation was rejected 1,790 to 1,616 in favor of a plank that permitted abortion in cases of rape, incest, or where the mother's life was in imminent danger.[34] The decision was "considered a victory for party moderates."[35]

The abortion controversy is significant for two reason. First, it shows that at least through the early 1980s substantive disagreements within the Republican ranks were limited. As observers such as Chandler Davidson have noted,[36] and as we pointed out earlier in the chapter, Republican splits during the party's formative and adolescent years were not based upon policy or philosophical disputes. Upstarts such as Henry Grover often criticized "establishment" figures like John Tower and Peter O'Donnell. But the establishment was not being outflanked on the right. Tower maintained one of the Senate's most conservative voting

30. Jimmy Banks, *Money, Marbles and Chalk: The Wondrous World of Texas Politics* (Austin, TX: Texas Publishing Co., 1971), chap. 16.
31. Ibid., p. 202.
32. Alexander P. Lamis, *The Two-Party South*, p. 202.
33. Jorjanna Price, "GOP State Convention: Clements Appeals to Delegates to Pull Together," *Houston Post*, 11 September, 1982, p. 18A.
34. Felton West and Jorjanna Price, "GOP Delegates Adopt Weakened Abortion Stand," *Houston Post*, 12 September, 1982, p. 2B.
35. Sam Kinch, Jr., "GOP Platform OKs Abortion in Some Cases," *Dallas Morning News*, 12 September, 1982, p. 1A.
36. Chandler Davidson, *Race and Class in Texas Politics*, pp. 201–6.

records, and he and O'Donnell were ardent supporters of Barry Goldwater's successful drive to win the 1964 Republican presidential nomination by articulating an unabashedly conservative message.[37] Second, the abortion debate was a harbinger of things to come. By the 1990s it was probably the most divisive issue for Republicans nationally and in Texas.

1994

By the time Democrats gathered for their 1994 convention in Fort Worth, harmonious meetings had become the norm. As expected, events went smoothly again. Bob Slagle was reelected to his eighth term as state chair, and there were the customary partisan speeches.[38] The convention adopted a platform that Democratic activists anywhere in the country would likely have supported. Universal health care and environmental protection were endorsed. Consistent with contemporary fashion (at least among Democrats), a multifaceted approach to crime was proposed, including prevention, increased law enforcement, meaningful punishment, and an end to early release of violent offenders. On the social issues, full access to abortion and family planning information and services was advocated, along with an end to discrimination, including discrimination against homosexuals. In a transparent slam against the Republicans, the platform noted that disagreements among party members are inevitable and should be tolerated, while "stealth candidates," who would impose an agenda of intolerance, should be opposed.[39]

When Republicans assembled in Fort Worth a week after the Democrats, expectations were decidedly different. A newspaper headline read, "GOP Primed for Another Family Feud," and a Republican consultant said, "It's not every day you see a train wreck."[40] Journalists and others seeking political controversy and drama now looked for it among the Republicans.

Attention was focused on the race for party chair. There were three candidates: Tom Pauken, a Dallas attorney, whose support had forced the incumbent chair, Fred Meyer, to the sidelines; U.S. Representative Joe Barton of Ennis, and Dolly Madison McKenna, a Houston businesswoman. The conflict was a case of "something old, something new." What was familiar was that the two strongest candidates, Pauken and Barton, shared a staunch conservative philosophy. Their backers agreed on the issues, but were split on insider-outsider lines. Barton was the

---

37. Roger M. Olien, *From Token to Triumph: The Texas Republicans Since 1920*, pp. 187–8.
38. Gardner Selby, "Fisher Says He Has 'Stuff of Victory'," *Houston Post*, 4 June, 1994, p. 25A.
39. Thomas L. Whatley, *Texas Government Newsletter*, 11 July, 1994.
40. Gardner Selby, "GOP Primed for Another Family Feud," *Houston Post*, 9 June, 1994, p. 25A.

choice of much of the party's establishment, including Senators Phil Gramm (who was something of a mentor to Barton) and Kay Bailey Hutchison, and Fred Meyer. Although Pauken had the support of former Governor Bill Clements and several past state party chairs, he and his backers viewed themselves as insurgents waging a grassroots campaign against the hand-picked choice of the state's top Republican Party leaders.[41]

There were two elements in the party chair contest that were not seen earlier in our survey. First, one of the contenders had clear policy differences with the other aspirants. McKenna ran as a moderate on social issues and differentiated herself from her rivals by taking a pro-choice stand on abortion. Second, perhaps the most important subtext of the race was the domination of the convention by delegates from the Christian right. An estimated 60 percent to 70 percent of delegates fit this category, and a large proportion of them were attending their first state convention. In relative terms, they gave less attention to economic issues and more attention to social issues than the delegates who had traditionally dominated Republican conclaves.[42]

Against this backdrop, it is not surprising that the favorite of the Christian right, Tom Pauken, won the race. After a preliminary tally showed Pauken with 54 percent, Barton with 39 percent, and McKenna with 8 percent of the vote, Barton and McKenna agreed to end their candidacies.[43] The platform also reflected the strength of religious conservatives. It called for a reversal of *Roe v. Wade*, with abortions to be banned except to save the mother's life. It advocated selection of judges "who respect traditional family values and the sanctity of human life." Special protection for homosexuals was rejected, and the rights of home schoolers were championed. Despite protests from McKenna backers, the platform sailed through, and a statement acknowledging that Republicans have differences was overwhelmingly rejected.[44]

The Republican divisions should not be overstated or understated. On one hand, Republicans were in agreement on a broad range of issues, including questions of taxing and spending, approaches to crime control, and an emphasis on local control of schools. On the other hand, it is significant when a party's two top candidates feel obliged to distance themselves from their platform on a highly visible issue. Both Senator Hutchison and gubernatorial candidate George W. Bush were clearly

---

41. Gardner Selby, "GOP Primed for Another Family Feud," and "GOP Taps Pauken for State Party Chair," *Houston Post*, 12 June, 1994, p. 1A.
42. Lori Stahl and Sam Attlesey, "GOP Prepares for Convention," *Dallas Morning News* 9 June, 1994, p. 22A.
43. Sam Attlesey and Lori Stahl, "Pauken To Lead as Social Right Dominates GOP," *Dallas Morning News* 12 June, 1994, p. 1A.
44. Wayne Slater, "Moderate GOP Delegates Criticize Party's Tough Anti-Abortion Stance," *Dallas Morning News* 10 June, 1994, p. 42A; Thomas L. Whatley, *Texas Government Newsletter* 4 July, 1994; Attlesey and Stahl, "Pauken To Lead."

uncomfortable with the abortion plank. Hutchison said that government should not restrict abortion in the first two trimesters of pregnancy, and Bush ducked questions by stating that the abortion issue had been "settled" by the Supreme Court.[45] As their campaigns progressed, Hutchison and Bush maintained their positions, to the displeasure and consternation of the Christian right. Several conservative Christian groups went so far as to suggest that they might form a third party at some future time.[46]

1996

Texas Democrats were in an upbeat mood as they assembled in Dallas for their 1996 convention. Their optimism had several sources. President Bill Clinton was neck-and-neck with challenger Bob Dole in state polls, and the party was hopeful of carrying Texas for the first time since 1976. In the U.S. Senate race, challenger Victor Morales had gained favorable coverage for his outsider's effort to defeat Phil Gramm. Schoolteacher Morales had already beaten two veteran U.S. Representatives to gain the nomination, and Gramm was thought to be vulnerable following a humiliating defeat in his quest for the GOP presidential nomination. New state party chair Bill White, who had been selected by the State Democratic Executive Committee to succeed Bob Slagle after the latter's resignation in 1995, had made progress in modernizing Democratic operations.[47] Finally, Democrats took pleasure in Republican splits, in contrast to their own internal unity.

Expectations were for a harmonious Democratic convention, and the expectations were fulfilled. The faithful cheered as Hillary Rodham Clinton and other party luminaries recited the Democratic achievements and aspirations and gave the Republicans low scores. Victor Morales made a triumphant entrance into the convention hall in the white pickup truck that had become the symbol of his underdog campaign. Bill White was unanimously elected to a full term as party chair, and the platform sailed through without significant controversy.[48]

Pragmatism and centrism were the convention's subtexts. The theme in both convention speeches and informal in discussions was the party's support for mainstream values. The platform was a two-page document that stressed economic issues with broad appeal to the middle-class. It

---

45. Wayne Slater, "Moderate GOP Delegates." Consistent with the Supreme Courts ruling in *Planned Parenthood v. Casey* (1992), both candidates voiced support for parental consent for minors seeking an abortion.
46. Thomas L. Whatley, *Texas Government Newsletter* 29 September, 1994.
47. Philip Seib, "Texas Dems Focus Efforts on the Middle." *Dallas Morning News*, 12 June, 1996, p. 27A.
48. See Sam Attlesey and Lori Stahl, "Morales Revs Up Democrats, Vows To Unseat Gramm." *Dallas Morning News*, 9 June, 1996, p. 1A; and Clay Robison, "Morales Speech Lifts Democrats in Dallas," *Houston Chronicle*, 9 June, 1996, p. 1A.

called for tax cuts for couples earning less than $75,000 a year, immunization and nutrition programs for children, and full commitments to social security, medicare, and college loan programs. Hot-button issues such as abortion were omitted, though some were covered in separate issue papers that were adopted with the platform.[49] Various speakers attempted to counter the view that Republicans were more concerned with moral issues than Democrats. Their message was that Republicans did not have a monopoly on religious values. Rather, being true to the Bible requires supporting social justice and helping the needy.[50] As Lieutenant Governor Bog Bullock put it, the GOP has "no copyright on our beliefs and religious preferences. The Republican Party has no hold on Christianity."[51]

There was no mystery behind the Democrats' togetherness. Convention-induced optimism could not gainsay remarkable Republican progress. The perception was growing among national observers that "Texas is now largely a Republican state."[52] Thus liberal stalwarts like Billie Carr and state AFL-CIO President Joe Gunn endorsed the party's centrist course. Carr acknowledged some nostalgia for the battles of the past but agreed it was time to move on. "The 1960s were a great time to get lost, but we can't stay there forever."[53]

Two weeks after the Democratic Convention, Republicans met in San Antonio. While the proceedings were not a carbon copy of 1994 (Tom Pauken was reelected state chair without serious opposition), its outlines were remarkably similar. Once again religious conservatives occupied most of the delegate seats, with estimates of their presence running to 80 percent or more.[54] As in 1994, social issues were the focus of attention. A preliminary skirmish occurred when the Log Cabin Republicans, a gay organization, attempted to secure a booth at the convention's exhibition hall. The request was rejected by party officials, and the decision was upheld by the State Supreme Court.[55]

The greatest controversy again revolved around abortion. The platform itself was not the problem. Delegates adopted a plank that called for banning abortion in all circumstances, even when the mother's life was in danger. Tom Pauken was among those who wanted to keep the

49. Alan Bernstein, "Party to Stress Secure Economy for Middle Class," *Houston Chronicle*, 8 June, 1996, p. 29A; "Morales Revs Up Democrats."
50. Alan Bernstein, "Texas Democrats Give Meeting Biblical Flavor," *Houston Chronicle*, 9 June, 1996, p. 1A.
51. Sam Attlesey and Wayne Slater, "First Lady Touts Clinton's Record at State Convention," *Dallas Morning News*, 8 June, 1996, p. 1A.
52. John E. Yang, "Democratic Retirements Open Door for GOP in Texas House Races," *Washington Post*, 26 December, 1995, p. A4.
53. Bernstein, "Party to Stress Secure Economy."
54. Sam Attlesey, "State GOP Convention Could Turn into Brawl," *Dallas Morning News*, 26 May, 1996, p. 48A.
55. Christy Hoppe, "Justices Bar GOP Gay Group," *Dallas Morning News*, 20 June, 1996, p. 25A.

exception to save the mother's life, but the plank carried as part of a staunchly conservative document that the convention overwhelmingly approved with little debate.[56] (Other noteworthy platform provisions included calls for abolishing the Internal Revenue Service, outlawing dispensing birth control devices to minors, repealing all gun control laws, opposing presenting homosexuality as an acceptable lifestyle, withdrawing the United States from the United Nations, and, in a change from a longstanding position, ending the party's support for initiatives and referendums.)[57]

The major fallout from the abortion issue in 1996 came over selecting delegates to the Republican National Convention. Religious conservatives launched a campaign to prevent people who were not sufficiently committed to the right-to-life cause from going to San Diego. Their most prominent target was Senator Kay Bailey Hutchison. Senator Dole and a number of Texas officials had called for affirmation of the party's pro-life stance while simultaneously acknowledging that not all Republicans accepted it.[58] But this position was unacceptable to many delegates. Said delegate Bill Price, president of Texans United for Life, "When it comes to killing unborn children, there really is no room for tolerance."[59]

The conflict was fierce. Phil Gramm, whose pro-life credentials were unimpeachable, denounced the behavior of Hutchison's opponents as "outrageous" and threatened not to accept a delegate seat at the national convention if his colleague was not also chosen. Hutchison said she was the target of a "kamikaze mission" by a "small group that is not in the mainstream of our party."[60] Eventually Hutchison was selected to go to San Diego, though the standing vote on which she and other at-large delegates were chosen appeared to be close. But overall the convention was a ringing success for religious conservatives. Besides leaving a very clear imprint on the platform, more than 80 percent of the 123 national delegates selected were considered among their number. Moreover, contrary to the wishes of the Dole campaign, Governor Bush was not selected to chair the Texas delegation to the national convention. Tom

---

56. Clay Robison and Alan Bernstein, "GOP Delegates Urged to Exclude Hutchison from National Slate," *Houston Chronicle*, 21 June, 1996, p. 25A; and Wayne Slater, "GOP Platform Adopts Hard Line on Abortion," *Dallas Morning News*, 23 June, 1996, p. 22A.
57. Slater, "GOP Platform"; and Clay Robison, "Initiative and Referendum Plank Draws Fire from State GOP Right," *Houston Chronicle*, 20 June, 1996, p. 32A. Support for initiatives and referendums was dropped out of fear that public opinion, swayed by "the liberal media," might use these approaches to endorse casino gambling, gay marriage, or other unacceptable ideas.
58. Craig Hines, "Dole Urges 'Civility' on Abortion," *Houston Chronicle*, 7 June, 1996, p. 1A.
59. Wayne Slater and Sam Attlesey, "GOP Abortion Foes Vow No Compromise," *Dallas Morning News*, 21 June, 1996, p. 1A.
60. Sam Attlesey and Wayne Slater, "GOP Debates Hutchison's Role," *Dallas Morning News*, 22 June, 1996, p. 1A.

Pauken won that honor, and Dick Weinhold, executive director of the Texas Christian Coalition, was named vice chair.[61]

Senator Hutchison was wrong. The delegates who opposed sending her to San Diego were not a small, unrepresentative minority of the party. Their issue views and general orientation to politics were reflective of a majority of Republican activists in Texas. For those drawn to politics because of their conservative Christian beliefs, the cause was more important than the party. To quote Bill Price again, "Principles are more important than playing political games."[62] Reflecting on the proceedings, one observer wrote that they seemed "much more an ideological revival service" than a political convention.[63] This situation is fraught with danger for the Republicans. We will have more to say about it in our conclusion.

Overview

There was a lot of change between 1962 and 1996. In 1962 the Democrats were the overwhelmingly dominant party in Texas. Their center of gravity was unmistakably conservative. Splits in the party were prominent, and they provided encouragement for Republicans: however, John Connally admonished Republicans not to get their hopes up. Democratic diversity was a source of vitality, according to Connally. If Republicans expected to see "blood running in the streets," at the Democratic convention, it was "a classic example of wishful thinking."[64] By the 1990s the tables had been turned. Now it was the Democrats who hoped to capitalize on Republican divisions. Ann Richards extended an invitation to disgruntled Republicans in 1994: "To those of you in the Republican party who, because of dogma and right-wing radicals in your party feel unwelcome, we are delighted to have you in the Democratic party."[65] The reason for the change is evident. One party was on the rise, while the other was increasingly on the defensive.

Legislative Voting Records

Changes in the party system may also be seen in the voting records of legislators. We can expect a time lag between grassroots developments

---

61. Sam Attlesey and Wayne Slater, "GOP Delegates Heavily Anti-Abortion," *Dallas Morning News*, 23 June, 1996, p. 1A; "Republicans in San Antonio: Preview for Bob Dole in August?" *Texas Government Newsletter*, 1 July, 1996, p. 1.
62. Clay Robison and Alan Bernstein, "GOP Delegates Urged to Exclude Hutchison from National Slate," *Houston Chronicle*, 21 June, 1996, p. 25A.
63. Jane Ely, "GOP Gathering an Old-Time Revival Service," *Houston Chronicle*, 23 June, 1996, p. 2C.
64. Allen Duckworth, "Connally Accuses Republicans of 'Thought Control'," *Dallas Morning News*, 17 September, 1962, sec. 1, p. 14.
65. Wayne Slater and Sam Attlesey, "Richards Solicits GOP Defections," *Dallas Morning News*, 5 June, 1994, p. 1A.

The Party System in Texas   171

in the parties and the voting behavior of legislators. Although the makeup of state conventions is quite responsive to the latest political trends (the ease with which Christian conservatives were able to take over the 1994 and 1996 Republican conventions is an example), there is considerable continuity in legislative membership. Incumbents are able to use their office privileges (for example, staff, travel, and postage allowances) and political skills to win reelection even when broader forces may be working against them.

The records of members of the Texas House of Representatives were evaluated according to their votes on issues selected by *The Texas Observer*, a liberal bellwether. The *Observer* chooses a dozen or so issues per session for rating legislators: agreement with the editor's position determines the score. More agreement means a higher score—and a more liberal voting record.[66] The voting behavior of members of both parties was analyzed for the 1977, 1985, and 1995 sessions. Although not all of the data are presented in detail, the findings were generally consistent with our previous results.

Figure 10.1 is a histogram showing *Texas Observer* scores for state Democratic representatives in 1977. Scores for the 132 Democrats are grouped in fifths (0–20, 21–40, etc.). The data show a conservative-leaning delegation. Forty-one members were in the most conservative category, and another thirty-five were in the second-most conservative group. The mean score was 41.27. Contrast these figures with the data from 1995, which are presented in Figure 10.2. The Democratic center of gravity has clearly shifted. Among the eighty-seven Democrats (the drop in their contingent is noteworthy), twenty-four were in the most liberal group, and twenty-three were in the second-most liberal class. The mean increased to 59.02.[67]

Data for the Republicans are less revealing. The small number of cases in 1977 makes analysis problematic. In 1985 the fifty-two Republicans had a mean *Texas Observer* score of 16.25. In 1995 the mean score for fifty-eight members was 6.37. In both years the majority of Republican legislators had scores in the 0 to 20 range; indeed, in 1995 every Republican was in this category. We might speculate that as the lag between grassroots political developments and legislative membership plays out, there will be some decrease in Republican harmony. However, there have been relatively few votes in the legislature on social issues, such as abortion and school prayer. As long as the legislature downplays these matters, Republican unity is likely to remain strong.

---

66. Absences were excluded from the calculations and did not lower a member's score, but any member who missed more than 50 percent of the votes in a year was omitted from the analysis.
67. In 1985, the mean *Observer* score for the ninety-six House Democrats was 61.03. See *The Texas Observer*, 28 June, 1985, pp. 68–9.

FIGURE 10.1

Texas Observer Scores for State Democratic Representatives, 1977

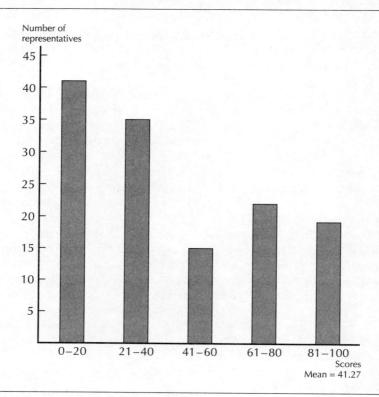

Source: *The Texas Observer*, June 17, 1977, pp. 8–9.

Conclusion

Republican growth in Texas has been remarkable. A generation ago the Republican Party was becoming competitive, but the operative word was "becoming." It still made good sense for ambitious young conservatives like Phil Gramm to seek their (political) fortune in the Democratic Party. Conservatives, while making overtures to moderates and liberals, were still the top dogs in the Democratic Party, and the typical Democratic representative in Austin or Washington had a voting record that leaned to the right. Today things are clearly different. Republican gains have put Democrats on the defensive. Although most officials are still Democrats, there is no doubt which party is on the rise. The Democratic Party is hardly homogeneous, but its drift toward the center has left

The Party System in Texas 173

FIGURE 10.2

Texas Observer Scores for State Democratic Representatives, 1993

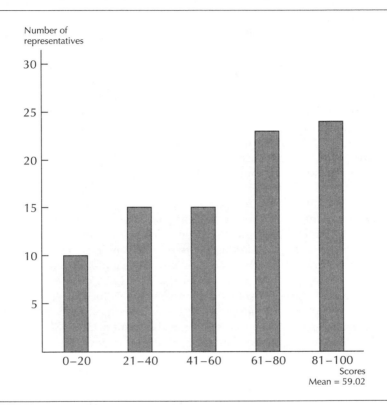

Source: *The Texas Observer*, June 16, 1995, pp. 20–22

some of its more conservative officeholders feeling rather lonely and uncomfortable and out of place.[68]

We do not mean to suggest that conservative Democrats are on the verge of extinction. They are not. The dominant figure in the 74th Legislature (1995–1996) was Lieutenant Governor Bob Bullock. Although he was considered a moderate liberal earlier in his career, by the mid-1990s Bullock was comfortable working with the state's business establishment on tort reform and a variety of other issues. House Speaker Pete Laney had never been considered anything but a conservative during his long

---

68. See Paul Burka, "Stuck in the Middle," *Texas Monthly*, November 1994, pp. 80–5. A regular feature of the news is the announcement that one or more Texas public officials have switched party affiliation from Democratic to Republican. Invariably the converts are conservative Democrats. For example, shortly after the legislature adjourned in 1995, two of the ten Democrats with *Texas Observer* scores in the 0–20 range announced that they were switching to the Republican Party.

legislative career, and he and his team were firmly in control in their chamber. Still, it is the long-term trend that is most significant, and that trend suggests that the Bullock-Laney team, which remained in office in 1997–1998, may be among the last of Texas Democrats with a traditional orientation to lead the legislature.

Republican growth has been accompanied by issue disagreements, especially on the social issues. Abortion is the leading illustration, and the conflict seen at the 1994 and 1996 state conventions may be a forerunner of future battles within the party. Thus, to the extent that growing harmony among the Democrats is a response to a decline in the party's support, pleasure over the unity must be tempered. Republican concern over intraparty divisions may be eased by the realization that the splits are a byproduct of the party's rise.

The significance of Republican fissures should not be underestimated. The party is being pulled in opposite directions. When it looks outward, the incentives are for relative moderation in trying to reach the vast pool of voters without consistent ideological views or a strong attachment to either major party. When it looks inward, there is pressure to hew firmly to the social conservative line. Somehow the party's leaders must convince the activists who control the state organization of the necessity of pragmatism in the political arena. In view of what we have seen at the party's recent state conventions, this is likely to be a daunting task.[69] Similar problems plagued the Democrats nationally and in many states for the better part of a generation beginning in 1968.

Additional light may be shed by consulting a venerable source. In the 1950s journalist and political commentator Samuel Lubell published an award-winning book called *The Future of American Politics*.[70] In it he set forth "a new theory of political parties." The theory is valuable in understanding what has been happening in Texas party politics. Lubell argued that political conflict in a particular era revolves around splits in the majority party. The minority party tries to take advantage of fissures in the majority coalition, and third parties tend to be formed by disgruntled elements of the majority. He added that while divisions in the majority can be a liability, they may "also serve as the great, unifying force" within the party.[71] Battles within the majority party may be especially intense because the participants know that whoever wins the fight will have the upper hand in gaining office and shaping public policy. In other words, higher stakes lead to sharper conflict. Moreover, as

---

69. See Mark J. Rozell and Clyde Wilcox, eds., *God at the Grass Roots: The Christian Right in the 1994 Elections* (Lanham, MD: Rowman & Littlefield, 1995), especially John M. Bruce, "Texas: The Emergence of the Christian Right," pp. 67–89; and Rozell and Wilcox, "The Past as Prologue: The Christian Right in the 1996 Elections," pp. 253–62.
70. Samuel Lubell, *The Future of American Politics*, second ed. (Garden City, NY: Doubleday Anchor, 1955), esp. chap. 10.
71. Ibid., p. 214

a result of the conflict the losing faction may become disaffected (temporarily or permanently), giving hope to the minority party. The winning faction will see its attachment to the majority party strengthened.

At the national level Lubell provided evidence in support of his theory into the Eisenhower era, and more recent developments also seem consistent with his interpretation. In the 1960s, for example, the Democrats were still dominant, and pitched battles were fought within the party over civil rights and the Vietnam War. By the 1990s neither party had a decisive edge, but the Republicans appeared to be on the rise. Conflicts within the Republican Party between libertarians advocating a hands-offs policy on abortion, gay rights, and other social issues and the Christian right were intensifying. Pragmatic conservatives like George Bush and Robert Dole were left in the uneasy middle. The shift in sources of third-party movements is also instructive. When the Democrats were ascendant, they emerged from divisions within the Democratic coalition. Strom Thurmond's States' Rights party (1948), Henry Wallace's Progressive party (1948), and George Wallace's American Independent party (1968) are cases in point. In the 1980s and 1990s the leading third-party efforts were mounted by John Anderson's Independent party (1980) and Ross Perot's United We Stand America party (1992) and Reform Party (1996): all three developed largely from splits among the Republicans.

The Texas tale is similar to the national story in its broad outlines. Before the Republicans were a major force in state politics, Democrats could afford to be at each other's throats. With people of widely divergent views calling themselves Democrats, and with the stakes being so high (whichever faction was dominant in the Democratic Party was sure to control state government), it was inevitable that intraparty battles would be intense. As Republican strength grew, Democrats became more conciliatory toward each other. Republican advances made it easier for new entrants to the political arena (whether homegrown or migrants from other states) to cast their lot with the Republican Party. A growing Republican grassroots base facilitated the party switch of John Connally, Phil Gramm, and many other one-time conservative Democrats. The flight of conservatives made it easier for Democrats to find common ground, but at the price of a smaller mass base. Republicans have grown, but have had to deal with sharp splits over policy issues. Like their national counterparts, Texas Republicans have witnessed bitter battles between the Christian right and their libertarian-leaning fellow partisans. Pragmatic conservatives like George W. Bush and Kay Bailey Hutchison have had the challenge of maintaining good relations with both camps. The last significant state-based third party in Texas was La Raza Unida. Its gubernatorial candidate, Ramsey Muniz, drew 6 percent of the vote in 1972, primarily from disaffected Mexican-American Democrats. It is a sign of the political times that recent third-party talk has been heard from Christian conservatives who believe that Texas Republicans have been insufficiently sensitive to their concerns. Political parties want to grow. If growth is the measure of a party's success, then Texas Republicans have earned high marks. However, they have also learned that the road to the top is not smooth: how they navigate the political highway hazards will help to determine their prospects and the Democrats' opportunities.

11
The Texas Trial Lawyers Association: Interest Group Under Siege

Charles P. Elliott, Jr.
Texas A&M University—Commerce

Texas politics, like politics in general, can be explained as a battle between competing interests over political rewards. In Texas, that interest group conflict often pits one business interest against another. However, business interests are often pitted against the interests of workers or injured parties. Because organized labor is a weak political force in Texas, labor unions are not significant players in the state's political battles. Consumer groups exist, but they usually have shoestring budgets and cannot assert their interests through campaign contributions. Trial lawyers, however, are the major interest group in battles that pit business interests against those of workers or injured parties.

Trial lawyers are also known as plaintiffs lawyers. They are the lawyers who represent individuals in suits against businesses, insurance companies, physicians, and other professions. The trial lawyers are often aligned with labor or with consumer groups because their interests are usually, but not always, compatible with those groups. That is, if laws make it easier for workers to sue employers, injured persons to sue companies producing harmful products, or consumers to sue companies that produce badly designed or faulty products, not only are the individuals advantaged, but so are the lawyers who represent them.

Trial lawyers are usually paid on a contingent fee basis: the lawyer makes no money unless he or she wins the case. If the case is successful, the lawyer will usually get from 33 percent to 40 percent of the settlement or judgement in the case, plus any expenses that have been incurred. As a result, trial lawyers have a financial interest in promoting laws that make it easier for individuals to sue and win against businesses, insurance companies, and professionals because those groups are most likely to have the resources to pay substantial settlements.

Some trial lawyers have been very successful and they have been willing to contribute their resources to political and lobbying campaigns. The trial lawyers are well aware that Texas is a conservative, pro-business state. They also know that, without well-organized labor groups, lawyers are the primary sources of funds for political efforts to pass legislation favorable to those who may sue business.

Because the political interests of trial lawyers are often contrary to the interests of businesses, they are seen as anti-business. Trial lawyers tend to be aligned with liberal Democrats, who often have labor, consumer, and environmental interests, rather than with conservative Democrats or Republicans, who tend to be aligned with the business community.

This chapter examines some of the activities of the Texas Trial Lawyers Association, the leading organization of trial lawyers in the state. It discusses their political activities as well as their problems in promoting their interests in the pro-business environment of Texas.

Texas politics changed dramatically from the early 1960s to the mid-1990s. Even casual observers are aware of the growth of the Republican Party, the liberalization of the Democratic Party, and the arrival of two-party politics in Texas. What may not be so widely recognized is the proliferation of interest groups and the changes in the ways in which they operate. Although an examination of the changes in interest group politics is beyond the scope of this chapter, it is instructive to trace the history of one such group, the Texas Trial Lawyers Association (TTLA).

In the 1960s the TTLA was enormously successful in dominating the legislative process in those areas of public policy it deemed vital to its interests, but by 1995 it was being seriously challenged by groups new to the Texas political scene. This evolution can best be understood by comparing two reform movements separated by a quarter of a century: workers' compensation reform efforts from 1965 through 1969 and the battles over the civil justice system in the 1980s and 1990s.

WORKERS' COMPENSATION REFORM ACT OF 1969

By 1965 most informed observers agreed that something was seriously wrong with the Texas workers' compensation program and the way it was being administered by the Industrial Accident Board. Employers were unhappy with the high cost of insurance premiums; organized labor was unhappy because benefits were too low; and injured workers were deprived because weekly benefit payments were often withheld by insurance carriers, and medical benefits were frequently terminated prematurely.

No one tried to remedy the situation until it came to the attention of Governor John Connally and his staff in the mid-1960s. During his many years as Senator Lyndon Johnson's right-hand man and as Secretary of the Navy under President Kennedy, Connally had developed a close working relationship with the Texas business community. It was during the Connally administration that Texas business and political leaders began to realize that future economic development could be facilitated by cooperation between the State of Texas and business interests.

The public side of this cooperation involved considerable emphasis on improving higher education and promoting recreational opportunities in the state. A less-well-known aspect of business' concern with public policy focused on ways to contain the spiraling costs of workers' compensation insurance and to improve delivery of benefits.

The primary interest group involved in this effort was the Texas Employers Association (TEA), later known as the Texas Association of Business. The TEA decided that workers' compensation insurance costs could be contained if a way could be found to achieve final settlement of more claims by the Industrial Accident Board rather than having them go to the state courts. In those days, board action had become little more than a formality on the way to court, where cases were subject to trial de novo. The trial de novo provision allowed board awards to be appealed to a state district court, where they were tried as ordinary civil cases. In such trials, all evidence was developed anew and there was no review of board proceedings or evidence developed by the board. From 1965 to 1967, 85 percent of board awards were appealed because they averaged $861 per claim, while appeals resulting in court judgments averaged $2,662.[1] Businesspeople believed that this approach was driving up the cost of workers' compensation insurance. TEA and its allies sought ways to change the law to make board awards final in most cases.

In 1965 a coalition of business and organized labor went to the legislature with a reform proposal that included abolition of trial de novo for workers' compensation claimants who appealed board awards. The proposal failed in the 1965 legislative session and again in 1967. Those promoting change concluded that the reason these efforts had failed was that the Texas Trial Lawyers Association (TTLA) had not been included in the coalition that developed the proposal. The TTLA, a small group of attorneys interested in workers' compensation law, had a few of its own members and many sympathizers in the legislature. No reform was possible as long as the trial lawyers and their allies could prevent abolition of trial de novo. The attorneys argued that claimants were not being treated fairly by the board, and that trial de novo was needed to protect their rights.[2]

It was readily apparent to objective observers, that trial de novo was not only a way to protect the rights of claimants, but also a lucrative source of income for attorneys engaged in the practice of workers' compensation law. Court awards were usually higher than board awards, and the attorney's share was also larger. Under the law in effect at that time, attorneys who represented claimants in workers' compensation cases received 15 percent of board awards and 30 percent of court awards.

---

1. Charles P. Elliott, Jr., *The Texas Industrial Accident Board: An Administrative Case Study* (Ph.D. thesis, University of Texas at Austin, 1972), pp. 49, 52.
2. Ibid., p. 99.

Governor Connally, the TEA, and the Texas AFL-CIO regrouped after the 1967 legislative session. The governor seized the opportunity to appoint new members to two of the three positions on the Industrial Accident Board. One of these appointees was Tony Korioth, a former member of the state legislature and a member of the Texas Trial Lawyers Association. Korioth, with the blessings of the governor, immediately added the Industrial Accident Board and the TTLA to the coalition working for change.

The expanded coalition arrived at a reasonable compromise that did not threaten the interests of claimants or their attorneys. The proposal set the attorney's share at 25 percent of any settlement, regardless of whether it came from the board or a court. A new device, called a pre-hearing conference, was instituted to bring together a hearing officer from the board, representatives of the insurance carrier, and the claimant's attorney. The goal of the pre-hearing conference was to mediate the differences between the insurance company and the claimant and to construct an agreement that could be incorporated into a formal settlement decision by the board, thereby reducing the number of cases appealed.

The new coalition worked out the details of the bill in advance, and when the legislature convened in January 1969, they found four sponsors—two in the senate and two in the house. One in each house came from the liberal side and one from the conservative side of the membership. The coalition secured the support of the lieutenant governor and the speaker of the house, and the legislation passed unanimously in the Texas senate and with one dissenting vote in the house of representatives.[3]

The real significance of these early attempts to restructure the Texas workers' compensation system is not found in the particulars of the solution but in the way that it was derived. Meaningful reform was not possible without the cooperation of the TTLA and its sympathizers, and the reform effort could not have been successful as long as those seeking change insisted on the elimination of trial de novo. Reasonable compromise was achieved when the reformers abandoned their attempt to eliminate trial de novo and offered the TTLA an approach that did not substantially impair the lawyers' interest in the system. In short, the TTLA and its allies could veto any change in the workers' compensation system which they found unacceptable, so their interests needed to be protected in order to achieve substantial change.

Comprehensive Tort Reform Bill of 1987

The Texas Civil Justice League (TCJL) was formed in 1986 to promote business interests in the civil justice system, and the legislative session

---

3. Ibid., p. 105.

of 1987 marked the TCJL's first attempt at tort reform in Texas. The reform effort was unsuccessful in the regular session, but a bill limiting punitive damages passed in the first special session and was signed by Governor Clements.

Punitive damages have always been the wild card in the civil justice system and a source of uncertainty for business. Businesses can make reasonable predictions about liabilities for measurable economic losses which may result from a course of action, but punitive damages are unpredictable and create great uncertainty.

For plaintiffs, punitive damages serve as a means of punishing corporations (which cannot be held criminally liable) for courses of action corporations undertake knowing there is danger to others. The TTLA argues that the uncertainty of punitive damages is constructive because it discourages courses of action businesses know to be potentially dangerous, and that juries must be free to award extremely large amounts in punitive damages in order to discourage misbehavior by multi-billion dollar corporations.

In 1987 the TTLA decided that the best response was to seek compromise with the TCJL instead of simply resisting proposals for change. The primary effect limits punitive damages to amounts no greater than four times actual damages. The TCJL was new at tort reform and apparently unaware that actual damages could include not only direct economic losses, but other damages such as loss of consortium, disfigurement, and loss of future earning capacity. Because the TCJL was caught off guard and agreed to the arrangement while not realizing that fact, the law did not provide the relief the business community wanted.

Because the 1987 act did not satisfy business, it set the stage for future attempts to more effectively limit punitive damages. What is notable, however, is that the TTLA, in its first encounter with well-organized opposition, recognized the need for compromise on civil justice matters. The Texas Civil Justice League was only modestly successful in its first attempt at reform, but it learned much from the experience.

Workers' Compensation Act of 1989

For a few years after the enactment of the workers' compensation reforms of 1969, the percentage of cases in which board settlements were appealed declined, and it appeared that the new arrangements would solve some of the problems in the system. The amount of weekly compensation was increased by the 1969 act, and improved administrative procedures delivered help to claimants much earlier than before. However, as time passed, the proportion of appeals of board decisions began to rise, and the anticipated savings on workers' compensation insurance did not materialize. By the mid-1980s, business interests began to experience substantial increases in the cost of insurance, and they once again sought relief from the legislature.

By the time the legislature convened in regular session in January 1989, workers' compensation reform was near the top of the agenda. Not only had severe strains developed in the workers' compensation system, but the Texas Civil Justice League, supported by the business community, was committed to changing the workers' compensation system to make workers' compensation insurance less expensive.

The TCJL initially set out to educate Texans on problems in workers' compensation and Texas tort law, and was successful in convincing a great many people that the civil justice system in general and the workers' compensation program in particular were contributing to rising insurance costs. From 1985 until 1989, workers' compensation insurance premiums in Texas had increased 148 percent and were among the highest in the country, while benefits paid to injured workers were among the lowest.[4]

In the last two years of his second term, Governor William P. Clements put workers' compensation reform on his list of legislative priorities. When the 71st Legislature failed to resolve the issue in the regular session, Governor Clements called it back into special session for that purpose in the summer of 1989. At the end of the thirty days, the bill failed to pass because it was stuck in conference committee. The governor was determined to resolve the issue, and called a second special session for November.

The house of representatives was receptive to proposals for changes in the workers' compensation system, and the changes passed the house easily. In the twenty years since the last round of changes was made, workers' compensation had become a public issue chiefly because of the escalating cost of the insurance and the public education program by TCJL. In addition, the composition of the house of representatives had changed substantially. Even though the number of attorneys in the house had not fallen dramatically, the number of people who came into the legislature with a pro-business point of view had increased substantially. A major reason for the increase in pro-business representation was the deliberate effort of Republican Party leaders to recruit legislative candidates willing to support policies favorable to business.

The combination of public attention and greater representation for the business viewpoint resulted in house passage of a completely new approach, which substituted a nine-member Workers' Compensation Commission for the three-person Industrial Accident Board. Trial de novo was also abolished as a means for claimants to appeal awards made by the commission.

The senate was another matter. The interests of the TTLA were

---

4. Texas Government Newsletter, (Austin, Texas) Volume 17, Number 22, 17 July 1989 and Number 36, 13 November 1989, and Bland, Sullivan, Biles, Elliott, and Pettus, *Texas Government Today*, 5th edition (Pacific Grove, CA: 1992), p. 178.

strongly represented in the senate by Senator Carl Parker of Beaumont and Senator Ted Lyon of Rockwall. Lieutenant Governor William Hobby supported most elements of the reform proposal, but initially opposed abolition of trial de novo.[5]

Those defending the old system counted heavily on Hobby's support for trial de novo, and sought to protect their interests by negotiating behind the scenes in the senate. They were not prepared to debate the issue in public, nor were they prepared to compromise, especially on trial de novo. They seriously underestimated the impact of rising costs of workers' compensation insurance and the intensity with which the business community approached the issue.

Workers' compensation reform was stymied in the senate through the regular session of the 71st Legislature and through most of two special sessions. The first session had expired without change, and early in the second session the senate appeared to be hopelessly deadlocked. Few observers thought that the impasse could be broken. However, in December 1989, Lieutenant Governor Hobby reversed himself on trial de novo, and the reform act was passed. Trial de novo was abolished on appeal for most cases, and the workers' compensation system in Texas was converted to a system in which awards made by the Workers' Compensation Commission would be final in all but a very few cases.[6] Lieutenant Governor Hobby never publicly explained his change of position on the issue, but Senator Lyon's view was that the legislature had been struggling with the issue all year, and the lieutenant governor simply wanted it resolved one way or another.[7]

The TTLA and organized labor had lost the big one. From 1990 on, the system would be administrative, not judicial, and attorneys would have little or no part to play in that system. It took a few years to finalize the remaining cases filed under the old law, but once they were gone, there was no incentive for attorney involvement in workers' compensation cases.

Complete restructuring of the workers' compensation system could not have occurred twenty years earlier. In 1969 any changes in the system required the acquiescence of the Texas Trial Lawyers Association. In 1989 the TTLA no longer exercised the kind of power it had two decades before.

By 1997 it was possible to assess the impact of the 1989 legislation. The legislation removed all incentives for attorney involvement in workers' compensation claims. For claimants this meant that they no longer had the assistance of attorneys for pressing their claims. For plaintiff's attorneys whose practices were based on compensation and personal in-

---

5. "Working Class Heroes," *Texas Observer*, 15 December 1989, pp. 3–5.
6. Randall W. Bland, Alfred B. Sullivan, Robert E. Biles, Charles P. Elliott, Jr., and Beryl E. Pettus, *Texas Government Today*, fifth edition, p. 182.
7. Ted B. Lyon, Jr., telephone interview 15 May 1995.

jury work it has meant a devastating reduction in business, because workers' comp was their bread and butter.

However, the total reduction in revenue has been greater than the loss of comp alone. People whose initial contacts with attorneys occurred when they had workers' compensation claims would often go back to those same attorneys for other legal services. In particular, comp cases often led to third party cases filed by the injured party against the manufacturer of equipment involved in the original injury. For many personal injury attorneys, the loss of revenue from these third party claims was even greater than the loss of revenue from comp cases. As a result, most personal injury attorneys have been forced to reduce their staffs and move into new areas of practice. These restructured practices will almost surely be less profitable.[8]

On the other side of the issue, business interests appear to have achieved the result they wanted. By early 1997 workers' compensation insurance rates declined by 21 percent from the base rate set by the Department of Insurance in November 1990. At the same time, claims incurred or paid declined by 50 percent.[9] This kind of success undoubtedly spurred the appetite of the business community and caused them to ask for further changes in the civil justice system.

PRODUCTS LIABILITY ACT OF 1993

Although it did not attract the same level of attention as the debate over workers' compensation in 1989, passage of the Products Liability Act of 1993 was driven by the same kinds of business concerns and some of the same groups that were involved in 1989. While the significance of the 1993 act is not of the same magnitude as the 1989 changes in workers' compensation or the changes in tort law proposed in 1995, the act was part of a long-term effort by business to lower operating costs by reducing its legal exposure, thereby reducing the cost of product liability insurance.

The battle shaped up with the Texas Civil Justice League taking the lead in support of the legislation and the Texas Trial Lawyers Association in opposition.[10] A number of product liability bills were introduced, but most of the conflict was avoided early when the protagonists were able to compromise. Both groups supported the act as it passed.

The most important provision of the 1993 Products Liability Act requires plaintiffs who sue a company for manufacturing an inherently

---

8. Joseph Calve, "Poured Out," *Texas Lawyer*, Volume 12, Number 40, 16 December 1996, p. 1.
9. Telephone interviews with Pam Beachley of the Business Insurance Consumer Association, 17–18 February 1997.
10. Robert C. Newberry, "Products Liability Bill Will Tie the Hands of the Injured," *Houston Post*, 17 February 1993, p. 15A; telephone interview with Willie Chapman, Texas Trial Lawyers Association, 17 March 1995.

dangerous product to prove that a safer alternative design was available at the time of manufacture and that it was economically feasible. Alcoholic beverages, tobacco, and firearms manufacturers are exempt from liability when their products are used as directed.[11]

In 1993 the TTLA took an approach that suggested that they had learned from their experience in 1989. From the beginning, they assumed that the issue was a serious one, and they were willing to compromise. They accepted a limited change in tort law, and were able to head off other proposals that were more objectionable.

Comprehensive Tort Reform of 1995

Buildup to the 1995 Session

The election on November 8, 1994, produced a Republican sweep all across the United States and resulted in Republican control of both houses of Congress for the first time in forty years. Texas elected its second Republican governor since Reconstruction. In the 73rd Legislature (1993–1994), there were thirteen Republicans in the Texas senate and fifty-six in the house. In the 74th Legislature (1995–1996), there were fourteen Republican members in the senate and fifty-eight in the house.

The small number of legislative seats gained by Republicans does not tell the whole story. The real impact can be understood only by looking at which Republicans replaced which Democrats in the Texas senate, the bastion of resistance to tort reform. In 1992, Florence Shapiro, a Plano Republican who supported tort reform, defeated Senator Ted B. Lyon, Jr., of Rockwall. Democratic losses in 1994 included Senator Steve Carriker, defeated by Republican Tom Haywood; Bill Haley, who left the senate in mid-term and was replaced by Republican Drew Nixon, who defeated a Democrat supported by the TTLA; and Senator Carl Parker, defeated by Republican Michael Galloway.

All of the Democrats were supported by the TTLA, and all of the Republicans were supported by the Texas Civil Justice League and/or Texans for Lawsuit Reform (TLR), a new and very aggressive tort reform organization. The losses were key ones for senate Democrats. Most of the effective opponents of tort reform were gone after the 1992 and 1994 elections. In addition, the TLR was emboldened by the fact that it had actively supported the Republican winners, all of whom had run as supporters of tort reform.

Gubernatorial candidate George Bush also pledged his support for tort reform. Bush received strong support from the well-established Texas Civil Justice League. Texans for Lawsuit Reform received an enormous boost from Republican election victories and began promoting an ambitious tort reform agenda.

---

11. Products Liability Act of 1993, *Vernon's Texas Codes Annotated: Civil Practice and Remedies*, chapter 82, section 82.005.

The elections of 1994 produced five effects that made tort reform virtually impossible for the TTLA to prevent in the 74th Legislature:
1. They demonstrated public support for tort reform.
2. They demonstrated the political strength of Texans for Lawsuit Reform and the Texas Civil Justice League.
3. They removed first-line Democratic senators who might have successfully resisted tort reform.
4. They convinced remaining senate Democrats and Lieutenant Governor Bullock that resistance to tort reform could be politically dangerous.
5. They inspired the two tort reform organizations to press for more drastic measures than might have otherwise been the case.

Principal elements of the reform agenda included sanctions for frivolous lawsuits; limitations on exemplary (punitive) damages; limits on recovery under the Deceptive Trade Practices Act; severe limitations on contingency fees; limitations on where lawsuits can be tried (venue); plaintiff's bond requirements in medical malpractice suits; abolition of joint and several liability; and limitations on admissibility of expert testimony. Proposals to limit contingency fees and abolish joint and several liability were the most objectionable to the TTLA and others wanting to protect claimants' interests.

The contingency fee bill proposed limits of 10 percent of the first $100,000 of a judgment and 5 percent of any amount in excess of $100,000. Such limits would effectively eliminate all contingency fee arrangements and would have the practical effect of denying access to the courts for claimants who could not afford to pay attorneys in advance.

Another bill proposed to abolish joint and several liability and substitute a system of proportionate liability. Joint and several liability is a means by which the resources of all parties associated with the responsible party are lumped together for the purpose of awarding judgment to the plaintiff, and the entire amount of the judgment must be borne by any or all of those parties. Abolishing joint and several liability and replacing it with a system of proportionate liability would, in many cases, mean that the injured party would have to bear all or part of the cost of his or her own injury if one or more of the parties to the tort could not pay its share of the judgment.

The tort reform bills were sent by Lieutenant Governor Bullock to the Senate Committee on Economic Development, chaired by David Sibley, instead of to the Jurisprudence Committee. Sibley, a moderate Republican from Waco and a strong supporter of tort reform, was one of a number of Republicans appointed by Bullock to chair senate committees.

Labor, the TTLA, the National Breast Implant Coalition, and other groups opposing tort reform knew in advance that reform would be on the agenda. They were prepared to accept changes such as the prohibition on frivolous lawsuits, and they were willing to compromise on other matters. However, they had counted on Senator Carl Parker and some of the other Democrats defeated in November to soften the reforms and prevent the reform advocates from dominating the process the way that they had the workers' compensation issue in 1989.

The Process Unfolds

Senator Carl A. Parker was uniquely powerful in the senate, and Lieutenant Governor Bullock may have been counting on having Parker to lead the forces of moderation and take some of the sting from the reform legislation. Most legislators had accepted the inevitability of reform and were looking for ways to moderate some of the more radical elements in the bills that were being promoted by Texans for Lawsuit Reform. Many assumed that this task would fall to Senator Parker. However, Parker's defeat the previous November left Lieutenant Governor Bullock without an opposition leader on the tort reform issue in the senate. Subsequently, a Parker protege, James Fields, was brought into the process as general counsel for the Economic Development Committee chaired by Senator Sibley.

Few expected Fields to sidetrack reform efforts, but those who feared total destruction of the civil justice system hoped that he would be a moderating influence. Outside observers speculated that moderate reforms would be adopted and would be sufficient to keep the issue off the agenda of the 75th Legislature in 1997.

This approach was a variation on the old "inside" mode of operating, which the TTLA had used to protect its interests and the interests of claimants for several decades. The major difference in 1995, however, was that the TTLA and its friends knew that they would have to compromise with the reform movement if they were going to be able to save anything, and they so indicated early in the session.

After the senate passed the frivolous lawsuit and the exemplary damages limitations bills fairly early in the session, the reform process seemed to slow. By mid-March, 1995, it appeared that reform momentum was diminishing. Senate leaders had helped the reformers realize some of their goals and wanted to move to other issues. The more radical factions in the movement may have become less effective because they had alienated some of their allies.

The Outcome

The results of tort reform efforts in the 74th Texas Legislature constituted a major victory for the tort reform movement in Texas and a significant defeat for the Texas Trial Lawyers Association and its allies. Measures adopted included venue restrictions, proportionate responsibility instead of joint and several liability, prohibitions on frivolous lawsuits, limits on recovery under the Deceptive Trade Practices Act, and limits on exemplary (punitive) damages. The medical malpractice bill requires plaintiffs to post $5,000 bonds or provide affidavits from experts to ensure that their suits are reasonable. Most of the goals of the tort reform advocates were realized, except for contingency fee limits.

It will be several years before all of the cases filed prior to 1995 finally clear the system. However, by early 1997, the outlines of the new civil justice system were evident. For two decades or more the Texas system was thought to be plaintiff friendly. But by 1997 the civil justice system was dramatically different:[12]

1. Workers' compensation is entirely administrative in nature.
2. Insurance companies have reduced settlement offers and slowed the negotiation process, thus putting the financial squeeze on plaintiffs' attorneys.
3. The legislature and the Texas Supreme Court have changed the rules of the game to benefit corporate defendants and their insurance carriers.
4. There are more lawyers and a shrinking pool of profitable cases.
5. The media have generated a distorted picture of personal injury practice by their treatment of cases such as the McDonald's coffee case.
6. Juries have become antagonistic toward plaintiffs, with fewer verdicts and smaller awards for them.
7. The tort system has been successful, in part, and manufacturers are making safer products.

There are indications that the reform process is not over. TLR has returned to the legislature asking for severe limits on contingency fees and virtually unlimited discretion for judges to dismiss cases with no opportunity for claimants to appeal.[13]

The New Political System in Texas

Public Debate

In the 1960s the workers' compensation system was of little interest to the general public. Concerned groups debated the issue in private and negotiated their differences behind closed doors. The news organizations did not cover activities in state government as thoroughly as they came to do in the 1980s and 1990s. None of the parties to the compromise of 1969 perceived any advantage in "going public" with its case.

The Texas Trial Lawyers Association, in particular, had a record of successfully defending its interests in the closed system of that period. At any given time, several TTLA members were also members of the legislature, and those attorneys in the legislature who were not TTLA

---

12. Joseph Calve, "Poured Out," *Texas Lawyer*, Volume 12, Number 40, 16 December 1996, p. 15.
13. Joseph Calve, "Poured Out," *Texas Lawyer*, Volume 12, Number 40, 16 December 1996, p. 16 and SB 220 HB 7, 75th Texas Legislature.

members were inclined to support the TTLA position on such issues. Even members of the defense bar shared an interest in such matters because defending against workers' compensation claims, product liability suits, and personal injury cases provided some of their income. In addition, the TTLA historically had made campaign contributions to candidates, both attorneys and lay persons, who agreed with them on such issues.

Other interest groups shared the TTLA's approach. Organized labor had little public support during this same period and was forced to do most of its political work by lobbying the legislature and keeping a low public profile. The Texas Employers Association, the insurance industry, and the Texas Medical Association had also enjoyed considerable success by working behind closed doors, so they saw little need to become embroiled in public disputes.

Major public issues at that time usually revolved around public education, higher education, taxation, and spending. Issues such as workers' compensation could be worked out more or less privately among the interested parties, and the absence of a competitive political party system meant that the state had no mechanism for structuring political conflict in a way that moved that issue into the public arena.

Two-Party Politics

From the 1970s into the 1980s, the Texas Republican Party began to grow. Many Texans routinely voted for Republican candidates for president of the United States and to reelect U.S. Senator John Tower. Republican presidents usually provided policy leadership of a type many Texans liked, and Senator Tower's interests focused more on matters of national defense than on party building in his home state.

The historical conservatism of the Texas Democratic Party had made it difficult for the Republicans to establish a toehold at the state and local levels. Most attorneys were Democrats because the Democratic Party dominated state politics, and virtually all judges in the state were Democrats. The usual practice was for judges to retire from the bench in the middle of their term, and Democratic governors replaced them with other Democrats.

With the election of William P. Clements in 1978 as the first Republican governor of Texas since 1873, party politics in the state began to change. Clements had cut his political teeth in the Department of Defense in the Nixon administration, and he personified a new type of Texas political leader. Not only was he Republican, but he was an urban businessman. His fortune was built on the Texas oil industry, but by the time he was elected governor, he was a successful international businessman with strong ties to the national Republican Party and the urban business community, which was typically Republican.

The Republican Party in Texas grew by carefully organizing supporting interests and aggressively recruiting Republicans to run for the legislature. Political debate was no longer confined to the cloistered halls of the state capitol, and in that debate, Republicans regularly took the side of the business community. They also began to increase their numbers in the legislature. As Republicans fielded candidates for the legislature, they discovered that one of the public policy areas which was ripe for change was the Texas civil justice system.

Even though the Democrats in the legislature had traditionally been interested in promoting a sound business climate, the issue was of even greater interest to Republicans. Because there was no advantage for the Republican Party in perpetuating a system of political bargaining behind closed doors, as had been the practice, they took more issues to the public. They championed causes that appealed to business and, by adopting some traditional populist rhetoric, they began adding conservative Democrats to their voting base. Early recruits came from among the wealthier classes and from western Texas.

The Republican Party soon developed a two-pronged attack on the civil justice system: they elected more members to the legislature so that they could rewrite statutory law, and they elected more Republicans to the state courts so that they could rewrite the common law. Early victories in judicial elections came in urban areas, especially in Dallas County, and by 1995 the Republican Party had a majority on the Texas Supreme Court.

Attorney Advertising

Barely a year before the election of William Clements as the first Republican governor of Texas in more than 100 years, the Supreme Court of the United States announced its decision in the case of *Bates v. State Bar of Arizona*. *Bates* was the second major decision in a new category of constitutionally protected speech known as commercial speech. The effect of the *Bates* decision was to invalidate an Arizona State Bar rule that prohibited attorneys from advertising their services.[14]

The American Bar Association responded to the *Bates* case by amending its Code of Professional Responsibility pertaining to matters governing lawyer advertising. The ABA went further than the Supreme Court had in the *Bates* case by providing very lenient rules governing advertising. Advertisements could use the names of clients regularly represented if they gave their written consent. A basic prohibition against false or misleading advertising remained, as did a prohibition against solicitation directed to a specific client.[15]

Attorneys, as a professional group, have never enjoyed a good reputation in this country. It is difficult to ascertain the exact origins of this

---

14. *Bates v. State Bar of Arizona*, 433 U.S. 350 (1977).
15. Norman Redlich, Bernard Schwartz, and John Attanasio, *Constitutional Law*, 2nd edition (New York: Matthew Bender, 1989), pp. 1394–5.

low regard, but it may be rooted in the failure of laypersons to understand that everyone is entitled to legal representation, and the attorney who defends an obviously guilty client is not condoning a client's behavior. The lack of respect for attorneys may also be related to the fact that when people need legal counsel, they are usually involved in something unpleasant.

A general suspicion of lawyers was probably reinforced by (to many) tasteless advertising in the Sunday television supplements of newspapers and often crudely made television commercials that encouraged injured people to consult a particular lawyer to make certain that their rights were properly protected. It is also likely that the proliferation of attorneys in the United States during the past two decades has been a major reason why many attorneys have turned to advertising. In any case, advertising by lawyers has not improved the reputation of the profession, and has probably contributed to a public reaction against them.

Public Awareness

Two developments in the 1970s and 1980s engaged the interest of the news media and the general public. One of these involved a number of unusually large awards in suits against automobile, pharmaceutical, and asbestos manufacturers. Especially prominent among the widely publicized cases was the McDonald's coffee case. The other development was the formation and growth of tort reform advocacy groups.

Several legal cases, involving asbestos-related illnesses, improperly tested drugs, and defectively designed automobiles, as well as the McDonald's coffee case, resulted in extraordinarily large awards to the claimants in highly publicized product liability suits. Most people did not realize that such awards were exceptional, and were often reduced later by appellate courts. A case in point was a 1978 award in which victims and families of victims of a Ford Pinto rear-end collision were awarded $3.5 million in damages and $125 million in punitive damages when it was proven that the Pinto was unsafe and Ford Motor Company officials knew that it was unsafe when it was built. The presiding judge later ruled that the jury award of punitive damages was excessive, and he reduced the award from $125 million to $3.5 million.[16] Another example was the McDonald's coffee case, in which a jury's award of $2.7 million to a woman who had been severely burned was reduced by the judge to $640,000. Large initial awards were big news, but court-ordered reductions were not.[17]

Extremely high awards or settlements in a few such cases had disparate impacts. Although many might argue that "reining in" irresponsible manufacturers through threats of such high awards was well done,

16. *Facts On File Yearbook, 1978,* pp. 185, 264.
17. Joseph Calve, "A Cry From The Heart," *Texas Lawyer,* Volume 12, Number 40, 16 December 1996, p. 16.

for some people, the awards merely reinforced their impression that attorneys are greedy and unscrupulous manipulators of the legal system. Others were encouraged to file lawsuits in hope of getting rich from them. For such people, the disappointment they felt when they could not find a reputable attorney to represent them, or when their settlement was less than expected, may have served to reinforce their negative feelings about the legal profession.

The development of organizations seeking support for tort reform began inauspiciously in 1960, with the founding of the Insurance Information Institute in New York City. Its original purpose was to collect, analyze, and distribute data about and for the American insurance industry. The early focus of this organization involved mostly technical matters of common concern within the industry. In the 1970s, however, the institute became interested in public policy matters and recent changes in tort law. The institute became a clearinghouse for information about the development of tort law and began to provide guidance for business groups that wanted to influence its development.

By the mid-1980s, tort reform was gaining momentum all over the United States. The American Tort Reform Association and the Texas Civil Justice League were both established in 1986. These organizations provided grist for business groups alarmed about the developing nature of tort law, and they began a campaign of public education to persuade the general public to support reforms that would be beneficial to the business community. Their work was augmented in Texas in the early 1990s by the formation of Texans for Lawsuit Reform, the most vocal advocate of the reforms introduced in the 74th Texas Legislature in 1995. These groups were able to take advantage of public awareness of some large jury awards and the generally poor reputation of lawyers to rally public support for substantial changes in the civil justice system in Texas.

Conclusion

The Texas Trial Lawyers Association was not completely defeated in the 74th Legislature because it was able to compromise on many of the proposals and eliminate some of the most objectionable details. However, it is clear that the ability of the TTLA to resist major alterations in Texas tort law has been substantially reduced since the 1960s. Whatever its remaining strength, it is an interest group that still operates within the legislature and depends on behind-the-scenes bargaining to protect its interests.

One of the results of the reforms adopted by the 74th Legislature is that small businesses and consumers will have fewer opportunities for redress in the courts. It is clear that those who supported tort reform legislation in 1995 will push for additional changes in 1997. Whether the TTLA will lose again in the 75th Legislature remains to be seen.

Systemic changes such as public debate of tort law issues, growth of the Republican Party, unpopularity of lawyers, well-financed and well-organized opposition groups, and publicity associated with some very large awards in a few major cases have all worked against the Texas Trial Lawyers Association and its political tactics. Unless the TTLA can adapt to the new political environment by learning how to mobilize public opinion to support its goals and seeking new coalitions with some of the newly emerging public interest groups, it is likely to continue losing important battles in the Texas Legislature. Most observers of, and participants in the tort reform efforts of the 74th Legislature assumed that the reformers had accomplished most of their goals and were unlikely to pursue additional reforms. This reaction is not uncommon, and, indeed, there seems to be a kind of life cycle for reform movements in Texas. The cycle has four distinct phrases:

Phase 1: Ideas are floated in the media and in the legislature but do not often result in concrete policy.

Phase 2: The issue begins to resonate with the pubic. Established interest groups pick it up, or new groups organize to promote the issue and move it into the political mainstream. In this phase, bills are introduced in the legislature. Interest groups and legislative sponsors are not usually successful at this stage, but many proposals become familiar elements in political debate.

Phase 3: If the interested parties have some success in phase 2, in phase 3 proponents achieve widespread attention. They have a chance of winning at least tentative support from the speaker, the lieutenant governor, and the governor. A sure sign of the maturation of the issue is its inclusion as a plank in the platforms of legislative and gubernatorial candidates, as was the case with tort reform in 1994. This phase often produces at least modest success in the legislature. For many issues this success removes some of the urgency for reform.

Phase 4: The public and its leaders begin to lose interest in the topic, often assuming that they have solved most of the targeted problems. Additional bills to fine tune the laws may be introduced, but major changes are unlikely. Proponents' chief concern is to protect the gains they have made.

Consistent with the formula, tort reform advocates achieved most of their goals in the 74th Legislature, and the issue seems to have been replaced by other concerns in the 75th Legislature in 1997. However, TLR came back to the 75th seeking passage of those parts of its agenda which did not pass in the 74th. Their prospects were diminished somewhat. While tort reform groups did not lose any ground in the 1996 elections, neither did they gain much. Governor Bush made their work harder when he put the weight of his office and personal prestige into a tax reform effort. He proposed large reductions in property taxes and elimination of the franchise tax. He would replace the lost revenue with an increase in the sales tax and a net receipts tax on business. These would require complete restructuring of the financial base of the independent school districts and force the state to assume a greater share of the costs of public education. Powerful interests arranged themselves on both sides of the issue, and their struggles absorbed a major share of the legislature's energies for the session. In addition, many of the legislators who helped enact tort reform in the 74th Legislature were satisfied that they had accomplished most of what was needed and were reluctant to reenter that particular thicket in the new session.

To all of these difficulties must be added the fact that the TCJL did not, in the early days of the session at least, commit its support to new efforts. The feeling seems to be that TLR is greedy, and its unusually aggressive approach has alienated former allies and stiffened the resistance of old adversaries. In addition, TLR made several huge campaign contributions in some legislative races in 1996, and even friendly groups are afraid that they have bid up the cost of electioneering in the future.[18]

---

18. Wayne Slater, "Top legislative donor fights to limit lawsuits," *Dallas Morning News*, 3 February 1997, pp. 1A, 6A.

PART IV

Policies

12
Taxes in Texas

Bernard L. Weinstein
University of North Texas

As mentioned in the discussion of the Texas Constitution, the framers of the Constitution of 1876 constructed a document that decentralized power in government. Fundamentally, they believed in the Jeffersonian axiom that the government which governs least governs best. They wanted minimal governmental powers so that they could be free to run their lives with little interference. To the framers, minimal government also meant low taxes.

Things have changes substantially since those days. Texas is now the second-most populous state and has large urban centers such as Dallas and Houston; no one would now describe Texas as a rural agricultural state. Yet the bywords of low taxes and minimal government remain. Texans are so fearful of the potential for higher taxes that there is now a provision in the Texas Constitution that will require a constitutional amendment before a personal income tax is imposed.

It is often argued that Texas's low taxes are good for business, that a favorable business environment has been created that encourages the growth of existing businesses and the relocation of businesses fleeing high taxes in other states. As the following chapter points out, however, whether taxes are really low in the state depends on which tax is examined. Although Texas does not have a personal income tax, property and sales taxes have almost reached their upper limits. At the same time, there are pressures for additional public services. In 1990, Texas ranked thirty-second among the states in average teacher salaries, nineteenth in per capita expenditures for public schools, and thirty-seventh in expenditures for public schools per pupil. It seems obvious that there will be continued pressure for additional resources for public school education.

In 1989, Texas ranked fifth in the number of social security beneficiaries. The large numbers of older persons will place pressure on the state for public services. Although, as the chapter on welfare points out, drastic measures are being taken to lower public welfare costs, Texas has large numbers of public aid recipients. In 1989, 4.9 percent of Texans were public aid recipients, and Texas ranked twenty-ninth among the states in public aid recipients as a percent of the population. Texas also ranked fourth among the states in 1990 in crime rate per 100,000 persons and eleventh in violent crime rate per 100,000 persons. The demand for personal security also costs money in terms of more prisons and more police.

As pressures to increase state expenditures build, the national government is downsizing, and turning over more government programs to the state. In the past, much of the cost of government programs was paid for by the national government. State and local governments are going to have to pick up more of those costs.

Texans cannot depend on severance taxes, taxes on the production of oil and gas, which were once major sources of income for the state. Not that many years ago, nearly one-third of the state's budget came from such taxes. However, oil and gas production has declined dramatically in Texas, and now those severance taxes account for only 4 percent of the state's income.

As this chapter suggests, limits on the potential revenue from severance taxes, property taxes, and sales taxes, coupled with the pressures for additional public expenditures and services, will create an economic crisis in Texas. Shortfalls in revenues will not be met by increased economy in government, state lotteries, or casino gambling. When that crisis happens, Texans should be prepared for a state income tax.

Texas is the second-largest state in the nation, with a population that exceeds 19 million, and its state and local governments require huge sums of money to provide goods and services to its citizens. For example, the state budget for the 1996–97 fiscal biennium was $79.9 billion, up from $20.2 billion twelve years earlier. As people and industry have moved into the state, and income levels have generally risen, the demand for publicly provided goods and services has grown. In addition, federal environmental mandates and increased educational and social service needs of Texas's rapidly growing population have raised the level of state spending.

During the "boom" years of the 1970s and early 1980s, Texas had no major tax increases. Rapid economic growth, along with rising oil prices and high rates of inflation, generated biannual windfalls for the Texas treasury. Revenues grew so rapidly during this period that the legislature had little more to do than parcel out the bounty among competing constituencies, most notably education and transportation. However, when boom turned to bust in the mid-1980s, and surpluses became deficits, tax hikes became commonplace: rate increases or base broadening occurred in virtually every year between 1984 and 1991.

In recent years, as Texas's revenue situation has improved, a new concern with fiscal responsibility has been manifest. Many of the state's business and political leaders have voiced concerns that state spending is growing too rapidly and that rising tax burdens are putting Texas at a disadvantage when competing with other states for new business. In an effort to retard the growth of state spending, in 1991 the Texas Comptroller of Public Accounts instituted the Texas Performance Review, which issues cost-saving recommendations on a continuing basis. Between 1991 and 1996, the comptroller's office claims to have saved the state's taxpayers more than $8 billion.

This chapter has a dual purpose: (1) to describe the current nature and structure of the Texas tax system and how it has changed over the past decade, and (2) to discuss a variety of public policy issues related to the tax structure, such as fairness, revenue adequacy, and economic development.

WHERE TEXAS GETS ITS REVENUE

Sales and Excise Taxes

Having neither a personal nor corporate income tax, the State of Texas derives most if its tax revenue from the general sales tax (see Table 12.1). The tax is applied to the sale of tangible personal property, unless specifically exempted. Major exemptions include groceries, prescription drugs, fuels, most utilities, sales for resale, and raw materials. Although in the past the tax has been levied primarily on goods, in recent years it has been broadened to include services such as amusements, laundry and dry cleaning, debt collection, and insurance services. In fiscal 1996, the tax brought in $10.8 billion, which amounted to almost 55 percent of all state tax receipts.

As of 1997, the state sales-tax rate stood at 6.25 percent, a rate matched or exceeded by only six other states. Cities and other local governments

TABLE 12.1

Texas State Tax Revenue by Source, Fiscal Year 1996

Type	Revenue ($million)	% of Total Tax Revenue
Sales Tax	$10,791.5	54.6%
Oil Production and Regulation Taxes	377.0	1.9
Natural Gas Production Tax	447.1	2.3
Motor Fuels Taxes	2,321.0	11.7
Motor Vehicle Sales and Rental Taxes	1,965.3	10.0
Corporation Franchise Tax	1,639.0	8.3
Cigarette and Tobacco Taxes	566.7	2.9
Alcoholic Beverage Tax	418.7	2.1
Insurance Company Taxes	626.6	3.2
Utility Taxes	241.0	1.2
Inheritance Tax	160.1	0.8
Hotel and Motel Tax	176.5	0.9
Other Taxes	32.0	0.1
Total	**$19,762.5**	**100%**

Source: John Sharp, Texas Comptroller of Public Accounts.

can impose sales taxes of up to 1 percent; but the combined state and local rates may not exceed 8.25 percent. Five other states have equal or higher combined rates.

Selective sales and excise taxes on motor fuels, motor vehicle sales, tobacco, and alcoholic beverages account for an additional 27 percent of state tax receipts. As of 1997, the state motor-fuels tax—which is based on the quantity purchased as opposed to price—amounted to 20 cents per gallon. (This is in addition to the federal gasoline tax, which is currently 18.4 cents per gallon.) The motor-fuels tax is about equal to the national average and generated 12 percent of state tax revenues in fiscal 1996. The motor-vehicle excise tax, which is levied on the net purchase price of cars and light trucks at the time of sale, is currently 6.25 percent and accounts for 10 percent of state tax receipts. By contrast, the national average vehicle purchase tax rate is 4 percent. Texas's cigarette tax, 41 cents per pack, is exceeded by only ten other states, but the $3 per gallon tax on spirits is one of the lowest in the nation.

Sales taxes of all types currently account for slightly more than 81 percent of state tax revenues, a higher percentage than in any other state. Furthermore, the ratio of sales taxes to total state revenue collections has risen significantly since 1980, when sales taxes accounted for only 62 percent of the revenue total.

Business Taxes

The corporate franchise tax and severance taxes constitute the major business levies, and together produce about 13 percent of state tax revenues. The franchise tax, first enacted in 1907, is Texas's general business tax and is imposed for the privilege of doing business in the state. Until 1991, the tax was based entirely on corporate capital assets and fell most heavily on capital-intensive manufacturing industries. The franchise tax was collected regardless of whether the company was profitable. Less capital-intensive service industries, which composed the largest share of Texas's employment, paid a relatively small share of the tax.

In 1991, the legislature amended the franchise tax so that it is now levied either on capital or earnings, whichever yields the greatest tax liability. Since this change was enacted, the number of companies paying the tax has increased and revenue has risen steadily. In fiscal 1996, the corporate franchise tax produced about $1.6 billion, compared to only $597 million in fiscal 1991. The current rates of the franchise tax are either 0.25 percent of net taxable capital or 4.5 percent of net earnings.

Until the mid-1980s, severance taxes—which are ad valorem, or at a rate percent of value, levies on oil and gas production—were a major state revenue source, accounting for nearly 30 percent of state tax collections. However, with the downsizing of the energy industry in conjunction with lower oil and gas prices, the importance of severance taxes to the state revenue has diminished dramatically. Severance taxes now account for only 5 percent of state tax collections and generate barely a third of the money they did at their height. The tax rates—of 4.6 percent on oil and 7.5 percent on natural gas—haven't changed in nearly thirty years.

Other State Revenue Sources

Tax collections account for less than half of Texas's state revenue stream (see Table 12.2). The state relies heavily on federal funds for a wide range of human services programs, and these grants-in-aid account for almost 30 percent of all state revenues—$11.6 billion in fiscal 1996. Texas also derives considerable income from investments and royalties on state-owned lands. Licenses, fees, and permits have increased in importance in recent years and now account for 9.5 percent of all state revenues. The Texas State Lottery, which has been operating since 1992, brought in nearly $1.7 billion in fiscal 1996 and accounted for 4.2 percent of state revenues.

Local Taxes

The ad valorem property tax is the workhorse of local government finance and produces nearly as much revenue as all state taxes combined. Cities, counties, school districts, and special districts collected about $16 billion in property taxes in fiscal 1995, and school districts accounted for

TABLE 12.2

Texas State Revenue by Source, Fiscal Year 1996

Type	Revenue ($million)	% of Total Revenue
Tax Collections	$19,762.5	48.8%
Federal Funds	11,657.7	28.8
Interest Income	2,075.8	5.1
Licenses and Fees	3,841.4	9.5
Contributions to Employee Benefits	94.9	0.2
Sales of Goods and Services	197.7	0.5
Land Income: Rent, Royalties, and Sales	223.0	0.6
Settlement of Claims	14.7	0.1
Other Revenue Sources	902.4	2.2
Net Lottery Proceeds	1,718.3	4.2
Total	**$40,488.3**	**100%**

Source: John Sharp, Texas Comptroller of Public Accounts.

FIGURE 12.1
Growth of the Property Tax Levy by Unit Type, 1984–1995

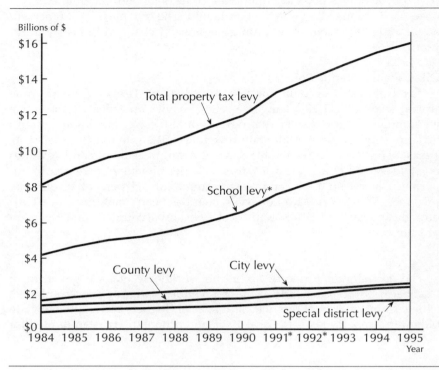

Source: John Sharp, Texas Comptroller of Public Accounts, Annual Property Tax Report—Tax Year 1995.
* 1991 and 1992 include Country Education Districts

58 percent of the total (see Figure 12.1). Over the past decade, total property tax collections have risen by more than 100 percent, mainly because of increases in school levies resulting from legislative and judicial mandates.

Most cities in Texas impose a 1 percent sales tax, and some municipalities collect additional sales taxes for public transportation, economic development, and property tax relief.

THE WAY WE WERE: TEXAS TAXES BEFORE THE OIL BUST

In the 1970s and early 1980s, tax policy and revenue generation were not the dominant public policy issues that they have become today. The legislature's main concern then was how to dispose of the multi-billion dollar surpluses that were accumulating each biennium.

This fiscal "nirvana" stemmed from several sources. First, rising commodity prices, especially for oil and gas, were generating severance tax windfalls for Texas and other energy-producing states. For example, in 1970 severance taxes on oil and gas yielded $269 million, or 15 percent of Texas's tax collections. By 1982, these taxes were bringing in $2.4 billion, which amounted to 28 percent of state tax receipts. Sales taxes levied on oil-field equipment also rose dramatically, as did local property taxes levied on drilling and pumping equipment and oil and gas leases. The national demand for Texas's oil and gas meant that the bulk of the severance and energy-related sales and property taxes collected in the state could be "shifted" forward to consumers in other parts of the country: that is, Texas was able to pass on a large portion of its tax bill to others in the form of higher energy prices.

High overall inflation rates in the 1970s and early 1980s also benefited the Texas treasury. Then, as now, the general sales tax was the major revenue producer for the state. As prices of consumer goods rose at double-digit rates in some years of the 1970s and 1980s, sales tax receipts increased. Retail sales were also driven higher by several million people who moved into Texas from other parts of the country to capitalize on the economic opportunities afforded by the energy industry boom.

Unfortunately, the good fiscal times came to an abrupt end with the collapse of commodity prices in the mid-1980s. West Texas intermediate crude oil (WTI), which had risen as high as $40 a barrel in 1982, dropped to less than $10 a barrel in 1986. Obviously, the 4.6 percent severance tax produced a good deal less revenue on $10 oil than it did on $40 oil. Lower prices for crude oil and natural gas were quickly followed by cutbacks in exploration and production, which exacerbated revenue shortfalls. The fallout from the drop in energy prices between 1982 and 1986 soon spilled over into the banking and real estate industries, and Texas slipped into a severe recession that lasted until the end of the decade. The dramatic change in Texas's economic fortunes resulted in frequent tax increases and permanently altered Texas's revenue mix.

By 1996, the severance tax contribution to Texas's finances had dropped in both absolute and relative terms, yielding a mere $824 million and accounting for only 4 percent of the revenue mix. Sales taxes, by contrast, had risen to 55 percent of the total. A number of revenue sources in 1996—such as the parimutuel betting tax and the lottery—didn't exist a decade ago (see discussion below).

Another noteworthy change in Texas government financing is the considerably greater reliance on federal aid. In 1982, federal aid amounted to 18 percent of state revenues, but by 1996 the percentage was 29 percent. This increase in federal aid is partly a reflection of the growing

TABLE 12.3

Texas State and Local Government Tax Revenue
as a Percentage of Personal Income, 1980 & 1992

	1980		1992	
	Amount	Rank	Amount	Rank
State & Local	9.75%	43	10.93%	30
State Taxes	5.75%	46	5.67%	43
Property Taxes	3.38%	24	4.29%	14

Source: Center for the Study of the States, State University of New York.

numbers of welfare and Medicaid recipients in Texas, but it is also a result of concerted efforts by Texas representatives to increase Texas's share of the federal aid pie.

How Texas's Tax Burden Compares to Other States

Despite several hefty tax increases in recent years, Texas's state tax burden, expressed as a percentage of personal income, is forty-third in the nation, and is the lowest of the ten largest states (see Table 12.3 and Figure 12.2). However, the low state tax burden has resulted in a high and rising local tax burden. For example, in 1992 Texas's local property tax burden was fourteenth in the country, up from twenty-fourth in 1980. When state and local taxes are combined, Texas ranks thirtieth in the nation compared with its forty-third placing in 1980.

Unlike most other states, where state government generates the bulk of tax revenues and shares a portion of these funds with localities, Texas relies principally on local governments for revenue collection and service delivery (see Table 12.4, p. 207). Whereas the property tax typically accounts for 30 percent of state and local tax revenues, in Texas the figure is closer to 40 percent. Because Texas does not levy a personal income tax, the contribution of sales taxes to the revenue mix is 35 percent compared to the national norm of 24 percent.

Another consequence of Texas's "upside-down" revenue mix and the lack of a personal income tax is an extremely regressive overall tax system, meaning that burdens on low-income families are greater than those on high-income families. For example, according to an April 1991 study conducted by Citizens for Tax Justice, Texas's poorest working families spend 17.1 percent of their incomes on state and local taxes while the rich spend only 3.1 percent. Middle-income Texans pay about 8.4 percent of their incomes on state and local taxes. Only Washington state, one of four other states without a personal income tax, has a higher tax rate on the poor, and only four other states impose lower taxes on the wealthy than Texas.

FIGURE 12.2

State and Local Revenue per $100 of Personal Income, 1992

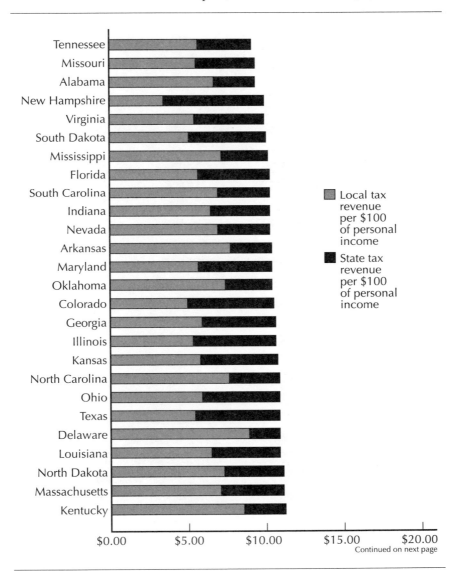

Continued on next page

Equity, Balance, and Adequacy of the Texas Tax System

No one likes to pay taxes, and there is disagreement about the proper amount of taxing and spending at every level of government. However, because taxes are necessary if any democratic society is to benefit from

FIGURE 12.2 (cont.)

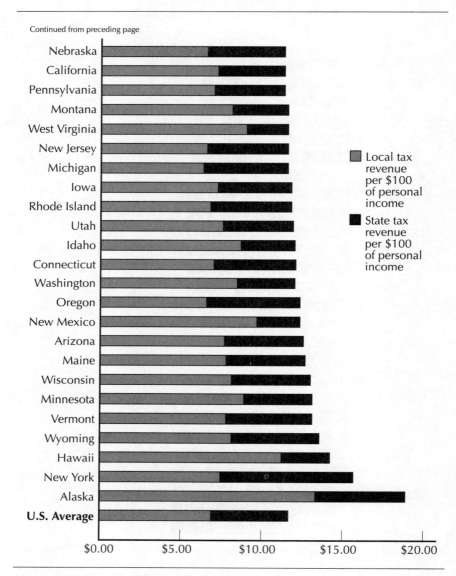

Source: Center for the Study of the States.

public goods, they should be designed, imposed, and collected in a nondiscriminatory fashion.

Economists generally agree that a good tax structure will exhibit the following characteristics.

TABLE 12.4		
Sources of State and State/Local Tax Revenues: Texas Versus the United States, Percent Distribution		
State	Texas	U.S. Average
Sales*	62%	33%
Excise**/Corporate***/Other	38	36
Personal Income	0	31
State and Local		
Property	39%	30%
Sales*	35	24
Excise**/Corporate***/Other	26	25
Personal Income	0	21

* Includes motor vehicle taxes
** Includes motor fuels, cigarette, alcholic beverage, and other excise taxes
*** Includes corporate franchise tax

Sources: John Sharp, State Comptroller of Public Accounts; U.S. Bureau of the Census.

1. *Equity.* The notion of equity, or fairness, means that tax burdens should be based either on benefits received or on the ability to pay. It also implies that tax burdens on low-income individuals should be less than those on high-income individuals. In addition, an equitable tax system should be uniform in its application and should not discriminate among different types of business organizations.

2. *Balance.* A good tax system should reflect a balance between households and businesses and should avoid overreliance on any particular tax or group of taxpayers. The tax system should also reflect a mixture of tax bases with the broadest coverage at the lowest rates possible.

3. *Adequacy.* Any tax system should be capable of generating the revenues required to finance government in a stable and predictable manner without resorting to frequent rate hikes. In addition, the tax structure should be such that revenues will grow in tandem with growth in the state's economy.

Texas's tax system meets none of these criteria. As discussed above, poor Texans pay more taxes relative to their incomes than do rich Texans. Another inequity is found in the disproportionate share of state and local taxes paid by business. According to a study by the State Comptroller of Public Accounts, businesses in Texas pay about 54 percent of

TABLE 12.5		
Estimated Percent of Total Texas Taxes Paid by Businesses and Individuals, 1994		
Tax	Business (%)	Individual (%)
Property	67	33
Sales	47	53
Motor Fuels	40	60
Motor Vehicle	36	64
Corporate Franchise	100	0
Natural Gas	100	0
Oil	100	0
Insurance	100	0
Cigarette/Tobacco	0	100
Alcoholic Beverages	0	100
Utility	100	0
Inheritance	0	100
Total State and Local	59.6	40.4
State	54.1	45.9
Local	65.1	34.9
Sources: John Sharp, State Comptroller of Public Accounts: U.S. Bureau of the Census.		

all state taxes and 65 percent of local taxes (see Table 12.5). This inequity occurs because the business sector pays about 67 percent of local property taxes, nearly one-half of all state and local sales taxes, and 40 percent of the motor-fuels tax. In addition, Texas is one of the few states imposing the sales tax on the purchase of manufacturing equipment. Another inequity stems from the fact that the franchise tax applies only to corporations and not to other forms of business.

The absence of a personal income tax causes a major imbalance in Texas's state and local tax structure, and an overreliance on property and sales taxes. It also imparts a high degree of inelasticity to Texas's tax system. For example, during the late 1980s and early 1990s when the Texas economy experienced falling oil prices, declining property values, and generally low inflation rates, state and local revenues stagnated. Faced with huge shortfalls, the state legislature was forced to hike sales, gasoline, and excise tax rates as well as dozens of fees simply to maintain the current level of service delivery. At the same time, most municipalities and school districts in Texas saw their property-tax rates skyrocket to compensate for declining real estate values.

The lack of a personal income tax in Texas has also limited the ability of the state to deal effectively with its public school funding inequities. School finance reform has been on the Texas political agenda for decades, beginning with a 1968 lawsuit in which a federal court found the school finance system unconstitutional because of inequities in the fiscal mechanisms used to generate revenues—namely, the local property tax. The inequities resulted from the fact that high-property-wealth school districts could impose low tax rates and actually generate more revenues than low-property-wealth districts imposing higher rates. Although the state could theoretically compensate for these disparities through grants-in-aid, in the absence of an income tax Texas did not have access to a substantial revenue stream that could be used for this purpose. Over time, the disparities between rich and poor school districts, in terms of both revenues and per-pupil spending, increased.

Several school finance reform bills were enacted between 1984 and 1992, but all were found to be unconstitutional because they did not deal adequately with the issue of fiscal disparities. In May 1993, the legislature approved and the governor signed Senate Bill 7, which established the current system of public school finance. Sometimes referred to as "Robin Hood," Senate Bill 7 transfers local property-tax revenues from high-wealth to low-wealth districts. For example, property taxes collected in an affluent Dallas suburb may actually be spent in a poor school district located in the lower Rio Grande valley. Even though significant disparities in per-pupil spending remain, the Texas Supreme Court, in a five to four opinion, upheld the constitutionality of Senate Bill 7 on January 30, 1995.

However, the Texas Supreme Court's opinion made it clear that the justices don't like the system the legislature has created, and warned "Our judgment in this case should not be interpreted as a signal that the school finance crisis in Texas has ended. . . . the existence of more than 1,000 independent school districts in Texas, each with duplicative administrative bureaucracies combined with widely varying tax bases and an excessive reliance on local property taxes, has resulted in a state of affairs that can only charitably be called a 'system.' "

Tax Policy and Economic Development: Corporate Welfare in Texas

Another aspect of inequity or unfairness in Texas's tax structure and policy can be found in the current use of state and local tax breaks as an economic development tool. Prior to the energy industry bust, state and local tax incentives were virtually nonexistent in Texas. Nonetheless, Texas experienced healthy job growth and business creation in conjunction with the commodity boom and huge numbers of new residents. However, when business formation and investment slowed in the mid-1980s, voices were raised in support of tax breaks to spur economic development. Responding to a growing clamor from chambers of commerce, real estate developers, and public utilities, in the late 1980s the legislature enacted a number of bills to permit local governments, including school districts, to abate property taxes for relocating or expanding firms. Enterprise zones, sales-tax exemptions, and other fiscal inducements were also enacted and presented to the public as ways to spur new business development.

At first, local governments and school districts were sparing in their use of property-tax abatements. For example, in 1990 the value of abated property statewide was only $1 billion out of a total tax base of about $700 billion. But by 1996, cities and school districts had granted abatements totaling $12 billion while the state's taxable property values had increased only marginally. It is not surprising that average property taxes for education have risen from about 1.5 percent of market value to 2.3 percent of market value since 1990, in part to compensate for the base erosion related to abatements.

Despite their growing popularity, there is little or no evidence that the granting of tax abatements to industry has resulted in net job creation or has been critical to decisions to relocate in Texas. There is no way to disprove the efficacy of tax incentives, because any firm receiving a tax break will attest to the importance of the break in the decision to expand or relocate. The process and economics of site selection, however, suggest that state and local tax breaks are unlikely to be significant factors in the investment decision.

For most companies, state and local taxes constitute a very small portion of operating expenses. By contrast, labor, materials, transportation, and utilities costs are much larger and far more crucial considerations for businesses scouting new locations. In addition, because state and local taxes are deductable, a company pays up to 38 cents more in federal tax for every dollar it doesn't pay in local property taxes, thereby reducing considerably the effective value of the abatement.

Tax incentives are not likely to disappear from Texas soon, mainly because businesses and politicians will continue to argue that such lures must be offered if Texas is to remain competitive with other states. Perhaps if the federal government reduced grants-in-aid to states offering abatements on a dollar-for-dollar basis, the practice would cease, but that is not a likelihood.

The Politics of Tax Reform in Texas

In the face of revenue shortfalls and school finance litigation, Texas has seen its share of tax reform study commissions and blue-ribbon panels. For example, in 1987 a nearly two-year effort was launched by the Select Committee on Tax Equity, which resulted in the most comprehensive assessment ever of the state and local fiscal system. Although the committee's report was long on detail, and thoroughly documented the shortcomings of the existing revenue system, it was short on recommendations, and silent on the matter of a personal income tax.

In the spring of 1991, Governor Ann Richards, Lieutenant Governor Bob Bullock, and House Speaker Gib Lewis appointed members to a Governor's Task Force on Revenue that was instructed to come up with a set of fiscal options for balancing the 1992–93 budget. The panel quickly split into "pro" and "anti" income tax groups, and the task force was unable to forge a consensus. At the end of the legislative session in 1995, Governor George Bush created yet another blue-ribbon commission to examine issues related to Texas's tax structure.

In response to the findings and recommendations of Governor Bush's commission, the 1997 Legislature considered the most radical overhaul of Texas's tax system in decades. As reported on by a special House Committee on Taxation and School Property-Tax Relief, the bill would cut residential school property taxes in half and increase the state's share of school funding costs from its current level of 47 percent to about 80 percent. The committee's proposals would also remove many sales tax exemptions, expand the state franchise tax to all companies except sole proprietorships, and increase the cigarette tax by 20 cents a pack. Taxes on alcoholic beverages and aviation fuel would also be increased. As of this writing, it is unclear whether the tax restructuring bill, as proposed, will become law. However, if it does pass, many of the inefficiencies and inequities that already exist in the Texas tax system will be amplified. Businesses will bear an even higher share of the tax burden than they do at present, while the overall regressivity of the system will worsen.

Why hasn't true tax reform taken hold in Texas? It is probably because the legacy of populism is alive and well, despite more than four decades of urbanization and industrialization. Elements of this populist tradition are a dislike and distrust of government and a seemingly ingrained belief that taxes, and especially a personal income tax, are somehow "un-Texan." This antitax sentiment is reinforced by a legislature that has become dominated by conservative rural and suburban interests and by the ascendancy of the Republican Party in Texas.

Texas's business and political leaders, while keeping the populist tradition, have been preoccupied for decades with creating and maintaining a favorable business climate for the state, which has meant keeping fiscal burdens relatively low in the belief that state and local taxes and spending are the primary determinants of a state's attractiveness to new and expanding businesses.

Will Texas ever see tax reform and the adoption of an income tax? Yes—and probably sooner than later. Between 1991 and 1997, a strong Texas economy plus the enactment of pari-mutuel betting and a state lottery helped to boost revenues so that fiscal crises were averted. The 1995 legislature was even able to increase spending for the 1996–97 biennium by about $9 billion without recourse to a tax hike. Within a few years, however, rising demands for state expenditure are bound to outstrip the ability of the existing tax structure to produce adequate revenues.

Texas's school finance problems are far from resolved, and federal courts continue to mandate higher levels of state expenditure for prisons and social services. In addition, Texas's population is expected to grow at nearly twice the national average for the foreseeable future, which in turn will generate demands for higher levels of public expenditure. There is also a growing recognition that Texas's underdeveloped public sector and low levels of spending on education and other human service programs may actually be endangering the state's long-term economic competitiveness. This problem will be compounded if the U.S. Congress continues to cut back on entitlement funding and grants-in-aid to state and local governments.

The next time Texas faces a substantial revenue shortfall, either due to a major recession or a confluence of the factors mentioned above, the state will have nowhere else to turn but the personal income tax, although there are legislators who would opt for a 10 or 11 percent sales tax instead. However, it is only through the direct taxation of income that Texas can avoid its recurring fiscal crises and also improve the overall equity, balance, and elasticity of the state and local revenue system.

13
Education Reform in Texas

Clark D. Thomas
U.S. Department of Health and
Human Services, Dallas

Texas has had a frustrating experience with public education. It is clear that any state's future lies in an educated citizenry, and yet Texas's children seem to be unable to compete in an increasingly high technology world economy. In areas of rural Texas, education seems to be the school time between football games, and some urban public schools have become threats to children's safety, due to increasing crime and violence, rather than challenges to young minds. One of Texas's largest school districts actually bragged about the great improvements in its Texas Academic Achievement Scores (TAAS) scores: eighth-grade students, for example, had average overall writing scores of 64, reading scores of 58, and math scores of 37: the overall score was 46. In contrast, a wealthy suburban district had eighth-grade writing scores of 98, reading scores of 98, math scores of 94, and overall scores of 91. It appears that it is only in well-to-do suburbs that Texas children's minds thrive, and there efforts to ban certain books, types of science, and even critical thinking are increasingly pervasive.

In the face of disappointments in the public school system, the state has experimented with numerous solutions to its crisis in education. Those efforts are discussed in the following chapter. What is most interesting, however, is how cautious policymakers have actually been in pursuing educational reforms. It is unlikely, for example, that educational reforms such as vouchers will be adopted in Texas. (With vouchers, the state would provide funds for students to attend schools of their choosing, and in theory, parents and children would tend to choose schools that offer the best educations for their children.)

Texas educational reforms have included attempts to centralize educational administration as well as more recent plans to decentralize educational administration. There have also been plans to improve education by spending more money on unsuccessful programs. The most radical educational reform may have been "no pass, no play," meaning that students could not participate in organized sports unless they had passing grades. Even that degree of change in Texas educational policy has been questioned by policymakers.

In thinking about education and educational reform policies in Texas, one should ask the following questions. Who benefits from the current educa-

tional system, unsuccessful as it may be? Are most educational reforms really drastic enough to dramatically improve the quality of education in Texas? Do most Texans really want a better educational system than they have now?

Cynics may answer that there is a lack of will, resources, and imagination to significantly improve education in Texas. If this is true, the future of Texas is not secure, and reforms such as discussed in this chapter will not adequately deal with the issues of quality public education.

It sometimes seems that education reform has always been a major topic of discussion in Texas: in fact, it has been a hotly debated public policy issue for about a decade. Prior to 1983, state government institutions in Texans had little interest in dealing with education issues. However, by the middle 1980s, the perception arose that there were problems with public education in the state. Serious questions about education quality and access to public education in Texas led to concerns that the traditional system was not working. Public schools had long had considerable autonomy, most administrative decisions being made at the local level. Political leaders and other public figures began to suggest that it was time for the state government to take a more active role in running Texas's schools. The result was the beginning of two very different reform efforts that would change both the way Texas schools were run and the perceptions that most Texans held about their state's public education system. By the end of the 1980s, the Texas Legislature, the Texas Supreme Court, and the specially formed Select Committee On Public Education (SCOPE) would all have a hand in shifting quite a bit of the control over Texas public schools from the local to the state level. This chapter considers how those actors got involved and the impact they have had on the way Texas schools operate.

Although state aid has been a significant source of funding for schools since the 1940s, even composing 51 percent of the state's budget in fiscal year 1984,[1] the Texas Legislature has concerned itself with little more than the funding formulas. Education policy was traditionally the responsibility of the education committees of each house, and bills reported to the floor passed with little input or opposition from the members as a whole.

By the 1980s, the legislature was unable to avoid the issue of education reform. Across the nation, more than one thousand pieces of state legislation affecting teacher policy alone were developed during the decade.[2] Many observers suggest that the impetus for this effort was the 1983 National Commission on Excellence in Education report, *A Nation*

---

1. Texas Research League, *Benchmarks: 1994–95 School District Budgets in Texas* (Austin, TX: Texas Research League, 1985).
2. B. Rodman, "Teaching's Status Still Cloudy Despite Reforms, Study Finds," *Education Week*, 20 April 1988, p. 4.

at Risk: The Imperative for Educational Reform.³ It begins with the statement, "Our nation is at risk. Our once unchallenged preeminence in commerce, industry, science, and technology innovation is being overtaken by competitors throughout the world."⁴ The report's attribution of this condition to an "act of unthinking, unilateral education disarmament" and the attention it brought to a decline in test scores, increases in functional illiteracy, and the decline in intellectual skills started the latest decade of reforms, and the "excellence movement" in education. Texas began to follow the trend when the legislature passed House Bill 246 in 1981. This bill sought to standardize the curriculum of the state's public schools by establishing twelve basic subject areas thought to be necessary to a sound education.⁵ It also addressed issues of attendance, discipline, and standards for academic advancement and graduation.

Excellence was not the only public education issue coming to a head in Texas at that time. Equity was also becoming a subject of heated policy debates. Efforts toward equality of educational opportunity began in earnest at the national level with the 1954 U.S. Supreme Court decision in *Brown v. Board of Education*, and continued with the Civil Rights Act of 1964 and the Elementary and Secondary Education Act of 1965. All targeted minority and economically disadvantaged children with the goal of increasing equity in education.⁶ The Texas Legislature first addressed the equity issue in 1915 by appropriating special equalization aid to encourage local tax efforts in rural school districts. The state's role shifted from promoting local efforts to providing funding for rural districts with the establishment of the minimum foundation plan (MFP) in 1949. The MFP, created under the Gilmer-Aikin Act, set minimum standards for state aid to education and became the basic method of state education finance allocation.

Several events, beginning with a California Supreme Court decision in *Serrano v. Priest* that found a similar foundation plan unconstitutional in that state, forced Texas to reconsider this allocation method. In 1971, a U.S. district court ruled Texas's education finance system unconstitutional in *Rodriguez v. San Antonio*. This decision was reversed by the U.S. Supreme Court in 1973. While the high court said that the finance system did not violate the federal constitution, it did find fault with the "chaotic and unjust" allocation method. Anticipating further challenges, the leg-

---

3. Donal M. Sacken and Marcello Medina, Jr., "Investigating the Context of State-Level Policy Formation: A Case Study of Arizona's Bilingual Education Legislation" (Educational Evaluation and Policy Analysis).
4. National Commission on Excellence in Education, *A Nation at Risk: The Imperative For Educational Reform* (Washington, D.C.: U.S. Department of Education, 1983).
5. Lyndon B. Johnson School of Public Affairs, "The Initial Effects of House Bill 72 on Texas Public Schools: The Challenges of Equity and Effectiveness," *Policy Research*, Project Report no. 70 (Austin, University of Texas, 1985).
6. "The Initial Effects of House Bill 72 on Texas Public Schools: The Challenges of Equality and Effectiveness."

islature passed several bills between 1975 and 1979 attempting to equalize funding for public schools. These efforts failed to prevent the expected legal challenge, which finally materialized in *Edgewood v. Bynum*, filed this time in state district court in May 1984. This case claimed that the Texas education system was in violation of the state constitution because children in poor school districts were not provided with educational programs that were substantially equal to those available to other students. In addition, because many of Texas's poorest school districts contain concentrations of low income and Mexican-American students, the suit argued that the state was practicing discrimination on the basis of wealth and national origin, in violation of the state constitution's equal protection provisions.[7]

It was within this context that the education reform decade truly got underway in Texas. The equity issue became important in response to the constitutional challenges to the existing funding system. Questions about the quality of education began to get serious attention when a gubernatorial candidate proposed pay raises for teachers. While the two issues arose in response to different pressures, and involve different problems and solutions, they also have much in common in the way they were handled by policymakers in the state and in their lasting impact on education policymaking in Texas.

Education Quality in Texas

Before the early 1980s, policymakers in Texas rarely worried about the overall quality of education in the state. The economy depended more on Texas's natural resources, particularly oil and gas, than on highly skilled labor. Employers tended to care more about how hard and long someone would work rather than whether he or she could read or solve complex mathematical problems. Legislators felt little need to do more than approve funding formulas each biennium.

In his bid for the office of Texas governor in 1982, Attorney General Mark White devised a strategy to unseat incumbent William P. Clements. His plan was to involve the state's powerful teachers' unions in his campaign by promising to propose an across-the-board pay increase for all public school teachers in the state. To avoid losing support from other areas, he argued that the state budget could fund the pay raises with no increase in taxes. The tactic worked. Two unions—the state affiliates of the National Education Association (NEA) and American Federation of Teachers (AFT)—representing 65 percent of the state's 170,000 teachers supported White's campaign, and began to register and mobilize voters, staff phone banks, and raise money. Their efforts were a key factor in an approximately 230,000 vote White victory. As promised, the new gov-

---

7. House Study Group, "Key Issues of the June 1984 Special Session," *Special Legislative Report*, 104, 16 July 1984.

ernor's "State of the State" speech in January 1983 called for a 24 percent pay raise for all public school teachers without additional taxes.

A rapidly deteriorating economy, the result of the national recession combined with an OPEC price cut driving down oil revenue, soon made it difficult for White to keep from breaking at least one of his two campaign promises. By March 1983, the Texas budget surplus had decreased by 45 percent and it became clear that the pay raise would be impossible without raising additional revenue. The new governor called for higher taxes on luxuries: he wanted to double taxes on beer, liquor, and video games. White also called for a five cent increase on a gallon of gasoline and in the cigarette tax.

Any increase in taxes, regardless of the source, was unpopular with the Texas Legislature. Two influential members of that body, newly elected House Speaker Gib Lewis and Ways and Means Committee Chairman Stan Schlueter, were adamantly opposed to raising taxes to fund an across-the-board teacher pay raise. Without their support, no revenue bill would make it to the floor of the house, and both men argued that many Texas teachers simply did not deserve a raise.

As it became clear that his plan would not survive the legislative session, White sought other ways to keep from losing the support of the powerful teachers' unions. In a compromise with Lewis, and at the urging of other powerful house members, the governor finally called for the legislature to approve a gubernatorially appointed panel to study the teacher salary issue. Certain that the findings of such a panel would justify his tax plan, White promised to call a special legislative session as soon as the group produced a report on the needs of teachers, and proposed an August deadline for the report.[8]

Such a strategy, while politically expedient, held several potential pitfalls. A panel loaded with teacher representatives and members of the education community would lack credibility, and the appointment of outsiders who might reflect the legislature's view on new taxes could result in failure to achieve the results White wanted. However, the governor needed the support of big business to pass the tax increases on which his teacher pay increases depended.

As the governor considered the makeup of his panel, the legislature was busy dashing all hopes of passage of teacher pay raises during the regular session. At the end of May, the Texas house adopted a $30.8 billion spending package that failed to include a provision for teacher pay increases. That same day, the last of the regular session, the house also passed Concurrent Resolution 275, creating the Select Committee on Public Education (SCOPE) in response to White's call for such a panel. The committee approved by the legislature differed from the one the

---

8. Richard Dunham, "Perot Holds Key to Teacher Pay Raises," *Dallas Times Herald*, 11 July 1983.

governor envisioned, in both composition and mandate. White had requested a commission that he would appoint to study teacher pay. The legislature created a twenty-two-member group to which the governor could only make five appointments. The remaining seats were filled by appointments made by the house and senate leadership and three members of the State Board of Education. Instead of concentrating on teacher salaries, the enabling resolution directed SCOPE to ". . . study the issues and continuing concerns related to public education in Texas."[9] This was a much broader mandate than requested by the governor. The legislature made clear its intent to evaluate the entire public education system before considering new taxes.

On June 16, 1983, White called a press conference in his office to announce the membership of the select committee and his appointment of Dallas businessman H. Ross Perot as its chair.[10] From the governor's perspective, this appointment had several advantages. Perot had a reputation of being anti-union, would likely draw the needed support of the business community, and would lend credibility to the committee that someone from within the education establishment could not. That Perot had been a staunch supporter of White's 1982 Republican gubernatorial opponent would head off the appearance of this being a political appointment.

The membership of the committee included the legislators and several prominent citizens, but there were no teachers. White explained the absence of working educators by saying that there was not enough flexibility to allow appointment of teachers from a variety of disciplines. He emphasized, however, that teachers would be called upon to advise the group as it carried out its evaluation.

While "blue-ribbon" panels often include prominent members only to enhance credibility, Ross Perot made it clear from the beginning that he intended to be an active participant in SCOPE's activities. He told members he wanted the select committee to do more than simply "rubber stamp" the governor's pay raises, and expected to draft legislation that would improve public education in Texas. He also took his role as chair seriously, using it to influence the direction of the committee, often providing members with agendas only the day before meetings were scheduled.[11] Perot also chose to hold SCOPE meetings in Dallas hotels rather than state office buildings, complete with catered meals provided at his expense.

Meals were not the only items Ross Perot paid for. He also commis-

---

9. Select Committee on Public Education (SCOPE), *The Recommendations of the Select Committee on Public Education.* 19 April 1984.
10. John C. Henry, "Perot to Lead Education Committee." *Austin American Statesman*, 16 June 1983, p. B1.
11. Thomas Toch, *In The Name of Excellence: The Struggle to Reform the Nation's Schools, Why It's Failing and What Should Be Done* (New York: Oxford University Press, 1991).

sioned a Dallas consulting firm to design a teacher career ladder and financed an opinion survey of Texas teachers. He brought in, on his private aircraft, education experts from across the country to provide insight. Michael Kirst, John Goodlad, and Mortimer Adler, who were involved in the national education debate, advised Perot on the direction his committee should take. Sally Walters, Perot's secretary at Electronic Data Systems, was reassigned to handle committee business, and Perot's personal attorney Thomas W. Luce took a seven month leave of absence from the law firm he had founded to coordinate the work of SCOPE's staff. The state had budgeted $68,500 to cover the committee's expenses: Perot spent an estimated $2 million of his own money on this effort.[12]

In addition to financing much of the committee's work, Perot was instrumental in keeping the public involved. His wealth and previous notoriety assured him access to the media, and he took advantage of many opportunities to expound upon SCOPE's efforts. It is also likely that his position as an outsider on the committee provided the added credibility that White had anticipated. While many of the other SCOPE members were also prominent in state politics and the media, Perot's position as chair blurred the distinction between committee business and his personal actions. His ability to make news simply by being Ross Perot afforded him the opportunity to publicize the education reform cause whenever he desired.

In August 1983, Perot and the committee hit the road. In two weeks, as many as fifty members and staff traveled around Texas, holding hearings in school cafeterias and gymnasiums or talking informally to school officials. Each stop generated considerable publicity and focused attention on the schools in each community on the tour. The committee apparently heard similar concerns from teachers and administrators at each school they visited. The emerging themes of these meetings—lack of professional opportunities for teachers, underfunding of school systems, and the need to reach students at an earlier age—made up much of the framework for the committee's efforts. Perot also found justification for his belief that extracurricular activities were taking too much time away from academics during the school day.

Ross Perot became quite critical of the existing public education system, and no one was immune from his attacks. He was particularly hard on athletic programs, pointing out extravagances like Astroturf in football stadiums, electric cleat cleaners and towel warmers, football teams employing up to twelve coaches, and indoor field houses.[13] These were, to him, very visible examples of misplaced priorities. In fact, Perot's characterization of the standards established by the University Interscholastic

---

12. Thomas Toch, *In The Name of Excellence: The Struggle to Reform the Nation's Schools, Why It's Failing and What Should Be Done.*
13. H. Ross Perot, "Academics and Athletics: There is Room Enough for Both," *Dallas Times Herald*, 23 October 1983.

League (UIL), the body headed by school superintendents that sponsored statewide competitions, as a "bad joke on the children of Texas," caused almost immediate action. The UIL proposed sweeping changes in its regulations, including a reduction in the amount of practice time for teams, a ban on "red shirting" seventh graders to gain an extra year of eligibility (and also resulting in the student repeating a grade), and a revision of the rules that required only a "D" average and the passing of only three of six classes for a student to remain eligible for participation in UIL sanctioned competition.[14]

Programs other than athletics also felt Perot's wrath. He questioned the necessity of programs in hardware sales, poultry production, and feedlot employment, and asked why 600 of Texas's 1,071 school districts spent all of their locally generated funding on extracurricular activities. He also repeatedly told the story of an agriculture student who missed thirty-five days of the 1982–83 school year taking a pet chicken to livestock shows across the state. Although originally accused of exaggerating or exploiting an atypical example, Perot was vindicated when a Houston newspaper, checking the veracity of his story, found that no students interviewed at the Houston Fat Stock Show had missed fewer than twenty days of school; one student had actually missed forty-two days.[15]

Perot's business background was evident as he addressed issues of budgets and accountability. Although education spending had increased from $1.7 billion in 1973 to $8.3 billion in 1983, Perot suggested that there was no evidence to indicate improved student achievement during the same period. He charged that the education establishment could not even provide an accurate accounting of how those funds were being spent. Frequently asking "Who's in charge here?," he provided his own answer. Perot charged that the only system of accountability in Texas education was in coaches' win-loss records, saying that a losing coach would either be "fired or be made principal." He characterized school administrators as members of a "good-old-boy network of old coaches standing around holding hands and humming status quo. . . . They're a great bunch of guys, but their priorities are in letting kids play, not in making them learn."[16] Perot also charged that the way Texas trained teachers was in trouble. He noted that the education school at the University of Texas at Austin employed a 231 member staff, but only turned out 500 new teachers annually, saying that "If they were paving roads instead of educating teachers, they would be arrested for fraud and sent to prison."[17]

14. Thomas Toch, *In The Name of Excellence: The Struggle to Reform the Nation's Schools, Why It's Failing and What Should Be Done*.
15. Thomas Toch, *In The Name of Excellence: The Struggle to Reform the Nation's Schools, Why It's Failing and What Should Be Done*.
16. Paul Taylor, "Perot Electrifies State of Education," *The Washington Post*, 31 May 1984, p. 16.
17. Richard Dunham, "Perot Produces Sharp 'Readin', Ritin' Rhetoric," *Dallas Times Herald*, 3 October 1983.

Perot called for change, but the changes the select committee considered were hardly what Governor White had in mind. Rather than endorse teacher pay raises, SCOPE issued 140 other recommendations for reform of public education in Texas. One of the most controversial changes became known as "no pass, no play." A passing grade would increase from 60 to 70, and students with a grade below that level would be prevented from participating in extracurricular activities. Other recommendations addressed student attendance and performance. Students who missed more than five class meetings in a single semester would not receive credit for that term. No students would be exempt from final examinations, regardless of performance or attendance during the semester. Interscholastic competition at the junior high school level would be eliminated. Local school systems would be required to provide annual performance reports to the state board and the public, and accreditation standards would be tightened, with state funding cut off to school systems that failed to meet them. Students would be required to take standardized tests every year. All principals would be placed on annual contracts and given an opportunity to participate in the hiring of teachers in their schools. The textbook selection cycle would be reduced from eight to six years.

The school year was to be extended from 175 to 185 days with two additional hours in each school day. School buildings would open at 8:00 a.m. and not close until 6:00 p.m., to provide a haven for "latchkey" children. Pre-kindergarten programs would be provided for all four-year-olds, and five-year-olds would attend full-day kindergarten. The recommendations also limited class size in grades one through four to fifteen students. Scholarships and loans would be provided to promising college students who agreed to become teachers, and a "career ladder" would be established in every school system as a method of merit promotion of teachers. A "peer review" evaluation process would decide the placement of teachers on the ladder. Salaries for new teachers would increase from $11,110 to $15,200, but the across-the-board raises that began this process did not emerge in the recommendations. Instead, the career ladder would tie pay raises to performance, and every teacher would pass a literacy test or be barred from the profession. Finally, the elected, twenty-seven member state board of education was to be replaced by a nine-member panel appointed by the governor to staggered six-year terms.[18]

A Texas Research League study had recently reported that only 45 percent of every education dollar was spent on core academic programs, while nineteen cents were going toward vocational education.[19] The state's portion of this funding had increased from $80 million to more

---

18. SCOPE Recommendations.
19. Texas Research League, *Benchmarks: 1993–94 School District Budgets in Texas* (Austin, TX: Texas Research League, 1984).

than $240 million between 1974 and 1984. Perot had already expressed his displeasure with such programs, and the committee used this report to justify elimination of the state's subsidy of vocational classes. The final SCOPE report would insist that any vocational program with fewer than twenty students be discontinued.[20]

After some adjustments to reduce initial costs of the plan, the Select Committee on Public Education released its final report on April 19, 1984. When Perot addressed a news conference in Dallas that day, he was joined by the state's entire elected leadership. This was seen as a significant endorsement of the most comprehensive plan for education reform Texas had ever seen. Although it was far from what he had asked for when the select committee was formed, Governor Mark White expressed enthusiastic support from the plan. His staff quickly developed a plan to fund the recommendations. The new tax package called for $4.89 million in new revenue over the next three years.

THE TEXAS LEGISLATURE

Although they were members of the select committee, neither the house nor senate education committee chairs had supported the majority of the SCOPE reforms. William Haley, house Public Education Committee chair, was a former history teacher who still had the interest of teachers at heart. His counterpart in the senate, Carl Parker, was a longtime supporter of labor concerns. Both men expected to have an opportunity now to deal with the SCOPE recommendations and the governor's tax package in a venue where they held considerable power. However, William Hobby, who as lieutenant governor presided over the senate, and house speaker Gib Lewis had also been members of the select committee. Members of Hobby's staff were instrumental in drafting the SCOPE recommendations into proposed legislation, and Lewis was responsible, in a large part, for the creation of the committee. Both men had expressed support for the final report and had an interest in the fate of the proposals in the legislature. Neither would stand by quietly while their respective education committees disassembled the reform plan.

Hobby was concerned that the education committee in the senate would oppose many of the key SCOPE recommendations. To counter this resistance and reduce Carl Parker's influence, Hobby took advantage of his constitutional authority to make committee and bill assignments. As soon as the bill was introduced, he called the thirty-one-member senate into session as a committee of the whole and assigned each member to one of four subcommittees. Parker was given the chairmanship of a subcommittee on the teaching profession, leaving him with only one-

---

20. SCOPE Recommendations.

fourth of the jurisdiction he would have had otherwise and with little input on the more important aspects of the bill.[21]

Hobby then took an active role in lobbying for the SCOPE plan. He personally testified in senate hearings and promoted the bill with Speaker Lewis in a televised advertising campaign. These commercials aired as a part of a $300,000 media promotion financed by Governor White. Hobby also met privately with a number of senators, seeking their support for the measure. He was apparently successful: the senate passed the SCOPE bill by a vote of twenty-two to nine on June 23, 1984.

In the house, the progress was not as smooth. Lewis referred the proposed legislation to the Public Education Committee, chaired by Haley. Vice-chair Ernestine Glossbrenner was a member of the Texas State Teachers Association (TSTA), the Texas affiliate of the National Education Association. The TSTA took credit for her election as well as those of several other committee members.[22] Thus, the committee was more sympathetic to the views of affluent suburban school districts, which opposed provisions for aid to poorer districts, and the views of teachers who were only interested in across-the-board raises.

The house committee delayed the legislation for almost two weeks before finally meeting on June 17 to mark up what was now known as House Bill 72. By the end of the fifteen-hour meeting, most of the important SCOPE recommendations had been eliminated from the bill. The teacher testing provision and mandatory preschool for four-year-olds were removed. The teacher career ladder became insignificant, and the plan to change the state board from an elected to appointed membership had disappeared. Texas newspapers called this the "Father's Day Massacre."

Gib Lewis, fearing the demise of most of the reforms he favored, called Haley to his office on the following morning and reportedly suggested that he would lose his committee chairmanship if House Bill 72 came to the full house floor in that form.[23] Haley apparently got the message. Saying that he did not agree with many of the changes made by his committee, he introduced a substitute bill that same day.[24] After some debate and compromises over issues of state aid formulas and the state school board, the SCOPE bill passed earlier by the senate was incorporated into House Bill 72 and introduced on the house floor that afternoon. It passed on June 23 by a vote of 119 to 29.[25]

Ross Perot realized that the supporting tax bill was as important as

---

21. Thomas Toch, *In The Name of Excellence: The Struggle to Reform the Nation's Schools, Why It's Failing and What Should Be Done.*
22. Thomas Toch, *In the Name of Excellence: The Struggle to Reform the Nation's Schools, Why It's Failing and What Should Be Done.*
23. Ibid.
24. Audio tape of floor debate, Texas House of Representatives, June 23, 1984.
25. Texas House Journal, 23 June 1984.

the legislation containing the SCOPE reforms. Without new taxes, there would be no money to implement the changes. He also knew that, with the corporate support he had generated before the special session, he could apply pressure to legislators whose support faltered.

SCOPE supporters gained leverage with more than just the education community by proposing an increase in gasoline and other transportation-related taxes to fund the reforms. Texas law requires that 25 percent of the state gasoline tax be spent on public schools. The remainder of the proposed increase included a $1.4 billion commitment to new highway construction. This tactic brought the state's highway lobby, the Good Roads and Transportation Association, into the debate on the SCOPE side. Truckers' groups, paving contractors, highway engineers, and other transportation-related groups were also interested. If the tax bill passed, they stood to gain money and jobs, and if SCOPE's reforms failed, they were sure that Perot would be able to kill the accompanying revenue measure. Thus, they supported both bills.

The tax bill passed on July 3, the last day of the special session. The first tax increase in Texas in thirteen years boosted levies on car rentals, gasoline, tobacco, hotel rooms, license plates, malt liquor, commercial franchises, and tractor-trailer rigs. New taxes were levied on computer software, newspaper subscriptions, cable television, dry cleaning, massage parlors and escort services, non-farm use of fertilizer, and automobile parking and storage. The combined increases and new taxes were projected to raise $4.7 billion in new funds between 1985 and 1987.[26]

With House Bill 72 and its funding in place, Perot and the supporters of SCOPE's proposals could declare victory. The final legislation passed in June was very similar to the preliminary report issued by the committee in April. Almost all of the committee's recommendations survived. Extracurricular activities were to occur before or after school. The passing grade was raised from 60 to 70, and promotion of students with an average below 70 to a higher grade was prohibited. The one-time teacher test was included, with a March 1986 deadline for its implementation. No pass, no play survived, as did the provision requiring no credit be given to students who missed a class more than five times without a valid excuse.

The bill also limited first- and second-grade classes to twenty-two students by 1985, to be followed by third and fourth grades by 1988. Mandated standardized tests in reading, writing, and math were included for grades one, three, five, seven, and nine, and language and math skills tests for grade twelve. Eleventh graders would be expected to pass a basic skills test before they could graduate. School systems would be more accountable for outcomes, with mandatory performance reports presented to the state board each year.

---

26. Thomas Toch, *In The Name of Excellence: The Struggle to Reform the Nation's Schools, Why It's Failing and What Should Be Done.*

Education Reform in Texas 225

The one area that suffered the least under the new plan was vocational education. The legislature required minimum enrollment limits for vocational education classes, but rejected most of the other SCOPE recommendations. Legislators did not limit state subsidies to vocational education, but provided for a 45 percent increase in state dollars for every student enrolled in such classes. In affirmation of the influence of the vocational educators' lobby, they were also given eleven- and twelve-month contracts as well as double the planning time of other teachers during the school day.

While Ross Perot and the Select Committee on Public Education saw the majority of their recommendations become reality in the 266-page bill, Governor Mark White and the Texas teachers' unions were not as pleased with the outcome. Not only did the teacher test pass, so did a four-rung career ladder and a statewide teacher-evaluation program. And while the bill, projecting a need for 14,000 new teachers by the year 2000, increased starting salaries from $11,000 to $15,000 a year, there were no across-the-board pay raises.

Although it was far from what he had intended, the governor had little choice but to support the recommendations of his select committee and sign the reforms sent to him by the legislature. He had appointed the committee chair and promised to act on education reform when a bill came to his desk. He did not get the teacher pay raises he promised in the beginning and he did not get through his term without raising taxes. He did end up with some credit for the major overhaul of Texas's public education system. Although it was perhaps a historic achievement, education reform was not what his supporters had signed on for. When the governor's term expired, Texas teachers remembered his promises. Without their support, and facing economic conditions far worse than when his term began (a condition he and Perot had hoped education reform would help to avoid), Mark White failed to win reelection. William P. Clements became the new governor of Texas.

EQUITY IN EDUCATION

The greatest impact of Select Committee On Public Education was in structural changes in the way Texas's public schools operated; however, House Bill 72 also provided for an increase in state financial aid to poorer school districts. Several hundred million dollars were included in the bill to go to these districts in an effort to equalize funding to the state's schools, but critics of the plan claimed that the changes in the state funding formula were not extensive enough.

In May 1984, several school districts had gone to court to have the Texas public school finance system declared in violation of the state constitution. The argument again centered around the differences between the funding of the richest and poorest school districts. At the time, taxable property values per student ranged from $25,000 to $10 million. The consequence of this was that per-student expenditures ranged from approximately $1,600 to more than $10,000 across Texas's school districts.[27] This meant that students had very different opportunities for a public education depending upon which district they happened to live in. Even though House Bill 72 sought to adjust the inequities, low-property-wealth districts opted to continue the suit, saying that the finance system was still "intolerably illegal."[28] After a trial that ended in 1987, the district court ruled that the existing system was in fact unconstitutional, because it discriminated against the state's poorest school districts. The judge commented that these were often the districts charged with educating children with the greatest need. He ordered the state to stop funding its schools until the violations were corrected. A court of appeals reversed the ruling, but the Texas Supreme Court reversed that judgement, saying that the school finance system was not "efficient" as required by article VII, section 1 of the Texas Constitution (Edgewood I, 777 S.W.2d). This, in effect, upheld the original order for the legislature to correct the funding inequities between the richest and poorest districts.

Senate Bill 1 was passed in the summer of 1990 to correct the inequities in funding. It increased the amount of state aid going to poor districts without a similar increase to the wealthy districts. The actual amount of state funding depended upon the taxable property wealth in a particular district. Although the new appropriation totaled $528 million new state dollars in fiscal year 1990–91, the school districts went back to court, charging that the legislature had really done little to change the structure of the finance system. The Texas Supreme Court agreed, again ruling the system unconstitutional.[29] Writing for a unanimous court, Chief Justice Tom Phillips argued that the new law still left property-rich districts with considerably more money than poorer districts, and ordered the district court to reinstate its original order to stop funding the schools until the system was fixed.

After considerable discussion, the legislature passed Senate Bill 351 on April 11, 1992, just four days before the court-imposed deadline. This new bill was a major change in the way local property wealth was used to calculate the local obligation for school funding. It created 188 county education districts (CEDs) to handle taxing responsibilities. The boundaries of most of the these districts were drawn along county lines, but high-property-wealth counties were matched with less-well-off counties within the education districts. All the local school districts within a

27. State Comptroller, "School Doors Open to Major Changes," *Fiscal Notes*, October (Austin, TX: Office of the State Comptroller, 1984).
28. "Key Dates in Texas School Finance Case," *Dallas Morning News*, 31 January 1985, p. 5a.
29. Edgewood Independent School District v. Kirby, 804 S.W.2d 491, 496 Tex. 1991.

county education district would then depend on the same property wealth, taxed at the same rate, to generate local school funds. The idea was to reduce the funding gap between the wealthiest and poorest school districts in an effort to satisfy the court's equity argument.

Four days after the Texas Legislature passed Senate Bill 351, State District Judge Scott McCown decided that the new school finance plan would stand as constitutional unless challenged. Almost within the hour, several school districts and individuals announced that they would appeal the judge's ruling and fight the new finance plan. The challenge came from both wealthy and poor school districts, both of which argued that the plan was still not constitutional.

The Texas Supreme Court once again got involved. The court sustained the challenges of two plaintiffs, agreeing that Senate Bill 351 indeed violated the Texas Constitution because it created a state ad valorem tax, forbidden in article VIII, section 1-e. The justices also ruled that it created an ad valorem tax without the benefit of an election, in violation of article VII, section 3.[30] The Supreme Court once again directed McCown's district court to reissue its injunction, with another extended date to give the legislature time to act.

The legislature's initial response to this blow was to change tactics: if they could not fix the school finance system to fit the constitution, they would change the constitution to fit the finance system. Legislators first proposed a constitutional amendment that would have required high-property-wealth school districts to give up some of their property taxes. After a bitter battle in the house, Republican members were able to reach enough of an agreement to kill the plan. When they could not pass that constitutional amendment within the legislature, lawmakers next took their problem to the people. They asked voters to approve a new amendment that would authorize the legislature to create county education districts, which had the limited power to set, collect, and distribute ad valorem taxes. The voters summarily defeated the plan in a referendum election, and the legislature was once again forced to deal with the issue from within the existing constitutional constraints. Nearly 63 percent of the voters were opposed to the plan. This sent the issue back to the capitol one more time, and after considerable discussion and debate, legislators came up with Senate Bill 7 just under the June 1, 1993 deadline imposed by the Supreme Court.

Senate Bill 7 is the most recent legislation in a series of attempts to satisfy the Supreme Court, and possibly equalize public school funding in the process. This bill is similar to most of the previous attempts to revise the system in that it maintains the two-tiered structure known as the Foundation School Program. The first tier is designed to "guarantee

---

30. Carrollton-Farmers Branch Independent School District v. Edgewood Ind. Sch. Dist., 826 W.W.2d 489, 524 Tex. 1992.

sufficient financing for all school districts to provide a basic program of education that meets accreditation and other legal standards."[31] This means that for every student, a district is entitled to a basic allotment set by the legislature. The amount varies with the actual cost of running the schools. To actually receive the allotment, a school district must raise its local share of funding through local ad valorem taxes within a range of rates established by the legislature. When a district cannot raise the allotment from its own taxes at the required rate, the state will make up the difference.

The second tier sets up a system that is supposed to provide each district with the ability to "supplement the basic program at a level of its own choice."[32] The state guarantees that a district will receive a certain amount per student for every additional penny of tax effort above the tier 1 minimum it sets. When the district's additional tax effort does not reach that guarantee, the state will make up the difference.

This two-level approach is not significantly different from many of the funding schemes in place since the first state-level funding effort passed in the 1940s. Senate Bill 7 is different, however, in that the legislature capped a school district's taxable property at a level of $280,000 per student. This effectively prevents any school district from raising any more than a maximum amount based on its tax rate and a property wealth of no more than the $280,000 limit.

There are certainly school districts in Texas that enjoy property wealth well above this limit. Under SB 7 they are no longer able to take advantage of this additional wealth to supplement the foundation funding for their schools. This legislation requires that any district whose property wealth is greater than the limit must do something to bring the values down to within the cap. The legislature offered several options from which a school district could choose to meet the requirement. A wealthy school district could elect to consolidate with another school district, or it could actually "detach" or remove territory from the taxable property valuation process. A district could also contract with the state to provide funding for students outside the district, or consolidate its tax base with another school district. If a school district fails to choose one of the options provided by the legislature by a certain deadline, the commissioner of education is required to solve the problem for them, by detaching property from the tax roles of the wealthy district and annexing it to another school district. If that still does not reduce a district's property wealth below the cap, the commissioner is required to consolidate that district with one or more others. The purpose of the cap and the shifting of property wealth (on paper, if not in reality) is to reduce the spread between the per-student spending of the wealthiest and poorest school districts.

31. Texas Education Code 16.002(b).
32. Texas Education Code 16.301.5.

Senate Bill 7, like all of its predecessors, faced a challenge in the courts. Several school districts, wealthy and poor, fought this bill on similar constitutional grounds. In January 1995, the Texas Supreme Court ruled that the method of funding Texas's public schools established under Senate Bill 7 is constitutional: but that is about as far as the court would go. Justice Cornyn, writing for the majority, suggested that the only thing good about the law was that it just barely met the equity requirements in the constitution. He was careful to point out that the court still believed that the legislature has a long way to go toward developing a truly comprehensive change in the way the state funds its public schools.

Education Reform Ten Years Later

A decade after the first major effort toward education reform in Texas began, it is not clear exactly what the changes have accomplished. The intent of House Bill 72 was to improve the quality of education in Texas through a series of policy changes, but the outcomes are mixed. The state mandated reforms were implemented to different degrees across school districts, the teacher career ladder was never fully funded, the teacher competency test was given only once, and the teacher evaluation process seems to indicate that all Texas teachers are "above average." Student scores on standardized tests are higher than they were prior to the SCOPE reforms, but the tests have changed a couple of times and the scores are still lower than those of students in many other states. The no pass, no play provision seems to have been effective for some students, but there is evidence suggesting that it has not helped retain some of those at the greatest risk of dropping out of school.

Senate Bill 7 was the last in a series of legislations ostensibly designed to reform the way the state funds public education. The more immediate goal, however, was to simply satisfy the Supreme Court and keep the schools open. The new formulas narrow the gap between the amount of money wealthy and poorer school districts can spend per student, but they do little else in the way of reform. There are still more than 1,000 independent school districts in Texas, each of which relies heavily on its local tax base. The Supreme Court was careful to note that the plaintiffs failed in their assault on this final bill only because they were unable to present enough evidence that the state had failed to adequately provide facilities. It is clear from the language of the decision that the justices were not satisfied with the solution. It also seems likely that Senate Bill 7 is not the final stop on the road to public education finance reform.

Regardless of the substantive outcomes of the reform efforts undertaken during the last decade, the way Texans look at public education has changed forever. Prior to the early 1980s, education was not a priority. The state felt some responsibility under the constitution, and under finance laws passed much earlier, to provide funding for public education, but its involvement ended there. There was little interest in making major changes in the way public schools operated. By 1983, pressure from a variety of directions caused policymakers to look more closely at the problems and issues related to public education in Texas. Quality became an issue at the national level as it became apparent that standardized test scores and other achievement indicators were lagging behind those of other nations. State officials soon began to realize that scores in Texas were lagging even further behind the national scores. At the same time, economic conditions were changing within the state. No longer could the economy be expected to thrive simply because of the wealth of natural resources in Texas. It was becoming clear that Texas soon would have to compete for jobs by offering an educated workforce and quality schools, and funding those schools was becoming an issue at the same time. Foundation funding formulas had come under attack in other states, and although the U.S. Supreme Court had not ruled on the Texas system, it had implied that a state-level suit had merit. Policymakers and political leaders began to realize that change was necessary, and education reform suddenly became a priority.

For the first time, education became a major issue to the Texas public and the state legislature. Never before had so much pressure been applied from so many points on the political spectrum to force such sweeping change in public policy in Texas. Just as this pressure for change brought much more attention to public education in the state, it also altered the way education policy is made in Texas. Prior to the beginning of the decade, when members of the education community needed something from the Texas Legislature, they went to the appropriate committee, explained their situation, and often saw the results they wanted with little debate. The reforms that came in the 1980s did not originate within the education community, nor did they involve much input from educators. There were no teachers on the Select Committee for Public Education from which House Bill 72 originated, nor were educators directly involved once the school finance issue went to the courts. Legislators, judges, and a billionaire businessman from Dallas were the ones deciding what would happen to, and in, Texas's public schools.

What Next? or A Reformer's Work Is Never Done

By 1995, Ross Perot had moved on to other problems and projects, but the legislators and judges were still involved. Many of the reforms recommended by the select committee and implemented by House Bill 72 were still in place. The state had considerable control over curriculum, textbooks, accountability measures, administrative decisions, and education spending.

As the reform movement enters its second decade, the public education system in Texas remains a major topic of discussion among politicians and policymakers. Although the state Supreme Court has a major role, along with the legislature, in deciding where local districts get their money and how they spend it, there is again growing dissatisfaction with the quality of education in the state. The improvements from the efforts to centralize control at the state level have not been as great as expected, and many now argue that state control is part of the problem.

At the end of May 1995, at a middle school in eastern Texas, Republican Governor George Bush signed into law the latest education reform package developed by the legislature. The new legislation returns a great deal of power to local communities and reverses the ten-year trend of state control of public education. It allows local voters to adopt home-rule charters and free their school districts from many state requirements, including class-size caps at lower grades, and will allow them to create local campus programs that do not fall under strict state scrutiny.

The new law also allows students in low-performing schools to transfer to other schools in their district or nearby using tuition grants issued by the state. Although this falls short of the school voucher system popular in some other states, it introduces an element of competition into public education that supporters believe will be an incentive for lower quality schools to improve as they fear losing students to better schools.

Other changes include an increase in the minimum salary scale for teachers and more provisions for dealing with disciplinary problems. The most visible change in this round of reforms affects the same plan that received the most attention in 1984. The 1995 reform package takes much of the bite out of the controversial no pass, no play rule. The suspension period for failing students is cut from six to three weeks, and the original ban on participation in practices has been lifted.

This change is as symbolic as it is substantive. No pass, no play was the most visible and most controversial reform in the package that Ross Perot and the Select Committee On Public Education presented to the Texas Legislature in 1984. It headed the list of changes that signaled the beginning of a decade of strict state control over public education. The relaxation of the suspension period is another signal: this time it heralds the relaxation of state involvement in local decisions about what should happen in public schools.

WHAT DOES THIS MEAN?

The effects of the 1995 reforms, like those of the 1980s, can only be measured over time. It is impossible to judge now whether these changes will be the salvation of public education in Texas or will have unintended effects that will prompt new calls for reform in a few years, or even months. It is possible, however, to draw at least one conclusion.

It is unlikely that conditions will ever return to the way they were prior to 1984. The latest round of reforms may result in a continuing trend toward decentralization and greater local control of public schools.

Alternatively, dissatisfaction after a few years could trigger a new effort toward state control. Although the Supreme Court's ruling on Senate Bill 7 upheld the most recent variation of state funding formulas, the opinion also made it clear that the equity issue is far from settled. Ad valorem taxes are becoming less popular as a method of financing education, and there is little to suggest that anyone is completely satisfied with the most recent solution, so more changes are likely in this area. The one sure thing is that public education in Texas is changed forever. Gone are the days when public education policy was hammered out by the education committees in the legislature with little input from anyone but members of the education establishment. Regardless of the outcomes of the latest reforms, there will be more and they will evolve under much greater scrutiny than those that began the first round of change. Public education in Texas is now a significant public policy area and will continue to receive a great deal of attention.

14
Welfare Reform and the New Paternalism in Texas

EDWARD J. HARPHAM
UNIVERSITY OF TEXAS AT DALLAS

Public policy is often complex, and few public policy issues are as complex as public welfare. The issues of welfare reform in Texas are tied to the national debate over welfare reform. In addition, changes in Texas are governed in large part not by decisions of Texas policymakers, but rather by decisions of national policymakers.

In addition to problems in welfare policy involving complex problems of the relationship between states and the national government, there are difficult empirical and normative questions that are raised by public welfare. Among the key questions are whether and the extent to which society has an obligation to provide support to those unable to support themselves. To what extent is poverty an economic condition that can be redressed with money, and to what extent is poverty a "culture" that requires the development of a different work ethic among the poor? To what extent does the receipt of welfare benefits allow the state to control or retrain the poor toward more productive values? Is welfare a right?

Not only is there dispute over these questions, but the issue of welfare reform raises crucial questions about the role of government. In Texas, conservatives have tended to argue that the "welfare state," begun in the Roosevelt administration and dramatically extended during Lyndon Johnson's "Great Society," was a well-intentioned effort to eliminate poverty. They argue that its unanticipated consequence was to create a culture of poverty by destroying individual responsibility, the family, and by creating a class in society dependent on the government. Liberals have countered with the argument that poverty is less than it would have been without the welfare state. Both sides, however, are agreed that even with the New Deal and the Great Society, levels of poverty in Texas and the nation remain very high. Most liberals and conservatives also recognize that welfare policies need some reforms, if only because they believe that welfare has been destructive to the family unit.

In recent years, conservatives have been the dominant voice in welfare policy, and policies are being developed to reduce welfare dependency by breaking what is seen as the "culture" of poverty. Conservatives have distrusted government to the point that they have often suggested that gov-

ernment does not solve problems, it is the problem. However, these conservatives are turning to solutions that give government a far more intrusive role in the lives of poor people, in the belief that such an effort can solve the problem of the culture of poverty. Conservatives are requiring welfare policies that include compulsory work programs, limits on the numbers of children that women on welfare may have, and punitive measures aimed primarily at the fathers of children on welfare.

This chapter explores the welfare policies in Texas and details how the debate over welfare has affected policymaking in the state.

During the 1994 gubernatorial race, welfare reform seemed to come from nowhere to become a defining issue in the campaign. Republican candidate George Bush, Jr., accused Governor Ann Richards of allowing welfare rolls to swell to unprecedented rates. One Bush television commercial held Governor Richards responsible for the fact that welfare spending was up 142 percent and welfare rolls had grown by more than 200,000 during her first term in office. Something had to be done, Bush argued, to get people off welfare and back to work. The cycle of poverty perpetuated by a misguided welfare policy had to be broken, and a new ethic of individual responsibility had to be promoted. To this end, the Republican candidate offered a series of reform proposals that would increase job training and work requirements, prosecute deadbeat parents, and impose new limits on benefits.

Responding to the Bush criticisms, Richards declared welfare to be a non-issue. Texas offered such paltry benefits to welfare recipients that reform was largely irrelevant. "Welfare is driven by federal mandates. Reform must involve federal solutions," claimed Richards.[1] While accepting the idea of improving child support provisions in the law, she backed away from offering any other reform proposals at the state level.

Welfare reform was far from being a non-issue. It was a cornerstone to the Bush campaign, and became one of the key issues that dominated the 71st Legislature during its regular session. Joining newly elected Governor Bush in his efforts to reform welfare in Texas were many influential Republicans and Democrats in state government, including two of the leading Democrats in the state, Lieutenant Governor Bob Bullock and Comptroller John Sharp. Together they forged bipartisan legislation that sought a new direction for welfare policy in the state, one that broke with many of the assumptions of the past.

Why did welfare become such a defining issue during the campaign and the legislative session? What is the significance of the reform legislation that was finally put into place? This chapter addresses these questions by putting the recent debate over welfare reform in a larger political

---

1. Quoted in Jonathan Eig, "Bush, Richards Clash over the Need for Welfare Overhaul," *Dallas Morning News*, 29 September 1994, p. 1A.

Welfare Reform and the New Paternalism in Texas 235

context. A new consensus, or as I refer to it, a "new paternalism" has emerged at both the national and state levels over what the welfare problem is and what must be done to address it through public policy. The reform legislation in Texas is part of a larger movement to rethink the goals of welfare policy in the nation, and to move responsibility for the scope and direction of welfare policy away from the federal government and back to the states.

POVERTY AND WELFARE IN TEXAS

Welfare has never been a popular topic in Texas. The "go getter" mythology that has defined the state since its founding has always focused on the winners, not the losers. The heros of popular culture in Texas are wildcatters drilling for oil and risk-taking individuals who build business empires, not single mothers or others on welfare who have difficulty taking care of themselves or those close to them. Small government, low taxes, and a pro-business ethos have been the defining features of Texas's civic culture.

Nevertheless, poverty remains a troubling problem in Texas.[2] In 1996, 3.6 million people or 19 percent of the state's population lived below the official poverty rate as defined by the federal government. Almost 26 percent of those under the age of seventeen are considered to be poor, as are 20.3 percent of those over the age of sixty-five. In comparison, the national poverty rate in 1994 was 14.5 percent. The national poverty rate for children under seventeen was 21.8 percent and for individuals older than sixty-five was 11.7 percent.[3]

Approximately one-third of African-Americans and Hispanics in Texas are poor. In contrast, between 10 percent and 15 percent of Texas whites live below the poverty threshold. These percentages mirror rates for these groups at the national level.

Aggregate statistics only capture part of the story of poverty in Texas.

---

2. Defining poverty is a complicated and controversial affair. In the United States, poverty is defined in terms of an index developed by the Social Security Administration in 1964 and revised by federal interagency committees in 1969 and 1980. The "poverty index" is based on the Department of Agriculture's 1961 Economy Food Plan and takes into account the consumption requirements of families based on their size and composition. It is indexed to the rate of inflation. The poverty index is based solely on monetary income and does not take into account other in-kind benefits that people may receive such as food stamps, Medicaid, or public housing. In 1996, the poverty level for a family of three was set at $12,980 a year. In recent years, there has been growing dissatisfaction on both the right and left that the poverty index fails to capture the nature or extent of poverty in America. Nevertheless, it continues to be the dominant measure used by policymakers for thinking about poverty in America and Texas.

3. Data on poverty and welfare policy are drawn from one of the following sources: Texas Department of Human Services *Annual Reports*; Texas Department of Human Services *DHS at a Glance* (November 1994), Texas Comptroller of Public Accounts *Partnership for Independence* (January 1995); U.S. Bureau of the Census. *Statistical Abstract of the United States 1994*, 114th edition (Washington, DC, 1996); *Texas Almanac 1996–97* (Dallas, TX: Dallas Morning News, 1996).

There is also an important regional component. Over the past thirty years, Texas has become a dynamic urban economy with the accompanying urban problems of unemployment, underemployment, and poverty. In the metroplex region, the counties surrounding the Dallas–Fort Worth area, more than 628,000 people, or 12.6 percent of the population, live in poverty. In the Gulf Coast region around Houston, almost 828,000 people, or 19.1 percent of the population, are poor. Rural poverty is also a major problem. Some of the poorest counties in the nation are located along the Texas-Mexico border. Of the 1.58 million people residing in the southern Texas region around Brownsville, 37.7 percent live in poverty. More than 27.8 percent of the 726,000 people living in the Upper Rio Grand River region around El Paso live in poverty.

The Texas Department of Human Services (TDHS) is the most important state agency concerned with poverty. Along with a number of smaller social service and child support programs, the TDHS administers the major welfare programs sponsored by the state.

Since the New Deal, Aid for Families with Dependent Children (AFDC) has been the principal welfare program serving the poor in Texas. AFDC is a state and federal program that provides temporary assistance to families with low income. Monthly cash grants are provided to families with dependent children in which one or both parents are either absent or disabled. AFDC-UP, a complementary program begun in 1990, provides assistance to families in which both parents are present, but the primary breadwinner is unemployed.

Historically, the federal government has provided funding and minimum guidelines for the operation of state programs. Along with other states, Texas has retained the power to determine eligibility requirements and benefit levels under AFDC subject to the federal guidelines and standards. It has used this power to create one of the most stringent AFDC programs in the country. Eligibility requirements for welfare in Texas are strict. To qualify in 1994, one must have had less than $1,000 in assets, excluding a home and a car with an equity of $1,500. In addition, to qualify initially for minimum benefits in Texas, a single parent with two children can earn no more than $402 per month. In the succeeding year, this family would lose all its benefits if its monthly earnings exceeded $278. Nationwide the monthly income allowed for the first year was $778 and for the second year $529. Benefit levels were also low. In 1994, the typical AFDC family of a single mother with two children received a maximum grant of $188 per month.

Federal reforms passed in 1996 will fundamentally restructure Texas's main welfare program to the poor. For the 1998–99 biennium, AFDC will be replaced by a new federal block grant program entitled Temporary Assistance to Needy Families (TANF). TANF will provide the state with considerably more discretion in the formulation of welfare policy. The longterm effects of these reforms on state welfare policy, however, are not known at this time, although they are the subject of considerable speculation.

Medicaid is a state and federal program that provides medical insurance coverage for the poor. All AFDC recipients are eligible for Medicaid. As with AFDC, Texas determines Medicaid's eligibility criteria as well as the services provided, subject to federal guidelines. A formula (the federal medical assistance percentage, or FMAP) using Texas state per capita income compared to the U.S. average is used to determine the percentage of Medicaid expenses funded by the federal government. For 1994, Texas's FMAP was 64.18 percent.[4] The typical family of three on welfare in Texas received $286 in Medicaid payments per month in 1995.

Food Stamps is a federal program that provides food coupons to families with low income and assets. Households with individuals receiving AFDC or Supplemental Security Income, a national welfare program geared for disabled and elderly poor people, are eligible for food stamps, as are families whose income is below 130 percent of the poverty level. The typical family of three on welfare in Texas received $304 in food stamps in 1995.

Texas ranks near the bottom of the states in providing welfare to poor people. In 1992, Texas ranked forty-eighth in the nation with total per capita welfare expenditures of $420, compared to $614 for the nation as a whole. Only Mississippi and Louisiana, states much poorer than Texas with less-diversified economies, provide lower average AFDC payments than Texas.

The comparatively paltry welfare benefits provided by Texas supply one backdrop to the welfare reform debate that broke out in 1995. These figures alone, however, do not account for the way in which the debate took place or the final form that welfare reform assumed by the summer. To understand these developments, we must consider two other things: first, how a new understanding of the nature of welfare as a problem emerged in the 1980s; second, how this new understanding of poverty gave rise to a new set of policy initiatives meant to change welfare as Texas has known it since the 1930s.

Welfare and the New Paternalism

The origins of the modern welfare state lie in Franklin Roosevelt's New Deal. Prior to the 1930s, welfare was a state and local responsibility.[5] State and local officials were seen to be in the best positions to assess

---

4. The FMAP for other states ranges from 50 percent to 78.85 percent.
5. A notable historical exception to state and local funding of welfare was the Civil War pension system set up by the federal government for Union soldiers and their dependents. Funding and setting benefit level for the pension system were among the most controversial issues shaping national politics in the late nineteenth century. For a discussion of the com-

the needs of the poor in the community and to make sure that programs were run efficiently and fairly. The Great Depression of the early 1930s challenged much of this conventional wisdom. Local and state welfare programs were overwhelmed by demands for assistance. Calls for an expanded federal role in welfare mounted as the nation slipped into the darkest days of the depression in the early 1930s.

Early New Deal programs funneled more than $93 million of direct federal relief into Texas along with $21 million of surplus commodities by April 1935.[6] However, it was the Social Security Act of 1935 that changed forever the role that the federal government would play in welfare policy. In addition to establishing two social insurance programs, the Old Age Insurance (popularly known today as social security) and Unemployment Insurance, the act put into place a series of state and federal public assistance programs. Aid for Dependent Children (ADC, later AFDC for Aid for Families with Dependent Children), Old Age Assistance (OAA), and Aid for the Blind (AB) articulated a new role for the federal government in welfare policy. States continued to determine benefit levels and to administer public assistance programs. However, in exchange for federal financial assistance, they were expected to meet certain minimal federal standards.[7]

The basic strategy assumed by Texas through the mid-1960s in regard to public assistance policy was to appropriate the minimum amount of state dollars to get the maximum amount of federal money available. The expansion of existing programs to new groups of people, such as to the mothers of dependent children in 1950, and the establishment of new programs, such as social service programs in the early 1960s, were due largely to the initiatives of the federal government. Between 1945 and 1965, state AFDC expenditures rose slowly from $1.495 million to $3.899 million, and federal expenditures in the state rose from $1.242 million to $16.594 million.

Welfare policy in Texas underwent a fundamental change in the late 1960s and early 1970s due to a series of federal government initiatives. President Lyndon Johnson administration's "War on Poverty" transformed the way in which many Americans thought about the poverty problem, as well as the role that the federal government would play in

---

plex politics that surrounded Civil War pensions, see Richard Bensel, *Sectionalism and American Political Development 1880–1980* (Madison, WI: University of Wisconsin Press, 1984) and Theda Skocpol, *Protecting Soldiers and Mothers: The Political Origins of Social Policy in the United States* (Cambridge, MA: The Berklap Press of the Harvard University Press, 1992).
6. Edward J. Harpham, "Welfare Reform in Perspective," in Anthony Champagne and Edward J. Harpham, eds., *Texas at the Crossroads: People, Politics, and Policy* (College Station, TX: Texas A&M University Press, 1985).
7. For example, state programs had to operate throughout an entire state, a single agency had to administer the program, and opportunities had to be available for fair hearings and appeals. See Harpham, in Anthony Champagne and Edward J. Harpham, eds., *Texas at the Crossroads: People, Politics, and Policy*, p. 271.

supporting poverty programs. Cash payments to assist the poor no longer were seen to be enough. Something also had to be done to eliminate what many considered to be unfair barriers that trapped the poor. A series of initiatives aimed at rehabilitating the poor through job training programs and social services came to be sponsored by the federal government during the late 1960s.[8]

Other changes at the national level had enormous implications for welfare policy in Texas. In 1965, Congress established Medicaid, a state and federal program that would finance health care for the poor. A series of Supreme Court decisions between 1968 and 1971 affected welfare policy by explicitly forbidding certain practices such as man-in-the house rules or residency requirements that had been used by states to keep people off welfare rolls. Along with other amendments to the Social Security Act passed in 1970s that liberalized the benefit formula for state AFDC programs, the court decisions laid the basis for the enormous expansion of welfare programs in Texas.

Between 1967 and 1973, participation rates and expenditures surged. During this time period, the number of families on AFDC in Texas increased fourfold, from 23,509 to 120,254. The number of children receiving benefits rose from 79,914 in 1967 to 325,244 in 1973. Total state and federal expenditures on AFDC, meanwhile, escalated more than fivefold, from $31 million in 1967 to $163.5 million in 1973. Participation rates declined by 34.3 percent and expenditures by 30 percent from 1974 to 1979, only to begin an upward climb again in the early 1980s.

As the welfare rolls grew and expenditures on AFDC, Medicaid, and Food Stamps escalated in the early 1980s, concerns mounted among conservative Democrats and Republicans in Congress that something was going wrong. Providing assistance to help those in need was recognized as a noble goal. But there was the lingering worry that some recipients would abuse the welfare system, using it as a way to escape work entirely. As early as 1967, Congress began addressing this by passing legislation in the form of the Work Incentive Program (WIN). WIN sought to establish a set of incentives that would encourage people to get off welfare and back to work: welfare recipients who worked would be allowed to keep a greater portion of their paychecks; federal funding of day care for welfare recipients would be increased; and "workfare" provisions would allow states to drop people from AFDC rolls who refused to participate in work or training programs.

For liberals, the WIN program was needlessly harsh, and failed to take into account the economic realities lying behind poverty in America.[9]

---

8. Michael B. Katz, *In the Shadow of the Poorhouse: A Social History of Welfare in America* (New York: Basic Books, 1986); James T. Patterson, *America's Struggle Against Poverty 1900–1980* (Cambridge, MA: Harvard University Press, 1981).
9. James T. Patterson, *America's Struggle Against Poverty 1900–1980*, pp. 174–76.

Moreover, it broke with the assumption that had dominated welfare policy since the New Deal, that the primary purpose of welfare was to assist families with dependent children. The goal of WIN was not simply to assist people, but to get them to act in a particular way. WIN-type provisions were expanded in 1972 when recipient participation in work or training programs was mandated, and in 1974 when increased attention was given to job placement. At best, the WIN-type programs of the late 1960s and early 1970s were only marginally successful. Consequently, by the mid-1970s, WIN funds were frozen, and disillusionment set in that perhaps nothing could be done to solve the problems of America's welfare state.

A political stalemate brought welfare reform to an effective halt in the late 1970s. Conflicting demands on policymakers made it highly unlikely that any substantive reform of the existing welfare system might take place. On the one hand, liberals demanded that job opportunities for the poor be expanded and that benefits not be cut to those who needed them the most. On the other hand, conservatives demanded that reforms not entail increased expenditures. Reform proposals that addressed one set of concerns failed to satisfy others.[10]

As hopes of substantive welfare reform diminished, new ideas about welfare and the problem of poverty began to emerge. Disturbing questions were being raised about welfare in America: Why had the War on Poverty failed? Was it simply a question of inadequate funding or was something more fundamental at stake?[11] In the early 1980s, two popular books were published that argued that the traditional approach to welfare was not only misguided, but morally dangerous. In *Wealth and Poverty*, conservative publicist George Gilder argued that the welfare state was destroying the cultural capital that enabled people to escape poverty and facilitate the production of national wealth.[12] Charles Murray extended this argument in his 1984 book *Losing Ground*, in which he presented a detailed empirical analysis of the effects of the Great Society upon the poor.[13] According to Murray, the well-intentioned social policies of the 1960s had backfired, creating a dysfunctional underclass of people dependent upon welfare. Such policies may have made people, at least temporarily, better off financially, but they robbed people of the character traits and moral values that would enable them to succeed in

---

10. Martin Anderson, *The Political Economy of Welfare Reform in the United States* (Stanford, CA: Hoover Institution, 1978).
11. For a more in-depth discussion of the broader ideological implications of the debate over welfare in the 1980s and 1990s, see Edward J. Harpham, "From Public Welfare to Private Virtue: Shifting Liberal and Conservative Concepts of Social Well-Being," in Lawson Taitte, ed., *Moral Values in Liberalism and Conservatism*. The Andrew R. Cecil Lectures on Moral Values in a Free Society. Volume XVI. With an Introduction by Andrew R. Cecil (Dallas, TX: University of Texas, 1995).
12. George Gilder, *Wealth and Poverty* (New York: Bantam Books, 1981).
13. Charles Murray, *Losing Ground* (New York: Basic Books, 1984).

America's market economy, and destroyed the social taboos that motivated people to get off welfare and back to work.

Illegitimacy rates, in particular, were identified as a particularly insidious problem perpetuated by misguided welfare initiatives. In the years following the War on Poverty, these rates skyrocketed, becoming an increasing proportion of the total number of births in the United States. In 1970, 11 percent of all births were to unmarried women: 6 percent of all births to whites and 38 percent of births to blacks were to unmarried mothers. By 1985, 22 percent of all births and 15 percent of all white births were illegitimate: among blacks, the figure had grown to 60 percent. Such high illegitimacy rates insured that large numbers of individuals would be on welfare for years to come.

Murray's solution to the problem of welfare dependency was in stark contrast to the reform proposals of mainstream liberals and conservatives. Eliminate all welfare programs that fostered dependency, and allow the market to educate the poor as to the value of hard work and discipline. In short, he argued that policymakers must make a fundamental break with the past and develop a set of welfare policies based on a new understanding of government as part of the poverty problem.

Murray's empirical work was subject to scathing criticisms over the next few years. His methods, data, arguments, and conclusions were rejected as being insupportable. His conclusions and proposals were deplored as being unfounded or even morally perverse.[14] Murray's work, however, touched a nerve in the American psyche. The themes of welfare dependency and of the creation and perpetuation of an underclass by misguided public policy resonated throughout the work of both liberal and conservative scholars in the late 1980s and early 1990s. Such themes provided the foundations for what has been dubbed by many commentators as the "new paternalism" in welfare policy.[15]

At the national level, the first clear indication that the deadlock over welfare reform was about to be broken came in 1988, with the passage of the Family Support Act. In an attempt to stem the tide of rising illegitimacy rates and single-parent families among the poor, the act mandated two-parent family coverage for all state AFDC programs. Most of the money from the act, however, was allocated to work programs and support services developed by the states. The centerpiece of the reform was a new workfare program set up to replace WIN, titled JOBS. The program sought to help AFDC families become self-sufficient through a

---

14. See Edward J. Harpham and Richard K. Scotch, "Rethinking the War on Poverty," *Western Political Quarterly* March 1988.
15. See Lawrence Mead, *The New Politics of Poverty: The Nonworking Poor in America* (New York: Basic Books, 1992), William J. Wilson, *The Truly Disadvantaged: The Inner City, the Underclass, and Public Policy* (Chicago, IL: University of Chicago Press, 1987), and David Ellwood, *Poor Support* (New York: Basic Books, 1988).

series of education, training, and employment services, including child care for participating individuals, and transitional child care and Medicaid benefits for those who successfully got off welfare. New standards were drafted demanding that parents receiving welfare participate in these programs or lose their benefits.

Much hyperbole surrounded the passage of the Family Support Act. Some billed it as the most important piece of welfare legislation since the New Deal. Proponents such as Democratic Senator Patrick Moynihan of New York argued that, at last, something was being done to get people off of welfare and back to work. It was hoped that this new way of thinking about the problems of dependency and the underclass would bring welfare under control. The act was an important piece of legislation, and as Lawrence Mead noted, a "leading monument to the new paternalism in social policy."[16] However, there was less to the act than the fanfare implied. In fact, welfare was a much more intractable problem than the act's proponents were willing to concede, at least in their public rhetoric.[17]

After the passage of the Family Assistance Plan, welfare rolls continued to expand unabated at the national level. Between 1990 and 1992, the average number of monthly recipients on AFDC rose from 11.5 million to 13.8 million, and total federal and state expenditures rose from $21.2 billion to $25.0 billion. At the same time, Medicaid payments increased from $72.5 billion to $134.0 billion, and Food Stamp payments increased from $17.7 billion to $25.0 billion.

The explosion in welfare expenditures was even more telling in Texas. From 1984 to 1994, the participation in and cost of AFDC, Medicaid, and Food Stamps increased dramatically. During this time, the average monthly number of AFDC recipients rose from 337,400 to 786,400. Total state and federal expenditures rose from $188.3 million to $544.9 million. During the same period, the average monthly Food Stamp caseload rose from 394,000 families to 993,900 families, and the value of Food Stamps distributed rose from $664.9 million to $2.2 billion.

Long-term economic and demographic pressures played a major role in driving up welfare expenditures. As the population in Texas grew from 14.2 million in 1980 to 17 million in 1990, so did the total number of poor people residing in the state. The 1980s was also a period of technological transformation in the state and the nation. New jobs were being created and old jobs were disappearing, but not to the benefit of those at the bottom of the socio-economic ladder. The wages of higher-skilled labor tied to the emerging high tech economy were up during the 1980s and early 1990s, and the wages of less-skilled labor were down. According to a report released by the comptroller's office in January

---

16. Lawrence Mead, *The New Politics of Poverty: The Nonworking Poor in America*, p. 200.
17. See "Report Faults '88 Welfare Reform," *Dallas Morning News*, 30 March 1992.

1995, the average inflation-adjusted income of the poorest 20 percent of households in Texas fell nearly 15 percent from 1980 to 1990.[18]

Other demographic trends put added pressure on the state welfare programs. For example, the number of female-headed families with children under eighteen, perhaps the most important population targeted for assistance by AFDC, rose by one-third between 1983 and 1993. In addition, the number of never-married women with children under eighteen almost doubled during this period. Paralleling the problem at the national level, illegitimacy had become an issue of major importance.

A spiraling AFDC program was not the most pressing problem facing the state by the mid-1990s: the most expensive program by far had become Medicaid. From 1989 to 1993, the costs of financing health care for the poor escalated at an annual rate of more than 20 percent. During the 1994–95 biennium, $18.6 billion in state and federal funds were spent on Medicaid. Of all state dollars allocated during the biennium, 13 percent, or $6.7 billion, has gone to Medicaid.

Many factors lie behind the rapidly rising costs of financing health care for the poor in Texas. Health-care costs as a whole increased rapidly throughout the late 1980s and into the 1990s. Many Texans lacked health insurance coverage. In 1993, almost 22 percent of the state's population was not covered by health insurance, compared to the national average of 15.3 percent. Texas ranked third in the nation in the total number of Medicaid recipients, 2.1 million people, and federal mandates instituted in the late 1980s expanded the numbers of those who could qualify for Medicaid and the services that were to be provided for them.

The escalating costs of AFDC, Food Stamps, and Medicaid provide the backdrop against which the debate over welfare reform in 1995 took place.

Welfare Reform in 1995

During the 1992 presidential campaign, Bill Clinton argued that, if elected, he would "change welfare as we know it." As governor of Arkansas, Clinton was well acquainted with the problems that state welfare programs faced. He recognized how federal rules and regulations often made it impossible for states to respond creatively to the problems of poverty and welfare. However, during the first term of his administration, comprehensive welfare reform was pushed to the back burner behind Clinton's ill-fated health-care reform proposal.

---

18. See Texas Comptroller of Public Accounts, *Partnership for Independence* (January 1995). This surge of inequality following technological transformation paralleled that found in the nation in the 1980s and early 1990s. See Brian J. L. Berry, Edward J. Harpham, and Euel Elliott, "Long Swings in American Inequality: The Kuznets Conjecture Revisited." *Papers in Regional Science*, vol. 74, no. 1, pp. 1–21.

While comprehensive welfare reform flagged, administrative reform did not. Between 1993 and 1995, the federal government's Department of Health and Human Services encouraged states to engage in welfare reform on their own. States were allowed to establish time-limited pilot projects, usually only involving a portion of the state. These pilot programs had to be cost-neutral to the federal government. By granting states waivers to federal guidelines in the AFDC and Food Stamp programs, the Clinton administration stimulated experimentation across the nation to explore what reforms in welfare policy appeared to work and what didn't.

State reform efforts varied widely. Some states sought to modify AFDC rules restricting outside income to recipients. Others sought to remove some of the barriers that penalized welfare families from staying together or to create jobs for welfare recipients. Still others sought to adjust benefits to welfare recipients in order to influence their behavior. The most controversial reform proposals from various states were those that set term limits or family caps on AFDC benefits. By the end of 1994, twenty-five states were studying proposals requiring AFDC recipients to get a job after a certain period of time on welfare.[19] The new paternalism had become a major force across the nation.

Indications cropped up early during the Republican primary season that welfare reform would become an issue during the 1994 statewide elections. House Republican incumbent Harvey Hilderbran of Kerrville touted welfare reform as the key to breaking the cycle of poverty and decreasing the cost of government. Echoing the conservative themes of dependency, the underclass, and the need for a two-year time limit, Hilderbran said that welfare reform would be his number one legislative objective if returned to the state legislature. "I think it is only fair to ask welfare recipients to work in order to receive benefits. For too long, we have allowed many welfare recipients to give nothing back to their communities in return for their check."[20]

Hilderbran's concerns were echoed by George Bush during his race for governor. Throughout the spring and summer of 1994, Bush called for a rethinking of the assumptions underlying welfare in Texas along the lines of the new paternalism. Outdated thinking about welfare, Bush argued, was responsible for making people dependent upon the state for their own well-being and was one of the principal factors lying behind the explosion of the welfare rolls during the Richards years. Among the changes he called for were a strengthening of child-support procedures

---

19. For a detailed discussion of some of the nationwide welfare reform proposals see Texas Comptroller of Public Accounts *Fiscal Notes* (October 1994) and *Partnership for Independence* (January 1995).
20. Quoted in Phillips A. Brooks, "District 53 Candidates Focus on Welfare, Schools. Opponents Seek GOP Nomination in March 8 Primary," *Austin American Statesman*, 7 February 1994.

and penalties, the imposition of a two-year limit on benefits for recipients able to work, and a requirement that recipients accept a state-sponsored job after two years if they were unable to find work. In addition, he pushed for the creation of new child-care and job-training programs, the requirement that unwed mothers live with parents or guardians in order to receive benefits, the moving of family support programs from the state to the local level, and the institution of a fingerprinting program to prevent welfare fraud.[21]

Governor Richards refused to accept Bush's characterization of the problem, claiming that the issue of the underclass and welfare dependency was woefully overstated. The meager welfare benefits provided by Texas could hardly be considered an inducement for staying out of the work force. Moreover, most of the people who went onto welfare did so only temporarily. In the end, Richards argued, there was little that Texas could do to stem the surge in the welfare rolls because most of the increase had been mandated by the federal government. Beyond strengthening child-support provisions in the law and implementing a program establishing an electronic credit card for welfare recipients, she argued that Texas would be best served by waiting for substantive welfare reform at the national level.[22]

Richards may not have wanted welfare reform to be an issue in the gubernatorial race, but other more conservative Democrats did. Recognizing that welfare was an exploitable political issue, Lieutenant Governor Bob Bullock called upon the state Comptroller of Public Accounts, John Sharp, a fellow conservative Democrat, to study the problem of welfare in Texas and to develop a reform plan that could be considered by the state legislature when it reconvened in January after the elections. By the end of his own campaign, Sharp himself turned to welfare reform as a pivotal issue. Picking up on themes developed by Bush in his fight against Richards, Sharp identified some of the concerns that would lie at the heart of his office's welfare reform proposals. "Welfare regulations," he noted, "discourage self-reliance and encourage long-term dependence, and this has got to stop."[23]

Data released by the comptroller's office in October 1994 on participation in AFDC put the debate between Richards and Bush in relief. The data confirmed Richards's contention that many people went onto welfare because they needed it temporarily. Almost one-third of those who received welfare in 1993 in Texas had been on the rolls for one year or less. Almost half had accumulated benefits for less than two years. Moreover, benefits were quite low, particularly when compared to other

---

21. See Jonathan Eig, "Bush, Richards Clash over the Need for Welfare Overhaul."
22. See Wayne Slater, "Richards Protests Bush Attacks on State Welfare Spending. TV Commercials Defended as Accurate." *Dallas Morning News*, 23 September 1994, p. 30A.
23. Quoted in "Sharp Calls for Changes in Welfare." *Dallas Morning News*, 25 October 1994, p. 25A. See also Texas Comptroller of Public Accounts, *Fiscal Notes* (October 1994).

states. At the same time, the comptroller's office corroborated one of the central contentions of Bush's call for a new orientation toward welfare: there was a large group of people who appeared to have become permanently dependent upon welfare. One-quarter of welfare recipients in 1993 were "long term" recipients, having been on the rolls for five years or more.[24]

The publication of Comptroller Sharp's *A Partnership for Independence: Welfare Reform in Texas* in January 1995 set the terms under which welfare reform would be debated during the legislative session. The report contained a detailed analysis of poverty and welfare policy in Texas, focusing attention upon the facts that welfare often failed (1) to help those who needed it the most and (2) to encourage those dependent on welfare to become independent contributors to the state's economy. Four of the five stated goals of the program reflected directly the values of the new paternalism at the national level: enforcing personal responsibility and preserving the family, diverting Texans from welfare, keeping Texans off welfare once they left it, and cutting the bureaucracy while reducing fraud.[25] Among the 100 reform proposals contained in the report were many that had been supported by conservative reformers in other states or by Bush during the campaign, including a twenty-four-month welfare limit, granting communities more local control over job training and work force development programs, and the implementation of an automated fingerprint imaging program similar to one about to go into effect for driver's licenses.

Broad-based bipartisan support in both houses of the legislature soon developed for many, but not all, of the Sharp proposals. Bush, for example, wanted to subject all recipients immediately to a two-year benefit rule, whereas Sharp pushed for a trial program limited to 10,000 recipients. Other differences of opinion as to how sweeping reform should be and what direction it should take soon divided the bills introduced into the house and the senate.

Originally, the house bill co-sponsored by Republican Harvey Hilderbran, chairman of the house Health and Human Services Committee, and Democrat Mark Stiles, chairman of the house Calendars Committee, was the more sweeping of the two versions of the bill. Much of the bill had broad-based support, including provisions to revoke driver's and professional licenses of individuals who were delinquent in their child-support payments, to provide job training, Medicaid, and child care to recipients who were establishing themselves in jobs, and to fund pilot programs for education and training that sought to promote self-sufficiency. There were also highly contentious issues in the bill. As re-

---

24. See *Fiscal Notes* (October 1994).
25. The other stated goal was helping Texans with disabilities to get off state welfare and on to the Federal Supplemental Security Insurance program.

ported unanimously out of the house Health and Human Services Committee, the bill placed a cap on cash benefits paid under AFDC. No additional benefits would be available for children born to an AFDC mother who had been receiving benefits for more than ten months. In addition, cash benefits to parents were limited. Depending on the recipient's education and work experience, cash benefits could be limited to a period of six months to five years. Recipients would be required to sign a "responsibility" agreement with the state. The explicit goal of these provisions was to force people to behave responsibly and to take control of their own financial well-being as quickly as possible.[26] It was the new paternalism in action.

Although there was broad-based support for the committee's proposals in the house, it was not unanimous. Claiming that reform legislation was being used as a vehicle for "bashing" the poor, Democratic Representative Ron Wilson of the house halted debate on the welfare bill through parliamentary maneuvering and sent the bill back to committee. Although the bill finally passed the house overwhelmingly, its treatment was less favorable in the senate.

Judith Zaffirini, a Democratic from Laredo, sponsored reform legislation in the senate. Zaffirini, a supporter of family-oriented legislation, including education and training programs for those on welfare, could not accept the tougher features of the new paternalism found in the house bill. As passed, the senate version of the bill included time limits as well as a "responsibility" agreement provision, but lacked caps on the number of children that a recipients could have while on welfare, and did not legislate permanent freeze-out periods for recipients who wanted to reapply for public assistance.

The fate of comprehensive welfare reform remained in doubt in the conference committee up until the very end. Conferees had little trouble compromising on most of the differences between the house and senate versions of the bill. There was, however, considerable disagreement on the issues of caps and the freeze-out period. Caps on the number of children a person could have were simply too contentious, and consequently were not included in the final version of the bill. The freeze-out period, meanwhile, went through one version and then a second. On Monday, May 22, the conference committee voted to impose a relatively light freeze-out period of three years. In a second vote taken the next day, the committee reversed itself and extended the period to five years.[27] The reason for the shift was political. Neither Bush, who supported caps

---

26. "Panel OKs State Welfare Reform. Sends Bill to House," *Dallas Morning News*, 10 March 1995, p. 12D.
27. Under the bill, an exception to the five-year freeze-out could be made if a person could prove that his family would suffer "severe personal hardship" without welfare cash benefits. See Sylvia Moreno, "Conference Committee Toughens Welfare Bill," *Dallas Morning News*, 21 May 1995, p. 20A.

and a permanent freeze-out, nor Hilderbran, who sponsored the bill in the house, could accept a watered-down version of the bill. Hilderbran threatened to work against final house passage of the bill if these provisions were not tightened. Meanwhile, the governor hinted at a veto and a special legislative session to rewrite the bill.

The final version of welfare reform legislation passed the senate 30 to 1 and the house 128 to 9 on May 26. In line with the new paternalism, the law provided for a number of "carrots and sticks" that it was hoped would mold the character of those on welfare and wean them from their dependency on government largess. Among the carrots were expanded education and job-training programs, as well as selected pilot programs that promoted work by allowing families to receive transitional medical and child-care benefits. Among the sticks were limitations on benefits to a maximum of thirty-six months, alimony for spouses who couldn't support themselves, revocation of various state licenses for failure to pay child support, and the creation of a five-year ban for reapplying for benefits once benefits ran out.

Assessing Welfare Reform

The recent round of welfare reform in Texas can be assessed along a number of different dimensions. Politically, the reforms reflect the fact that a bipartisan consensus along the lines of the new paternalism has emerged in Texas. Improving welfare policy no longer means simply getting more money to those who need it, but trying to mold the character and alter the behavior of those who have turned to the state for help. Leaders in both parties agree that new approaches to the seemingly intractable problem of poverty and welfare are needed. The question is, what type of programs will work best in Texas?

Like other states, Texas has "bought into" many of the ideas of the new paternalism and has sought to design combined carrot and stick policies that encourage people to get off welfare and become financially independent. There is no guarantee that either the permanent or the pilot programs passed in the current welfare reforms are, in fact, the best available. Experimenting with new programs, expanding those that work and eliminating those that don't, must take place if welfare policy is to be pushed in a new direction.

Designing new programs will demand that Texas will have to decide how to measure success in a welfare program. Are the goals of welfare reform to spend less money and drive down the rolls, or are they to bring illegitimacy rates under control and help welfare recipients become permanent members of the work force? What happens if policy changes do not bring about the desired result?

The recent debate over the effect of family caps on illegitimacy rates in New Jersey highlights the complexity of these questions. Family caps on new children were introduced in New Jersey in 1992 in an effort to stem the tide of increasing illegitimacy rates among women on welfare. Early findings in 1993 seemed to indicate that the caps were having their desired effect: births among women who were aware that their benefits would decrease were down by 29 percent. A more recent study, however, finds that there has been no reduction in the birthrate among women on welfare due to the family cap. Individual policymakers have responded to these findings in one of two ways. Either they have argued that family caps don't matter and thus are needlessly harsh, or that family caps are not tough enough to get the desired result.[28]

One final factor needs to be taken into account when evaluating the current round of welfare reforms in Texas: the federal government. The reforms that have taken place in Texas are in large part due to the willingness of the federal government to grant the states more autonomy in the conduct of welfare policy. In the summer of 1996, President Clinton signed the Personal Responsibility and Work Opportunity Reconciliation Act, a piece of legislation that embodied the central assumptions of the new paternalism. Replacing AFDC with a block grant program that encouraged states to get welfare recipients back to work, the act represented a fundamental break with the welfare policy of the past. In addition, the federal government has approved forty-three waivers to states seeking to escape various federal mandates regarding the administration and operation of welfare programs. One of the most controversial waivers, which was not approved, came from Texas, which had proposed to privatize the administration of the state's welfare programs.

The full effect of these federal initiatives has yet to be felt, although preliminary findings are revealing. According to a report released by the Council of Economic Advisors on May 9, 1997, the number of welfare recipients in the United States had fallen by 20 percent between January 1993 and January 1997, a drop of 2.75 million individuals. These figures were mirrored in Texas. According to a Department of Health and Human Services report released in April 1997, in Texas the number of welfare recipients had dropped from 785,271 in January 1993 to 625,376 in January 1997. The welfare reforms passed in Texas in 1995 were not the end of the state's attempt to restructure welfare programs along the lines of the new paternalism, but only the beginning.[29]

---

28. Michael Kramer, "The Myth About Welfare Moms." *Time*, 3 July 1995, p. 21.
29. Date is from the Administration for Children and Families. U.S. Department of Health and Human Services' web site www.acf.dhhs.gov/news/casae-jan.htm. See also Saul D. Hoffman, "Could It Be True Afterall? AFDC Benefits and Non-Martial Births to Young Women," *Poverty Research News, The Newsletter of the Northwestern University/University of Chicago Joint Center for Policy Research*, vol. 1, no. 2, Spring 1997.